Holiday camps in twentieth-century Britain

Manchester University Press

STUDIES IN POPULAR CULTURE

General editor: Professor Jeffrey Richards

Already published

Holiday camps
in twentieth-century Britain
Packaging pleasure

SANDRA TRUDGEN DAWSON

Manchester University Press
Manchester and New York

distributed exclusively in the USA by Palgrave Macmillan

Published by Manchester University Press
Oxford Road, Manchester M13 9NR, UK
and Room 400, 175 Fifth Avenue, New York, NY 10010, USA
www.manchesteruniversitypress.co.uk

Distributed exclusively in the USA by
Palgrave Macmillan, 175 Fifth Avenue, New York,
NY 10010, USA

Distributed exclusively in Canada by
UBC Press, University of British Columbia, 2029 West Mall,
Vancouver, BC, Canada V6T 1Z2

British Library Cataloguing-in-Publication Data
A catalogue record for this book is available from the British Library

Library of Congress Cataloging-in-Publication Data applied for

ISBN 978 0 7190 8071 5 *hardback*

First published 2011

The publisher has no responsibility for the persistance or accuracy of URLs for external or any third-party internet websites referred to in this book, and does not guarantee that any content on such websites is, or will remain, accurate or appropriate.

Typeset in Adobe Garamond with Gill Sans display by
Koinonia, Manchester
Printed in Great Britain
by TJ International

STUDIES IN
POPULAR
CULTURE

There has in recent years been an explosion of interest in culture and cultural studies. The impetus has come from two directions and out of two different traditions. On the one hand, cultural history has grown out of social history to become a distinct and identifiable school of historical investigation. On the other hand, cultural studies has grown out of English literature and has concerned itself to a large extent with contemporary issues. Nevertheless, there is a shared project, its aim, to elucidate the meanings and values implicit and explicit in the art, literature, learning, institutions and everyday behaviour within a given society. Both the cultural historian and the cultural studies scholar seek to explore the ways in which a culture is imagined, represented and received, how it interacts with social processes, how it contributes to individual and collective identities and world views, to stability and change, to social, political and economic activities and programmes. This series aims to provide an arena for the cross-fertilisation of the discipline, so that the work of the cultural historian can take advantage of the most useful and illuminating of the theoretical developments and the cultural studies scholars can extend the purely historical underpinnings of their investigations. The ultimate objective of the series is to provide a range of books which will explain in a readable and accessible way where we are now socially and culturally and how we got to where we are. This should enable people to be better informed, promote an interdisciplinary approach to cultural issues and encourage deeper thought about the issues, attitudes and institutions of popular culture.

Jeffrey Richards

For Anna
and in memory
of my parents,
Charlie and
Dorothy Trudgen

Contents

List of illustrations

All illustrations are reproduced by kind permission of Butlin's Skyline Ltd.

Acknowledgements

As a child, I grew up surrounded by holiday camps and summer holiday-makers on Hayling Island. Family members, friends and neighbours found employment in them over the years as the camps were one of the principle employers on the island. The camps' centrality to the lives of many islanders has changed in recent years as the economic basis of Hayling has altered and yet, as I found when researching this book, the memory of them is still palpable. There are many people who absolutely must be thanked for their help and encouragement with this project, including those islanders who offered their memories. I wish to thank long-time island residents Joan Harrison and Olive Houghton, as well as Anthony Hutt, Wendy Kilshaw, 'A. J.' Marriott and Margaret White for their willingness to share reminiscences of holiday camps with me.

This book began as a PhD dissertation and I am enormously indebted to Erika Rappaport, Kenneth Moure, Lisa Jacobson and Eileen Boris, for their criticism, patience and support, and for all the dinners and conversations. My thanks also go to John Walton and Dick Hebdige who both gave me early encouragement to pursue the topic of holiday camps. My friend and colleague Carolyn Herbst Lewis read (and re-read) all the chapters without complaint, made substantial edits and offered insightful commentary and I am deeply grateful. Tony Lewis found obscure holiday-camp references in his vast knowledge of British popular culture, and Benton Lewis provided the best kind of distraction. My deepest thanks, however, go to Patrick Dawson who patiently waited while I wrote. And this book is for Anna Dawson who was constantly in my thoughts throughout the research and writing phases and who finally arrived to share our lives.

Funding for this book came from a variety of sources including a number of research grants from the Andrew W. Mellon Foundation, the Regents and the History Department of the University of California at Santa Barbara, as well as the Institute of European Studies at Berkeley. Various libraries, archivists and librarians have all been essential to this project. My thanks go to the Bodleian library, Oxford, especially the staff and archivists of the John Johnson Collection. The librarians of the British Library at St Pancras and the newspaper archive at Colindale were especially helpful. The archivists and librarians at Southampton University Special Collections, the Local Studies Collection of Portsmouth Central Library and the Hayling Island Library were amazing. Patrick Dawson and Gary Johnson at the Davidson Libraries at the University of California at Santa Barbara also deserve mention, as does the staff of the National Archive: Public Records Office at Kew, the Hampshire Records Office and the Wessex Film and Sound Archive in Winchester. I am also especially grateful to Vanessa Toulmin at the National Fairground Archive at the University of Sheffield for her help and expertise. eBay provided a surprising wealth of sources and contacts, underscoring the enduring nostalgia for holiday camps. Moreover, an unexpected call from Tony Cook brought a new dimension to the project.

The first chapter of the book appeared in an earlier form as an article 'Working-class consumers and the campaign for holidays with pay' in *Twentieth Century British History*, 18: 3 (2007) and is re-used with kind permission. I am also grateful to Butlin's Skyline for permission to use Butlin advertising. My appreciation goes to everyone at Manchester University Press, who have been professional, courteous and kind to work with.

Finally, this book is dedicated to my family and to the memory of my mother, a faithful Hayling Islander, who sadly died before this book was completed.

General editor's introduction

The long-running television comedy series *Hi-de-Hi!* indelibly inscribed on the popular consciousness an image of the holiday camps, with their chalet living, loudspeaker announcements, regimented activities, cheerful yellow-coat/red-coat entertainers, and bathing beauty, glamorous grandmother and knobbly knees competitions. Sandra Dawson's absorbing study, thoroughly researched, expertly analysed and immensely readable, explores the factual history behind the image. She establishes the context by analysing the campaign for holidays with pay, a campaign which, culminating in the 1938 Holidays With Pay Act, provided a significant spur to the development of the holiday-camp industry. She examines in detail the distinctive culture of the holiday camps with its implications for gender, class and national identities. She explores the various strategies employed by the major holiday-camp companies, Butlin's, Warner's and later Pontin's, to promote the holiday-camp experience. The Second World War had a major impact on the industry and Sandra Dawson assesses that impact. The return of peace presaged the 'golden age' of the holiday camp and Sandra Dawson successfully evokes that era which ended in the eclipse of the camps by social, economic and cultural changes in the 1960s and 1970s. The book is handsomely illustrated with contemporary postcards, photographs and posters and enlivened by first-hand testimony from guests and workers which together bring the holiday-camp experience to vivid life. This book perfectly complements two other volumes in the series, Susan Barton's *Working-class organisations and popular tourism 1840–1870* and John Walton's *The British seaside holiday: holidays and resorts in the twentieth century*. Together these three volumes constitute an authoritative account of a major British social and cultural phenomenon.

Jeffrey Richards
October 2009

List of abbreviations

BBC	British Broadcasting Corporation
BL	Bodleian Library
CEMA	Council for the Encouragement of Music and the Arts
ENSA	Entertainment National Service Association
HCPD	*House of Commons Parliamentary Debates*
HRA	British Health Resorts Association
HRO	Hampshire Record Office
ILP	International Labour Party
JJTC	John Johnson Travel Collection
NFPHC	National Federation of Permanent Holiday Camps
PCL LSC	Portsmouth Central Library Local Studies Collection
RAF	Royal Air Force
TNA: PRO	The National Archives, Public Record Office
TUC	Trades Union Congress
WSFA	Wessex Sound and Film Archive
WTA	Workers' Travel Association

Introduction:
creating a culture for leisure

New forms of mass leisure flourished in Britain between the First and Second World Wars, and Britons enjoyed a wider selection of commercial pleasures than ever before. Cinemas, amusement parks, dance-halls, variety theatres, and camping holidays offered a seemingly endless array of opportunities for fun and relaxation.[1] However, the ability to participate in these pleasures depended upon having the time and financial resources to afford them. In the first half of the twentieth century many working-class Britons lacked both. This prompted workers, unions, and members of the Labour Party to lobby Parliament to argue for annual paid holidays. The success of these efforts opened the way for vendors of mass leisure, who sought innovative ways to attract the growing market of pleasure consumers. This gave rise to the 'luxury' holiday camp, an all-inclusive, activity-driven pleasure package that soon became a popular form of commercial leisure in interwar Britain. Offering comfortable accommodation, three hot meals a day, childcare, and popular entertainment, these new-style holiday camps appeared along Britain's coastline close to the more exclusive seaside resorts of the 1930s.[2] Heralded as a revolution in leisure and as part of the tremendous growth of mass pleasure, the camps were marketed as an affordable holiday for British workers at a key moment of cultural and political change.

The history of holiday camps and paid holidays offers a fascinating lens through which to examine the importance of politics and pleasure to the notion of citizenship in twentieth-century Britain. This book builds on an earlier study by Colin Ward and Dennis Hardy that charts the nineteenth-century origins of holiday camps, as well as on recent works that link the consumption of pleasure to the development of class identity and citizenship.[3] While the Reform Acts of 1918 and 1928 increased the franchise and extended political citizenship to adult men and women in Britain, the expansion of paid holidays contributed to the idea of a new 'social' citizenship that helped to transform the identity of the worker from producer-citizen to consumer-citizen.[4] The mass luxury holiday camps built by Henry 'Harry' Warner and William 'Billy' Butlin in the 1930s demonstrated the possibilities of social citizenship at a moment when paid holiday time entered into the national debate alongside the needs of the working-class family.[5] While politicians acknowledged the right of workers to paid holidays, the lack of inexpensive accommodation threatened to complicate the response to the legislation guaranteeing that right. Warner and Butlin's commercial camps provided a model of inexpensive holidays and, as a result, the industry gained political legitimacy and a mass market. Building on earlier models, the new commercial luxury holiday-camp industry took advantage of the opportunity to market its potential to meet the needs of thousands of workers each week, at a critical moment just as the consumption of leisure became a marker of a new kind of social citizenship in Britain.[6] While the cost of a holiday lay beyond the wages of most manual workers, holiday camps were *perceived* as affordable and offered workers and their families the opportunity to exercise their rights and privileges as legitimate consumers of leisure.

This study illuminates the convergence of leisure with twentieth-century social policies, economics, culture, and war. The development of mass commercial holiday camps is significant not only to the history of domestic tourism, but also to the articulation of a 'democratic' twentieth-century British identity. Coming before the establishment of the comprehensive post-1945 welfare state, interwar policies redefined holidays as an important aspect of workers' well-being and an antidote to the debilitating effects of modernity. The mass holiday camps of the 1930s filled the need for inexpensive and 'democratic' sites of pleasure for workers' and families' recuperation and thereby gained political and social significance. As leisure time expanded during the Second World War, the cultural significance of holidays only grew. After the war years, holiday camps benefited from the policies of austerity and Labour's vision for postwar Britain as a nation with 'social balance'.[7] One all-inclusive cost for all campers, plus the ability to meet the needs of thousands of guests each week, gave holiday camps a commercial and political advantage over other players in the domestic tourist industry. With government support, the number of mass holiday camps expanded dramatically after the war to meet the needs of the increasingly affluent working classes.

The politics governing pleasure are vital to an understanding of perceptions of class identity and the major social and cultural shifts of twentieth-century mass consumption. Through an examination of the development of the major commercial holiday-camp chains established by Warner and Butlin, this study explores the way in which politics – broadly defined – shaped and was shaped by the new industry.

Chapter 1 examines the way interwar politics, the popular campaign for paid holidays, and the 1938 Holidays With Pay legislation contributed significantly to the growth of the nascent holiday-camp industry. This study engages with Susan Barton's recent work on working-class organisations and popular tourism.[8] Barton traces the emergence of popular tourism from the 1840s and argues that working-class organisations, friendly societies and unions played a significant part in the development of package vacations and annual paid leisure time. While Barton's work carefully documents trade union activity in the twentieth century, especially in the campaign for holidays with pay, this study offers an insight into the gendered dimensions of the same campaign in the 1920s and the 1930s. The campaign for paid holidays that was waged in the popular press helped to construct working-class families as consumers of leisure while simultaneously advertising the new holiday camps that promised to provide all-inclusive and affordable pleasure for British workers and their families. The report of the Holidays With Pay Committee and the 1938 legislation both document state support for the growth of commercial leisure. Recommendations from the committee urged the government to sanction the development of cheap forms of mass leisure like holiday camps to meet the needs of low-paid workers. Thus the report and the legislation helped not only to construct a market for mass pleasure sites such as holiday camps, but also to define the types of commercial leisure appropriate for workers. The campaign, the report, and the legislation deeply implicated the state in the 'construction' of a consumerist working class as well as the expansion of commercial class-based sites of leisure.

The allure of mass holiday camps also illuminates the gendered dimensions of social citizenship. As unions and marriage bars increasingly excluded married women from the workplace, the campaign for paid holidays highlighted the value of women's unwaged work. The plight of housewives, dependent on their husbands' wages for household expenses, became a symbol of working-class suffering. When Warner and Butlin advertised their camps as a holiday for housewives, they entered into the debate about the importance of women's unwaged work in the home without significantly challenging the gendered concept of the British worker/citizen as male. The provision of childcare, nurseries, meals, and housekeeping services in the camps created a space where married women could rest from their unpaid daily chores while the male worker could recuperate from the demands of modern labour.

Chapter 2 explores the distinctive culture developed in the mass holiday camps. After the Great War, amusement entrepreneurs began to see the working classes as a new market of consumers. Warner and Butlin successfully commercialised pre-existing working-class cultural forms such as self-parody, sport, variety performances, comedy, and community singing, and packaged them for the masses. The camps developed by the two men were part of what Alison Light has recently described as 'new commercial representations of "Englishness"' that were offered to 'heterogeneous and unpredictable new groups' in the interwar years.[9] Warner and Butlin successfully marketed their camps as a form of British culture for consumption even though the new consumers were often resistant. While the state expanded paid holidays and the domestic tourist industry responded with greater opportunities for pleasure, many Britons clung to the older leisure patterns of drinking at local pubs, taking picnics on day-trips to urban centres or the seaside, holidaying under canvas at makeshift campsites, hop-picking, or simply staying at home.

However, the expansion of the holiday-camp industry facilitated a cultural shift from homo-social to hetero-social leisure. As many historians have noted, leisure, especially working-class leisure in the first half of the twentieth century, was often sharply divided along lines of gender.[10] Sports such as football and cricket attracted male players and spectators, as did gambling establishments, whereas the cinema gained an increasingly female audience. Holiday camps incorporated these traditionally gendered activities into the daily entertainment programmes and reoriented them to appeal to both sexes. Sports teams were made up of both male and female guests, or topsy-turvy events were put on that inverted gender norms by requiring male players to dress as women and female players to dress as men. Evening entertainments also fostered a hetero-social culture of pleasure. Though traditionally considered the site of male sociability, bars in the camps offered adults of both sexes alcoholic beverages, gambling opportunities, competitions, music, and dancing.

Holiday camps were merely one part of a larger commercialisation of leisure in interwar Britain which led Butlin and Warner to develop distinctive advertising and marketing techniques to promote the uniqueness of their holiday camps. Chapter 3 looks at the way Warner and Butlin used extensive national advertising campaigns in newspapers and magazines that emphasised both the activities and the atmosphere of the camps. Unlike earlier holiday-camp proprietors, Warner and Butlin bought larger advertisements, encouraged reporters to write about their camps, made extravagant claims, and persuaded overnight celebrities and popular entertainers to endorse their camps. In this way, their names and the luxury holiday-camp industry as a whole gained national exposure, and a degree of notoriety as well.

Chapter 4 describes the way the Second World War temporarily stalled the development of holiday camps but also set the stage for a postwar expansion of new leisure empires. Paradoxically, the holiday-camp industry of the 1930s was able to deepen its connections to the construction of citizenship and national identity even as a new war demanded high levels of production and austerity. The interwar camps had been built at key coastal locations and, as they were capable of accommodating large numbers, they now housed troops and served as a blueprint for civilian evacuation centres during the war. In fact, the war stimulated the construction of more camps to billet troops and civilians. As a result, the government built a political and economic infrastructure that ensured the expansion of the number of camps throughout the war years and their subsequent availability for leisure in the immediate postwar period. Warner and Butlin, who oversaw the building of wartime hostels and military training facilities, benefited greatly at the end of the hostilities. They swiftly transformed the wartime establishments into holiday camps to meet the needs of postwar domestic tourism.

Chapter 5 looks at the way the holiday-camp industry also benefited from the cultural policies of the wartime government. State efforts to maintain morale with quality radio comedy and to 'uplift' the masses with high-brow entertainment such as ballet, opera, and Shakespearean plays were actively translated into the postwar camp entertainment offered by Warner and Butlin. Radio stars, comedians, ballet dancers, and musicians entertained postwar guests. By continuing wartime modes of entertainment, holiday camps legitimated the cultural policies of the wartime government and maintained the national 'myth' of a common experience and 'all Britons pulling together'.[11]

The chapter goes on to examine the way the common experience of war influenced a political 'consensus' established by the major parties in 1945 that focused on the needs of the working family.[12] Labour's landslide election victory on a platform of socialism and restraint, continued rationing and austerity, and a postwar settlement paved the way for the establishment of an extensive welfare state. The provision of inexpensive family-centred sites of leisure was made all the more significant because of welfare policies, full employment, increased wages, and a prolonged scarcity of consumer goods. Ironically, leisure markets expanded at the precise moment that consumption was the most regulated, altering the landscape of domestic tourism. The rationing of consumer goods created an opening for holiday camps to provide inexpensive distraction, entertainment, and relief from domestic austerity. The postwar politics of want and austerity also enhanced the appeal of mass leisure as the most efficient way to provide for working families. Unlike small hotels, holiday camps complemented the ideology of the postwar settlement.[13] The Labour government, despite and indeed because of austerity and the perceived ethos of equality, gave special help to holiday camps, to the detriment of other forms of domestic tourism. As the camps grew at home, attempts by British entrepreneurs to convert their vision so as to appeal to an international market failed. As a result, they turned back to Britain and courted the working-class market more aggressively. By the late 1950s, holiday camps had entered British popular culture as a 'classless space' into which mainly 'lower-class' people went. Warner and Butlin had become household names and their holiday-camp chains were part of a multimillion-pound tourist industry.

The increased demand for inexpensive accommodation for holiday makers with limited means posed a serious dilemma for the leisure industry from the mid 1950s on – how to cater for millions of domestic tourists during a short summer season without adequate labour. Chapter 6 examines the way full employment depleted the labour pool, forcing the leisure industry to compete for skilled and unskilled workers with other, better-paying industries. Hotels and caterers looked to foreign labour to relieve the shortages in Britain. Many of the workers came from former colonies and a resurgence of racism created further problems for the leisure industry. Consumer resistance further depleted profits for the industry as Britons continued to spend their paid holidays at home, with families, abroad, or under canvas in makeshift campsites. The holiday-camp industry faced similar problems and marketed its camps as places both to holiday and to work.

The entertainment featured in the camps transformed mainstream popular culture as many cultural icons of the 1960s found their voice as entertainers in the postwar camps. Others used the camps as inspiration for films, songs, novels, and children's books. Furthermore, holiday camps successfully met the leisure needs of families with children. The postwar baby boom and welfare policies challenged the assumption that only adults were legitimate consumer-citizens in the 'new' Britain. By recognising a new and important consumer group – working-class children – the holiday-camp industry both shaped and was shaped by the politics of the welfare state. The camps offered full-service facilities for babies, children, and young adults and met the needs of this burgeoning market. However, while the holiday-camp industry remained popular until the 1970s, by the late 1960s more and more Britons were coming to prefer packaged pleasure abroad.

To gain an understanding of the obstacles and opportunities that the domestic tourism industry faced, this study draws upon a variety of sources. Parliamentary debates and government documents as well as national and local newspapers reveal the role of the government in the development of mass leisure, as well as pressures 'from below' that encouraged the government to secure paid holidays and to assist in the development of the camps. The national and local press offers a useful picture of contemporary support or critiques of the leisure industry in general and holiday camps in particular. Many of the larger debates by social critics are mirrored in multiple articles, suggesting that the concerns about forms of leisure affected more than just the intellectual elite.

Trade journals, association records, and official histories similarly illuminate the role of other branches of the leisure industry, such as hoteliers and traditional resorts, in the growth of the holiday camps. *The Caterer and Hotel Keeper*, the trade journal of the domestic tourist industry in Britain, published weekly articles that included local and national news of interest to members, including coverage of parliamentary debates, the proceedings of industry conferences and associations, and the personal achievements of industry members. *The World's Fair*, another weekly trade paper and the official organ of the Showman's Guild of Great Britain, advertised entertainment jobs and equipment, and disseminated information for show people and entertainers. Both of these journals provide a useful and sometimes highly detailed picture of the leisure industry and its personalities, illuminating their aspirations and disappointments, hopes and anxieties. The journals offer an 'inside look' at the production of service in the twentieth century and are therefore an important yet often overlooked aspect of consumer histories.

Additionally, films, novels, children's books, postcards, photographs, and letters all contribute to the cultural dimension of this book and demonstrate the importance of holiday camps in British culture and popular memory. Interviews with former guests illuminate what holidays meant to people who went to the camps, while the reminiscences of entertainers, staff, and entrepreneurs reveal that some of those meanings were often unintended. The varied sources examined in this book add a new dimension to the current literature on domestic tourism, leisure, and popular culture in twentieth-century Britain.

Notes

1 See, for example, J. Richards, *The age of the dream palace: Cinema and society in Britain, 1930–1939* (London, 1989) and S. Braggs and D. Harris, *Sun, fun and crowds: British seaside holidays between the wars* (London: Routledge, 2000).

2 See J. Walton, *The British seaside in the twentieth century* (Manchester: Manchester University Press, 2000), pp. 34–40.

3 C. Ward and D. Hardy, *Goodnight campers! The history of the British holiday camp* (London: Mansell, 1986), B. Beaven, *Leisure, citizenship and working-class men in Britain, 1850–1945* (Manchester: Manchester University Press, 2005), *The car in British society: Gender, class and motoring, 1896–1939* (Manchester: Manchester University Press, 1998), J. Richards, *Films and British national identity: From Dickens to Dad's Army* (Manchester: Manchester University Press, 1997), A. Davies, *Leisure, gender, poverty: Working-class culture in Salford and Manchester* (Milton Keynes: Open University Press, 1992) and P. Bailey, *Leisure and class in Victorian England: Rational recreation and the contest for control* (London: Routledge & Kegan Paul, 1978).

4 For the significance of the 1918 Reform Act see N. Gullace, *The blood of our sons: Men, women, and the renegotiation of citizenship during the Great War* (New York: Palgrave, 2002), p. 4.

5 Many hotels and boarding houses did not welcome children or saw them as a potential problem. See J. Walton, 'The Blackpool landlady revisited', *Manchester Region History Review*, 8 (1994), pp. 23–30.

6 M. Hilton, *Consumerism in twentieth century Britain: The search for a historical movement* (Cambridge: Cambridge University Press, 2003), pp. 108–166.

7 P. Catterall, 'The state of the literature on post-war British history', in A. Gorst, L. Johnman and W. S. Lucas, eds *Post-war Britain, 1945–64: Themes and perspectives* (London: Pinter, 1989), p. 221.

8 S. Barton, *Working-class organisations and popular tourism, 1840–1970* (Manchester: Manchester University Press, 2005).

9 A. Light, *Forever England: Femininity, literature and conservatism between the wars* (London: Routledge, 1991), p. 216.

10 For a discussion of working-class homo-social leisure see B. Beaven, *Leisure, citizenship and working-class men in Britain, 1850–1945* (Manchester: Manchester University Press, 2005), C. Culleton, *Working-class culture, women and Britain, 1914–1921* (New York: St. Martin's Press, 1999), ch. 5, A. Davies, *Leisure, gender, poverty*, and 'Leisure in the classic slum, 1900–1939', in A. Davies and S. Fielding, eds *Workers' worlds: Cultures and communities in Manchester and Salford, 1880–1939* (Manchester: Manchester University Press, 1992), pp. 102–132. For a discussion of middle-class homo-social leisure see P. Deslandes, *Oxbridge men: British masculinity and the undergraduate experience, 1850–1920* (Bloomington: Indiana University Press, 2005), pp. 121–153, and E. D. Rappaport, *Shopping for pleasure: Women and the making of London's West End* (Princeton: Princeton University Press, 2000), pp. 85–92.

11 Historians remain divided about the experience of the Second World War. See C.

Ponting, *1940: Myth and reality* (London: Hamish Hamilton, 1990), A. Calder, *The myth of the blitz* (London: Jonathan Cape, 1992), and M. Smith, *Britain and 1940: History, myth and popular memory* (London: Routledge, 2000).

12 M. Francis, 'Not reformed capitalism, but … democratic socialism: The ideology of the Labour leadership, 1945–51', in P. Catterall and H. Jones, eds *The myth of consensus* (Basingstoke: Macmillan, 1996), pp. 40–57.

13 For a discussion of the postwar settlement see T. O. Lloyd, *Empire, welfare state, Europe: English history 1906–1992* (Oxford: Oxford University Press, 1993), pp. 284–305. For a more critical discussion see N. Ellison, 'Consensus here, consensus there … but not consensus everywhere: the Labour Party, equality and social policy in the 1950s', in P. Catterall and H. Jones, eds *The myth of consensus* (Basingstoke: Macmillan, 1996), pp. 17–39.

Imagining consumers: working-class families and paid holidays

M r Charles Turner, a manual worker in the upholstery trade, dreaded holidays. Married with two children, Turner lived in a rented house in Stratford and brought home wages of £3 each week. Neither Turner nor his wife had ever experienced a holiday away from home. They could not afford to do so. In April 1938 the Turner family were three weeks behind in their rent and faced meagre meals as a result of the upcoming Easter Bank holiday. The two and a half days' unpaid public holiday meant that Turner's wages would be halved that week. 'You have no idea', he told a staff reporter for the *Daily Express*, 'how these unpaid holidays throw our budget out of gear. It takes us months to recover.' Turner went on to explain that when the upholstery factory closed for a week in August, and during the Christmas break, he suffered a loss of wages for the days he did not work. If only he could work during the holidays, Turner maintained, he could catch up on all his bills. As her husband expressed his frustration over unpaid holidays, Mrs Turner offered the reporter a meal of homemade meat pudding and a cup of milky tea. She apologised for the food and explained, 'We were going to have fish for lunch today but that would have cost one and six and we can't afford that this week.' The following week would be even worse. Of her husband's 30s wages, ten would pay the rent and the rest, Mrs Turner maintained, 'would just about buy us food for the week if we go slow'. The Turners, as the *Daily Express* reporter told readers, were just one of millions of families in Britain who suffered from unpaid holidays. 'Can we', the reporter asked, please 'make this the last holiday without pay?'[1]

Two weeks after the popular and conservative-leaning *Daily Express* published the article about the Turner family a long-awaited report by the Holidays With Pay Committee recommended that all full-time workers in Britain receive at least one week's annual paid holiday.[2] The suggestions from the Committee formed the basis of the Holidays With Pay Act passed later that year. For those nineteen and a half million manual workers in Britain who, like Charles Turner, earned less than £250 per year, the legislation marked the end of a twenty-year campaign for holidays with pay and the beginning of paid holidays.

The final legislation, however, did not guarantee paid holidays. The 1938 Holidays With Pay Act recommended, but did not mandate, one week's annual paid holiday to all full-time workers in Britain.[3] Anticipating the legislation, some employers had already made agreements with workers and unions for paid holidays.[4] Thus the 1938 Act merely nudged many employers in the direction they were already headed.[5] For this reason, many scholars have dismissed the Act as largely insignificant. Furthermore, the legislation did little to change the leisure habits of British workers until after 1945. The outbreak of war in 1939 interrupted the full implementation of the statute, and, as the predicament of the Turner family illustrates, the cost of holidays placed them outside the realm of possibility for most workers until labour shortages elevated wages in the post-Second World War era.[6] Other historians note that the campaign for paid leisure in Britain and the 1938 Act mirrored similar movements and legislation in other European nations.[7] The Holidays With Pay Act in Britain followed many similar types of legislation in other nations.[8] Thus many scholars consider the Act relatively insignificant except as a milestone in international labour history.

The report of the Holidays With Pay Committee, the Act, and the campaign leading to the passage of the legislation are much more significant than scholars contend. First, the popular campaign for paid holidays helped to construct working-class families as consumers of leisure. Central to this image was the idea of the 'poor suffering British housewife'. Second, the report of the Holidays With Pay Committee and the 1938 legislation document the way state policy supported the commercialisation of leisure in the interwar years. Recommendations from the Committee urged the government to sanction the development of cheap forms of mass leisure, such as holiday camps, to cater for low-paid workers. Thus the Act recognised the needs of workers to enjoy leisure time, but also met the needs of business to keep wages low and profits high. Third, the campaign for paid holidays and the resulting 1938 Act not only helped to create a market for mass pleasure sites such as holiday camps, but also helped to define the types of commercial leisure appropriate for a mass of workers. The campaign, the report, and the legislation, then, deeply implicated the state in the construction of a consuming working class as well as in the expansion of commercial class-based sites of leisure.

The suitability of such sites of workers' pleasure revolved around popular perceptions of the working-class household. As the Committee met to discuss paid holidays, several popular daily newspapers, including the conservative-leaning *Daily Mail*, *Daily Express* and *Daily Mirror*, the liberal-oriented *News Chronicle* and the Labour-supporting *Daily Herald*, printed a series of articles that emphasised the plight of the 'poor British housewife' who depended on her husband's wages to feed and clothe the family. Unpaid holidays, the papers explained, created hardship and more work for housewives who were forced to try to 'make do' without a pay packet from their husbands. At the same time, newspapers also advertised new and inexpensive holiday camps that catered especially for the needs of women and children.[9] When the Committee published its recommendations in April 1938, it pointed to large, organised holiday camps in order to model the potential for low-cost mass catering that would enable all members of the family to enjoy a respite from the chores of daily living. Holiday camps offered individual accommodation, three hot meals a day, childcare services, and constant activities and age-specific entertainment for an all-inclusive price. The Committee recommended the construction of more holiday camps to make 'use of the advantages of large-scale enterprise' to 'provide facilities for families at low weekly terms' to cater for the 'worker who wishes to take his family on an inexpensive holiday in which his wife can enjoy rest and recuperation and freedom so far as possible from arduous household duties'.[10] Thus the campaign for holidays with pay and the recommendations of the Committee encouraged the growth of the holiday-camp industry by focusing on the plight of the working-class housewife and her need for leisure.

Although most of the holiday camps were owned by individual entrepreneurs or unions, two new 'chains' emerged in the 1930s. The holiday camps operated by William 'Billy' Butlin and Henry 'Harry' Warner gained national recognition through advertising and their ability to accommodate thousands of campers each week of the holiday season. In part, this recognition was driven by middle-class anxiety that the droves of holidaying workers and their families would overwhelm the already congested seaside resorts along Britain's coast. Although some in the leisure industry clearly anticipated Holidays With Pay as a boon for British tourism, others deplored the invasion of their resorts by working-class people and looked to the holiday camps to provide contained and inexpensive pleasure for those unwelcome workers and their families. By featuring the mass holiday camps built and operated by men like Butlin and Warner, the Committee gave political legitimacy to the camps, as well as the promise of commercial success.

As the Holidays With Pay Committee debated the possible extension of paid holidays, members also grappled with the problem of a dearth of holiday accommodation. Mass holiday camps emerged in the 1930s and developed the capacity to cater inexpensively for thousands of guests each week. For many members of the Committee, holiday camps appeared to provide the commercial answer to an economic and political problem. The report of the Committee therefore recommended that the government encourage the growth of holiday camps as suitable sites for workers' holidays.

Through an examination of the popular campaign for paid holidays in Britain in the 1930s, the report of the Holidays With Pay Committee, and the provisions of the legislation, this chapter explores the complexities inherent in the negotiations surrounding holidays for workers. The demand for paid holidays is a story about how workers, trade unions, the tourist industry, and others redefined leisure as a right in the interwar years and how the battle for that right was in part a battle to recognise women's unwaged work in the home.

Background to the British holiday

Linked to local traditions and religious festivals, time away from daily work routines was an integral part of pre-industrial life in Britain.[11] In 1552, workers celebrated twenty-seven saints' days and feast days, some with and some without pay. Changes in the number of feast days and holidays took place during the reigns of George II and Queen Victoria and the introduction of the August Bank Holiday in 1871 established Britain's first secular holiday.[12]

For many working people, the unpaid August Bank Holiday represented the full extent of an annual summer holiday and came at the cost of much-needed wages. Yet even before the introduction of the August Bank Holiday, some workers saved money and organised holidays. As railway construction linked seaside resorts to urban centres, and wages increased, the Lancashire cotton industry closed factories and even whole towns for a week each August while workers holidayed en masse in seaside resorts. These 'wakes weeks' were not, however, paid holidays. Workers saved up to pay for the week when the factory closed for annual maintenance and the installation of new machinery. For most workers, the annual week's closure represented an opportunity for a holiday – but it also meant lower wages throughout the year.[13] Nonetheless, the wakes weeks contributed to the growth of cheap amusements and the development of northern seaside resorts such as Blackpool.[14]

In the nineteenth century, the Co-operative movement also emerged as a worker's self-help organisation, a political party, an alternative economic system to capitalism, and an early welfare organisation.[15] Co-operatives provided essential food and fuel at cost price, encouraged savings schemes for unanticipated emergencies like sickness and death, and, from the latter half of the nineteenth century, holidays.[16] In the scholarly debate over the significance of co-operation as a social or political movement, the ability of the working class to organise self-help in order to enjoy holidays is often overlooked.[17] As Susan Barton has illuminated, working-class co-operation enabled some workers to plan and save throughout the year for a few days at the seaside during periods of leisure enforced by factory slow-time.[18] Not all leisure was enforced, however. Some workers organised to ensure that they received holidays even against the wishes of their employers.

As more workers enjoyed day excursions to the coast they encouraged the growth of mass amusements such as magic-lantern shows, fairground rides, music halls, pier amusements, tea dances, and the development of popular resorts such as Blackpool in the north-west, Weston-super-Mare in the south-west, and Brighton in the south of England.[19] The expansion of the railways and road networks, combined with the availability of cheap half-day excursions to the coast by train or charabanc (a horse-drawn and later motorised bus) and the popularity of inexpensive camping holidays over the August Bank holiday weekend, provided an alternative form of pleasure for many urban workers.[20]

The desire for a day at the seaside and the availability of cheap amusements encouraged the growth and development of new resorts close to urban centres, such as Hayling, a small flat island off the south coast of Hampshire.[21] In response to the practice of Wednesday afternoon closing that gave shop workers a free afternoon, an 1878 London, Brighton and South Coast Railway handbill advertised 'Cheap Day Excursion[s] to Hayling Island every Wednesday' from London Bridge and Victoria stations.[22] As the railways capitalised on this section of the consumer market with weekly excursions, resorts responded with entertainment for the trippers and, in the case of Hayling, the *Hampshire Telegraph* reported on all such social events in a weekly column. The island provided fresh air and sea-bathing, as well as religious concerts and teas hosted by local churches.[23] These activities were deemed 'rational recreation' and orderly amusements that would restrain the behaviour of the lower-class excursionists, who might otherwise be tempted to consume alcohol at the islands' many public houses and become disorderly. The idea of rational recreation linked to temperance pervaded the organisations on the island. As tourism increased, philanthropic and religious groups planned the leisure of their working-class patrons in an effort to contain and exert an element of control over their pleasure.[24] By 1889, the island supplied the annual venue for young urban tourists and organised camping pioneers from St Andrew's Home and Club for Working-boys and the Metropolitan Companies of the Boys' Brigade over the August Bank holiday. Other religious groups, like the Band of Hope and the Christian Endeavourers from industrial Portsmouth, also planned local camping holidays and day trips to the island.[25] For workers, however, these day trips and excursions to the coast, although relatively cheap, came at the cost of a day's wages.

By the early twentieth century, profitable sites of leisure had emerged in coastal areas around Britain. The increase in commercialised pleasure made holidays and leisure time a focal point of class conflict. As those on the political left and right debated the effect of modern industrial methods on the health of the worker, the campaign for paid holidays garnered support from a coalition of disparate constituencies that resulted in the passage of legislation in 1938.

The interwar campaign for holidays with pay

The demand for paid holidays is the story of the way that leisure was redefined as a right, not a privilege, for all workers. The battle for that right went hand in hand with a new recognition of the home as a site of production, and one that highlighted the unwaged labour of women in the home. The demand for paid holidays for all manual workers began in the nineteenth century and accelerated with the activity of the trade union movement.[26] In 1911, the Trades Union Congress (TUC) adopted a motion in favour of paid holidays, and the following year George Lansbury, a socialist MP, introduced the first Holidays With Pay private member's bill into Parliament.[27] Despite the support of the TUC, the idea of paid holidays did not gain general acceptance among employers or workers before the First World War.[28] Employers refused to believe that paid holidays might increase production. For the unions, who focused attention and fought for basic social, political, and industrial rights, the idea of paid holidays seemed 'somewhat utopian'.[29] In addition, historian Pat Thane points out that the number of union members was relatively small and roughly one-quarter that of Friendly Societies before the First World War. The working-class membership of the Friendly Societies preferred to maintain pressure for higher wages and retain worker independence in spending rather than to support demands for paid holidays that might give employers more control over their pay packets.[30] After the First World War, however, union membership increased and annual paid holidays entered negotiations and workers' demands in the collective bargaining for an eight-hour day. As in the United States, workers and unions soon recognised the intimate connection between basic social rights and recreation, so that the idea of paid leisure time became anything but utopian.[31] Rather, unions and workers conceived of paid holidays as a necessary adjunct to the vote and as a symbol of social as well as political citizenship.

During the First World War, the government suspended all holidays, paid and unpaid. After the war, as unions fought for higher wages and a shorter work week, the Conservative-led coalition government painted a picture of a nation divided between 'the people' on one the hand, and 'union bullies' on the other.[32] Many contemporaries and historians, however, note a shift in attitudes to leisure.[33] Waged workers wanted annual paid holidays on an equal basis with salaried workers, who had enjoyed them for almost a century.[34] While many waged workers were highly skilled, salaried white-collar workers received one or two weeks' annual paid holiday because employers believed that 'brain work' required annual recuperative and paid holidays while waged work did not. Paid holidays were therefore a marker of worker value and class distinction.[35] The insistence on the right to annual paid holidays for waged workers was in part a demand to remove the class distinction between waged and white-collar workers. Ironically, at the same time, waged workers and their union leaders also pressured married women to leave employment and many industries, including the Post Office, introduced a formal marriage bar. The use of unskilled female workers to replace skilled men during the First World War threatened wages and further devalued workers' skills. While waged workers demanded equal class treatment in terms of paid holidays, they did not demand gender equality. Indeed, workers wanted to preserve a gendered *inequality* to ensure that men retained work and married women remained economically dependent on their husbands.[36]

Nevertheless, as workers and unions in different regions of the country agitated for higher wages, shorter working days, and paid holidays, the most successful results occurred in the printing industry. In 1918, the Printing and Kindred Trades Federation secured an agreement that entitled all employees in the printing industry to a week's annual paid holiday after one year's service. The importance of this ground-breaking agreement lay in the fact that it covered all categories of workers, unlike earlier agreements that targeted specific groups (such as white-collar workers) and excluded others (largely waged workers). This agreement then stood as a model of a democratic approach to the idea of annual paid holidays. The publicity surrounding this and other strikes garnered a degree of political support, including the introduction of a second unsuccessful Paid Holidays Bill by an Independent Labour Party MP in 1925.[37]

Despite the failure of the second Bill, the campaign for paid holidays continued, especially in the press. In April 1926, a letter published in the left-wing *Lansbury Labour Weekly* highlighted the impact of holidays without pay on the lives of many manual workers. The author of the letter, a rail shop-worker, insisted that many thousands of workers dreaded public holidays such as Christmas, Easter, and the August Bank holiday because they were unwaged days 'paid for by the starvation of ... mothers and children'.[38] For this worker, the Easter holiday resulted in a loss of 30s in pay. As a result, every weekly payment, including rent, was behind. The alternative for this worker was unthinkable – to pay the rent and allow his family to go without food. This letter focused the readers' attention on the plight of the worker's family and the fear of hunger. As such, the argument coincided with two other interwar debates – the idea of a living wage and the problem of alleviating hunger in a modern industrial nation.[39]

The campaign for a living wage, led by the Independent Labour Party (ILP) in the 1920s, focused on the problem of poverty and argued for a minimum wage of £4 per week. The issue was complicated by the debate over family allowances. Should the state intervene and pay mothers an allowance for each of her children, or would this policy lead to lower wages for male workers? Were family allowances a means by which married women could regain some economic independence, or would they serve to strengthen the marriage bar in some industries and decrease women's claim to equal pay? While unionists debated the potential problems, concern for the working-class family, particularly for the nutrition and health of poor children, led the Labour Party to support family allowances, despite opposition from the TUC.[40]

Anxiety about the nutritional state of the nation underscores one of the chief concerns of the interwar years.[41] Medical examinations of working-class school children in London in 1927 and in Jarrow in 1933 showed signs of calcium deficiency and the onset of rickets, despite the provision of school meals.[42] Economic depression, worker unrest, and high employment, as well as the instability of international politics, exacerbated anxieties about the physical state of the nation and, in particular, the ability of the working classes to provide for the nutritional needs of their children.[43] As historian James Vernon points out, the importance of food and the alleviation of hunger was intricately related to a broader shift in ideas of 'the social'. He claims that the 'techno-politics' of food and nutrition that encouraged reformers to promote school meals and the physical assessment of the working-class diet were perceived as essential aspects of the social concerns of modern government.[44] Through its attention to the hardships experienced by the worker's family when no wages were brought home, the campaign for paid holidays received more support from social workers and reformers concerned with the health of the nation and the impact of poverty on the family. The campaign for paid leisure was thus allied with the debate over the living wage and welfare, firmly situating hunger and want as problems of modernity.[45]

While social scientists and economists debated the effects of poverty on the health of the working-class family, others were concerned with the effects of modernity on the physique and psyche of the manual worker. Studies of industrial fatigue undertaken in the United States from 1917 on suggested that regular periodic rests increased production and improved the health of the nation.[46] While British industries implemented Taylorist rationalisation and Fordist principles of assembly-line production, as in the United States, they failed to institute regular breaks as suggested by the American studies.[47] High levels of unemployment and the failure of the nine-day General Strike in May 1926 seriously affected union activity aimed at combating the transforma-tion of industrial production.[48] Nevertheless, supporters of the campaign for paid holidays argued that workers required more than a day or a weekend to recuperate from the debilitating and dehumanising effects of modernity.[49] As the number of work days lost to sickness increased, a third attempt to secure legislation for paid holidays failed in 1929, largely because of the Wall Street crash and the ensuing worldwide economic depression.[50]

As the British economy began to show signs of recovery, the movement for paid holidays continued. In 1932, the *Labour Magazine* published an article by a medical doctor in support of paid leisure time for workers. Dr J. Mensch wrote, 'Holidays are necessary for all of us if we are not to stumble through life like beasts of burden or prisoners on the treadmill.' A holiday from the 'dulling round of habit', and the 'daily struggle for existence', he argued, is an 'immunization' from the depression caused by modern industrial work. The article continued to stress the health needs of the urban worker. Mensch argued that the modern factory worker 'breathes … noxious gases and coal, wood, or metal dust' that undermined 'their physical and mental efficiency', and reduced the 'capacity for resistance to depressing influences'. The modern worker therefore needed annual paid holidays away from the city in order to regenerate and not choke in the 'dust of materialism'.[51] Mensch underscored the irony of rationalisation and mass production. Modern processes considerably increased the speed of production and the amount of goods produced, yet the workers were literally 'choked' by the dust of the materials used for production.[52]

Novelist and social critic Aldous Huxley echoed this critique of Fordist principles of mass production. In his 1932 novel, *Brave New World*, Huxley transformed the physically and mentally depressed urban worker described by Mensch into an automaton, biologically predestined to undertake any level of menial task required, and programmed to work the necessary hours for maximum output.[53] Thus, production is efficient and never ending; consumption is never fully satisfied. In Huxley's dystopia, leisure is unknown to workers, who are identified only by their biological classification and job description. The 'savage', on the other hand, lived away from urban production and resided in rural areas untouched by Fordist determinism and distant from the Brave New World. As Huxley points out in his foreword to the second edition, those who govern the Brave New World are not madmen: their aim is 'not anarchy but social stability, carried out by scientific means'.[54] Highlighting the relative inactivity of the unions in the years after the General Strike, Huxley feared the effects of modern industrial production on the capacity of workers to foment political action and bring about social change.

The arguments expressed by Huxley and Mensch mirrored a wider international critique, and the movement for paid holidays in Britain was also part of a larger international workers' movement.[55] When workers in France and Belgium successfully united and struck for holidays with pay in 1936, their success encouraged the British movement.[56] Campaigners stepped up the pressure.[57] Writing in the *Fabian Quarterly*, Guy Rowson, Labour MP for Farnworth, reoriented the debate from a narrow focus on the health of the worker to one that encompassed the working-class family. Rowson maintained that because wives were in charge of family budgets, they suffered unduly from holidays without pay. For that reason he had no doubt that annual paid holidays would 'be regarded as a boon in thousands of working-class homes' because they would reduce the workload for wives.[58] Rowson, like many other middle-class supporters of paid holidays, recognised household budgeting as work, yet he also imagined that work as the undisputed domain of women. Just as proponents of family allowances assumed that mothers took responsibility for the nutritional state of their children, Rowson never doubted that household budgeting was done by women. His assumptions, however, also affected the way he imagined and promoted the working-class household as a heterosexual enterprise. The male breadwinner worked outside the home, and the female worked within the sphere of the home on a budget limited by, and contingent upon, the wages of her spouse. His assumption, based on nineteenth-century notions of separate spheres associated with middle-class values and ideals, did not take into account the reality of the labour market or the modern working-class home.[59]

In the interwar period the number of unskilled married and unmarried women workers in the new industries grew at a faster rate than the number of men employed.[60] The First World War also changed the gender balance in the population and some women were single parents as well as the head of their households.[61] Other working-class women took more seasonal and part-time work in hotel service or catering to supplement the family income. Some, like the infamous 'Blackpool landladies', created an industry within their homes, accommodating boarders and seasonal guests.[62] Other women cooked, cleaned, or took in laundry for an income, and expected working children to contribute to the family economy.[63] They did so in addition to their care-giving roles, with or without the wages of a male breadwinner.[64] Although some unemployed or disabled men helped with the housework and childcare, this was the exception rather than the rule, and a breach of accepted masculine roles.[65]

At the same time, Ross McKibbin argues, this gendered household was one to which working-class men and women aspired.[66] Thus Rowson's argument appealed to many workers. Nevertheless, for many working women and their families, the consumption of pleasure was a luxury when food, fuel, and rent constituted a large percentage of the weekly income. A study of working-class motherhood in London between 1870 and 1918 suggests that family survival was the mother's main charge among the poor, with food as the primary focus of concern.[67] For many poor women, motherhood demanded self-denial, resourcefulness, and inventive (or even illegal) procurement of food for the family. The Boer War and the First World War brought the health and fitness of the nation into sharp focus, so that by 1926 the Board of Education promoted housekeeping and family budgeting as a key element in the education of adolescent girls, and magazines such as *Woman and Home* and *Good Housekeeping* proclaimed housekeeping as both a 'craft and a profession'.[68] For working-class households, however, the constraints of low wages marked the limits of getting and spending. Thus Rowson's argument for paid holidays harnessed the popular image of the modern housewife as a domestic consumer, while at the same time it highlighted the financial and nutritional hardships experienced by many workers' wives.[69] Yet, by focusing on the plight of the 'poor housewife', Rowson failed to fully grasp the complex financial relationships within the working-class household. His argument also left little room to contemplate the possibility of female labour outside the home and male involvement in unpaid chores within. And yet it appealed to many workers and received support from constituencies on the political left concerned with the plight of the poor, and those on both sides of the political spectrum determined to maintain a patriarchal family structure. The dual images of the working male as the family breadwinner and the 'struggling' housewife as the 'victim' made a more salient and persuasive argument in a society that was critical of working married women and that failed to give workers annual paid holidays.

As Rowson led the political campaign for paid holidays, the popular press promoted the image of the struggling housewife and maintained pressure on Parliament to pass the legislation. In June 1937 the leftist *Daily Herald* published letters from readers that illustrated the problem of unpaid holidays. One author, calling himself 'Military Medalist' and the father of two children, asked readers to 'picture a good wife and mother going to an early grave; children growing up in C3 condition [unfit for national service], and [his] own mental torment', because of the lack of money for a holiday. Mrs Hewitt of Hebburn-on-Tyne claimed that holidays meant 'making one weeks' wages go the way of two', while the wife of a bricklayer in Lowestoft claimed that her last holiday was nineteen years previously, just before she married. Mr R. G. Woods of Bristol reiterated the problem of unpaid holidays in his letter to the *Herald*. Woods maintained that he and his wife dreaded bank holidays because they meant 'a "lock-out" with the worry of a light pay packet and "going short," and a new struggle to get straight'. Like many thousands of other working-class families, the Woods 'struggled on' without paid holidays and without an annual holiday away from home.[70]

Just before the Easter bank holiday, the more conservative *Daily Express* also conducted a campaign to illustrate Britain's backwardness on the issue of worker leisure. The paper claimed that twenty-four nations, including Chile, Venezuela, France, Finland, Norway, and the USSR, granted annual paid holidays to all workers, and others, including Sweden and Denmark, were considering the legislation.[71] The campaign continued as a *Daily Express* staff reporter brought a human-interest story to the campaign when he visited a Mr and Mrs Charles Turner, of Stratford, to illustrate the plight of a working-class family during the unpaid Easter holiday. Not only did the family eat poorly during public holidays, but also neither Mr nor Mrs Turner had ever 'been away' for a holiday in their lives.[72] Juxtaposed to a photograph of swarming Easter holiday crowds, this article once again placed the cares of the working-class household budget at the centre of the holidays-with-pay campaign.

During the Easter holiday weekend another *Express* reporter went to Brighton, a favourite seaside resort for many Londoners, to investigate how many of the visitors received paid holidays. Of every ten people interviewed, nine received pay for the Easter holiday. The reporter claimed, 'It was a tonic to find that nine out of ten of the people I talked to were being paid during Easter, "Otherwise", they said, "we wouldn't be able to come" to Brighton.' On the other hand, the reporter argued, 'It was depressing to meet the people who were trying to make the most of the sunshine and then going home to pinch and scrape this week.' The reporter described a meeting with Mr and Mrs Albert Johnson, who did not enjoy a paid Easter holiday. 'Feeding their baby boy ice-cream by the Palace Pier', Mr Johnson cheerily responded to the reporter's questions: 'No good being miserable about it, but when I only earn £2 15s a week the loss of two-and-a-half days' pay makes a big difference.'[73]

In response to the popular campaign, and in preparation for the introduction of a new holiday bill when Parliament reopened in the autumn, in 1937 the women of the Labour Party organised a 'Seaside Campaign' for holidays with pay throughout July and August.[74] The organisers displayed thousands of posters and distributed over one million leaflets in their demand for a universal legal obligation to provide paid leisure time for all workers.[75] In addition, Labour women convened over 150 meetings in over forty seaside resorts, including Southend, Swansea, Sidmouth, Deal, Newhaven, Brighton, Dover, Blackpool, Weston-Super-Mare and Great Yarmouth, and invited Labour MPs and mayors to speak in support of holidays with pay.[76] The campaign targeted those fortunate enough to enjoy a summer seaside holiday and emphasised the millions who could not.[77] The seaside holiday campaign grassroots workers were the volunteer women and the youth of the Labour Party. The speakers at the meetings were most often men – either elected and waged representatives or those standing for election. Thus even the work of the campaigners modelled the notion that women undertook unwaged work while men received the benefits of wages.

The seaside campaign initiated by the women of the Labour Party not only supported party policy but also reflected the broader aims of Labour women, who sought to 'enhance society's valuation of women's maternal and domestic role' throughout the interwar years.[78] While supporting the right to work and opposing the marriage bar, Labour women also recognised the contribution women's unwaged work made to the economy and wanted to make this visible. The arguments given for the need for paid holidays focused on the problems and stresses experienced by the working-class housewife faced with the responsibility of feeding her family during unpaid holidays.[79] Indeed, the importance of women's domestic role was emphasised by Labour women in an earlier investigation into the connection between unpaid holidays and the nutritional state of working-class families. In May 1936, a year before the seaside campaign, investigators presented their findings to the National Conference of Labour Women. Working-class women, they argued, should not be blamed for the poor nutritional state of their children. Instead, they should be lauded for their ability to overcome the exigencies of low wages, unemployment, and unpaid holidays that contributed to the dietary deficiencies of the British public. The only way to improve the health of the nation's children, the investigators claimed, was to accommodate the domestic needs of the housewife through increased wages and the provision of paid holidays for all workers.[80] By placing the plight of the working-class housewife at the centre of the debate over worker leisure, Labour women sought to elevate the value of the domestic and unwaged work of women.

The left-wing *Daily Herald* supported the Labour women's seaside campaign and joined the crusade. An investigative journalist for the *Herald* went to a working-class neighbourhood in London to ask residents about their experience of holidays. Significantly, S. E. R. Wynne began his article with a description of the outsides of the homes: 'Such very clean doors – the knockers polished so that I could see my face in them as I stood on the step. And the steps themselves were newly whitened.' Once over the difficult introductions, Wynne claimed, 'You would never suspect the stories behind those doors' when he asked simply, 'What do you do about holidays?' The replies to the question posed to six families in the same neighbourhood revealed a variety of answers and a range of experiences. Wynne employed nineteenth-century imagery of the clearly deserving poor (based on cleanliness) as a signifier of respectability. The vivid description of the spotlessness of the homes signalled to readers of the *Daily Herald* that these were respectable households, worthy of public support.[81] The first family, a 68–year-old non-unionised printer and his wife, claimed that they had had a holiday once. Mrs B qualified the answer and claimed she and the kiddies went to Ramsgate for a week during the war years, without her husband, when he earned 'good money in war work'. This year, however, as part of the Coronation celebrations, Mr B looked forward to a week's paid holiday.[82] The couple planned to go to Folkstone, where three years earlier Mrs B had supported them both as a waitress when Mr B lost his job. The second couple, Tom and his 'pale, thin, tired-eyed wife', never took a holiday. She explained to Wynne, 'He's a painter, you see. Works when he's lucky, nine or ten months a year and then gets stopped when the weather's bad.' The couple experienced financial hardship during bank holidays because 'Tom is just put off – 7s cut out of his £2 2s a week'. For Tom and his 'pale, thin, tired-eyed wife', a summer holiday was unthinkable on the wages he earned. The third family described in the article made their own holiday in the summer – fruit and hop-picking in Kent.[83] Although Mrs Bill claimed that the hard work and long days in the fields made the whole family 'feel good', Wynne surmised that 'Mrs. Bill was not quite [as] enthusiastic as she wanted to suggest. The accommodation, for one thing, is doubtful: huts where she does all the cooking with her own utensils, and has to bring her own bedding.' This was a working holiday, with Mrs Bill undertaking a double shift outside the comfort of her home. The reporter could not believe that hop-picking was a recuperative holiday for this or any other housewife. [84]

The next door revealed David, a tin-plater, recently moved from Wales to London for the sake of his wife's poor health. David's company offered one hour of holiday pay for each week worked – but only to men who joined the Territorial Army and spent their holidays in training camp. David told Wynne, 'I want to be fit to work, not fit to fight. I won't take their money.' In that case, Wynne concluded, the health of David's wife would probably not improve. The final knock revealed an unemployed man, Mr N, who supported his wife and three children through seasonal and part-time work as a barman and porter. This family felt fortunate, as a holiday benevolent fund meant that the two younger children would experience a seaside holiday this year. '"Thank God for that fund," say Mr. and Mrs. N, and they mean it … They are grateful, sincerely, poignantly … One day they hope for a job and a holiday for themselves', and so, claimed the reporter, should the readers of the *Herald*.[85]

As the *Herald*, and other popular dailies like the *Express*, detailed the predicament of many low-paid workers who did not receive holidays with pay, Rowson introduced a new bill in Parliament that obliged employers to grant annual paid holiday of a minimum of eight consecutive days for all workers. Most Parliamentarians supported the bill. It received a second reading in the House of Commons and went to a Standing Committee for further discussion. Despite Parliamentary support, however, Conservative members of the Committee removed the obligatory clause. When Rowson disowned the altered Bill, the largely Conservative National Government decided to avoid further controversy and dropped it entirely.[86]

The continued press support for paid holidays, however, forced the government to convene an investigation into the possibility of extending holidays with pay to all workers. The Holidays With Pay Committee, led by Labour MP Lord Amulree, met for over a year to explore the extent to which holidays with pay already existed and to look into the possibility of extending the provision to include the nineteen and a half million manual workers who earned less than £250 per year.[87] As the Committee compiled its report, the press and the leisure industry maintained pressure on the government and the Committee through the publication of excerpts from the proceedings and through their own analysis of the problems associated with an extension of paid leisure.

The Amulree Committee

Lord Amulree oversaw the Holidays With Pay Committee, which assembled information from a number of sources, including government statistics and reports, as well as interviews with union representatives and employers. While the members of the Committee grappled with the information, the publicity surrounding the Committee encouraged many employers to grant annual paid holidays to full-time manual workers in anticipation of the legislation that, they believed, would soon force them to do so. In 1936 an estimated one and a half million workers received annual paid holiday. Two years later, the figure was almost four and a half million, even without the support of legislation.[88] Indeed, the increase in the number of workers granted paid holidays seemed to support the Minister of Labour's assertion that there was a 'national desire' for a 'beneficent revolution' that would give all workers in Britain paid leisure time.[89] Despite the alleged desire, however, in April 1938, fifteen and a half million full-time workers still did not receive annual paid holidays in any form.

The Committee received evidence presented by the TUC that persuasively argued that the nervous strain caused by mechanisation decreased worker productivity.[90] Regular annual holidays, the TUC asserted, counteracted the damaging psychological effects of dull, repetitive work and improved industrial efficiency.[91] Modern work, the data suggested, required modern remedies that included annual paid holidays. Further, the evidence presented recognised that wives, mothers, and sisters of workers contributed to industrial efficiency through their unpaid management of the household. While the union representatives shied away from likening household chores to modern industrial production, they did suggest that unpaid housework could be as debilitating. As a matter of 'social justice', a TUC representative claimed, women who worked in the home deserved to benefit from the health and recreational value of holidays with pay.[92] Behind this argument lay the assumption that annual paid holidays not only renewed the health and efficiency of the worker, they also functioned to regenerate the working-class family and served as a demonstration of collective egalitarianism for waged and unwaged work.

That egalitarianism, however, was not an argument for gender equality, but it did mirror contemporary feminist demands for paid housework.[93] The TUC recognised the importance of women's unpaid contributions in the home. It did not, however, challenge gender roles or suggest that men should contribute to the management of the household in any way, except financially. The recognition of the importance of the unpaid role of women came at a time when some unions were engaged in a concerted campaign to exclude married women from the workplace. Not only did married women experience discrimination in the workplace due to lower wages and 'marriage bars', but after 1930 most became ineligible for unemployment benefits.[94] The labour market and the emergent welfare system in Britain, Susan Pedersen claims, 'developed along male breadwinner lines, disproportionately distributing income to men on the assumption that they were (or soon would be) supporting dependent wives'.[95] Social justice was not, in this sense, tied specifically to the idea that married women deserved full-time employment and annual paid holidays for themselves. Instead, the TUC's argument reinforced traditional gender roles that tied married women to economic and leisure dependence within the home through exclusionary practices in the workplace.[96]

Of course, the family holiday did not necessarily mean leisure for women. Although the TUC argued that women would benefit from annual paid holidays, cheap holidays often entailed more work packing and unpacking, worrying and looking after children, shopping, cooking, and making beds in a caravan, tent, or boarding house. In order to keep down the cost of the holiday, boarding houses often allowed guests to buy and even cook their own food during their stay.[97] The responsibility for the provision of food and meals for the family remained within the realm of women's work even on holiday. A series of articles in the *Daily Herald* suggested ways in which women could plan ahead so as to experience some semblance of leisure time with the family.[98] One article even gave suggestions to women about how to cope with the difficulties of cooking away from home.[99] Thus, while the TUC supported the rights of all workers to annual paid leisure time, the left-wing press exposed one of the major constituent parts of that 'so-called' justice, the unpaid labour of women, even on holiday.

As the Committee gathered information and took detailed testimony from union representatives and employers, the issues gained in clarity. Three areas of concern emerged: the interruption to domestic industries that workers' holidays would cause if taken at the same time; the question of how the annual paid holiday would be financed; and the lack of facilities at which the newly leisured workers could spend their holiday time. The concern surrounding the interruption of domestic industrial production faltered, as entire industries such as the Lancashire cotton industry proved that the closure of factories for a week in the summer allowed the industry to repair and update machinery and did not interrupt production. Furthermore, the cotton industry claimed that employee–employer relations were improved, as negotiations between the two groups settled the week of factory closure. Evidence also suggested that regular holidays reduced absenteeism and improved worker efficiency.

The question of how holidays with pay would be financed caused more problems. While wakes weeks provided the Committee with successful examples of factory closure during the summer holiday period without detriment to the domestic industries, these enforced holidays were paid for by employee contributions. One well-known industrialist, Sir Malcolm Stewart, suggested that holidays with pay should be the right of every worker and paid for entirely by employers. Holidays, in his view, were the responsibility of industry 'prior even to the interest of capital'.[100] The majority of industrialists, however, did not agree with Sir Malcolm. Profits remained the chief motivation and employer contributions to holidays with pay would potentially interfere with the profit margin. Those opposed to the idea of employer contributions claimed that the cost of holidays would be passed on to consumers as it was, in effect, a statutory increase in wages.[101] Others argued there would be an unequal burden on certain industries that could force closures and create unemployment. When employers suggested that holidays with pay should be left to voluntary arrangements, many union officials feared that paid leisure would not become universal. Some companies could not afford the cost of workers' holidays, while other companies would simply choose not to offer their employees paid holidays.[102]

Union representatives, however, agreed with Sir Malcolm and argued that if salaried workers received paid annual leisure as a right, why shouldn't manual workers? While industrialists supported the idea of employee wage deductions to finance annual holidays, union representatives disagreed. Employee contribution schemes maintained class distinctions between blue- and white-collar workers and, union officials argued, wage deductions interfered 'with the worker's own distribution of his income by forcing him to have a certain amount deducted from his wages for the purpose of holidays'.[103] When asked if the TUC would consider a system where the employer and the state contributed to a holiday fund, Sir Walter Citrine, the chief witness for the TUC, asked the Committee, 'Who is the State?' In answer to his rhetorical question, Sir Walter answered, 'We, the taxpayers' are the state. Thus, any scheme to include state contributions, according to Sir Walter, was simply another way to make taxpaying workers pay.[104]

After a year, the Amulree Committee remained undecided about how to fund holidays for all workers. Several possibilities existed, including a central fund administered and paid for in the same manner as unemployment insurance, by contributions made by the employee, employer, and the state.[105] Despite the indecision, all Committee members agreed on the principle of annual paid holidays for all workers.

The timing of that leisure and the provision of sites of leisure for the eighteen million prospective new holiday makers and their families presented the Committee and the leisure industry with a sizeable political and logistical problem. If the Committee recommended holidays with pay for all manual workers, sheer numbers threatened to overwhelm the British leisure industry, should the millions of newly leisured workers descend on popular resorts in the same month. Reports about congested resorts suggested that the traditional seaside venues were already experiencing severe problems during bank holidays.[106] An article in the *Economist* described the chief characteristic of British holidays as 'congestion'.[107] An extension of paid holidays would cause more disorder and strain the transport facilities even further. As a picture of crowds of people on the beach during the August bank holiday in the *Caterer and Hotelkeeper* illustrated, holidays with pay threatened to create more chaos on the roads, on the railways, and in the resorts. 'This crowded August scene at a British resort may be seen in other months', predicted Sir James Marchant, an eminent economist, in a speech to the Bournemouth Hotel and Boarding House Association. The leisure industry 'must prepare for a great rise in the number of holiday makers' in the coming season, Sir James insisted.[108]

The idea of leisure and chaos in the 1930s rested on the relationship between citizenship and aesthetic sensibilities. Those concerned with the public spaces of the nation, including beaches, parks, and resorts, saw the 'appropriate conduct and aesthetic ability' of citizens as crucial elements in the determination of who should be allowed access to those spaces. Those who claimed cultural guardianship of the landscape in the interwar years constantly questioned the kind of public to be permitted and cultivated. While the discussion about teeming resorts in August ostensibly focused on the prospect of even more crowds, should the government choose to extend holidays with pay, the issue was really one of citizenship. Arguments for citizenship, David Matless suggests, 'worked in relation to a sense of anti-citizenship'.[109] In the 1930s, the potential increase in numbers of 'citizen' holiday makers with acceptable 'aesthetic ability' also expanded the potential for an increase in vulgar behaviour and anti-citizenship.[110] Thus the issue of overcrowding signalled larger concerns of cultural trespass, public behaviour, and rights of access to national space.

The problem of overcrowding was a subject of great concern at the 1937 British Health Resorts Association (HRA) Conference, and discussions among delegates shifted the image of the worker from groups of individual consumers to crowds. While Association members agreed that holidays with pay had great economic merit and would increase workers' health and efficiency, the efficacy of annual holidays would be thwarted by overcrowded resorts and a lack of adequate facilities.[111] The August holiday, in particular, already caused overcrowding and increased prices, and led to staff shortages.[112] If, as many in the leisure industry hoped, the season was extended, prices would stabilise and seasonal staff, difficult to find because of the short season, would benefit from a longer work year and thus qualify for unemployment insurance.[113] In a speech to the HRA in Blackpool later that year, Mr Roland Robinson, MP for Blackpool, argued for a holiday season that spread from April to October. This, he assured members, would alleviate congestion, keep expenses relatively low, and extend the work season. 'So far as the English weather is concerned', Robinson continued, 'there is nothing to indicate that we can rely upon any better weather in one of these months than in another.' The problem, as Robinson saw it, lay in the habit of 'looking upon the August holiday as an essential part of our elementary education system', but, he argued, 'there is no reason why this should be'.[114]

The August holiday habit, however, proved more difficult to solve. Mr Brown, the Minister of Labour suggested a solution to the problem. Brown argued that schools should alter their traditional schedules to accommodate family holidays.[115] Workers traditionally followed the school examination and holiday schedule, taking holiday time during July and August, the two warmest months of the year. If schools changed their schedules, workers could holiday at other times of the year, and the resorts would not be overburdened.[116] The Department of Education proved intractable on the issue of changing either school holidays or examination timetables, despite a concerted campaign by the hotel industry, which lobbied Parliament and induced national newspapers to ballot readers on the subject.[117] If part of the justification for paid holidays rested on the idea of family regeneration, the inclusion of school children in holiday time mattered. An article in the *Daily Express* accused the school system of barring families from enjoying an annual holiday together. The following day the same paper attempted to persuade those without children to take a holiday in June or September, when the beaches were empty.[118] The *Express* advocated a staggered holiday policy, based on the presence or absence of children. However, the most expensive holiday months remained July and August, largely because of the weather. The *Express*'s idea thus consigned the single and the childless to colder weather but cheaper accommodation, while forcing families to holiday in the most expensive, if warmest, months.[119]

Some members of the Amulree Committee saw the debate over the timing of workers' holidays in terms of class. One vocal member, Mr Rosetti, Secretary to the Minister of Labour, claimed that the supporters of staggered holidays were class snobs who 'shudder at the thought of a huge crowd swarming on the beach'. While Rosetti believed the vast majority of wage earners enjoyed crowds, he claimed that workers on holiday should not 'suffer unduly' from congestion during July and August or be compelled to take holidays in the cooler months of May and June.[120] Rosetti's solution lay in the provision of alternative forms of holiday accommodation so that workers could enjoy the recuperative effects of an annual holiday in warm weather without undue expense or overcrowding. As some of the Committee made favourable references to the German model, *Kraft durch Freude* ('Strength through Joy') organisations, and the *Dopolavoro* ('After work') organisation in Italy, other members looked to union and commercial models in Britain and suggested the 'extension of holiday camps and similar facilities' as alternative sites of leisure for workers.[121] While Committee members pointed out that it was not 'desirable to "shepherd" people into common centres at holiday periods, the establishment of rationally organised holiday facilities', such as union and commercial holiday camps, 'would enable many who could not afford a holiday at all to … go away and recuperate under attractive conditions'.[122]

Indeed, the quality and attractiveness of inexpensive accommodation in Britain was a major cause of concern for the Amulree Committee. When invited to speak to constituents of the Heath and Resorts Association, Committee member Ernest Bevin frankly urged the resort industry to change its prevalent attitude to working-class patrons. Middle-class caterers, Bevin claimed, viewed working people as 'vulgar' and considered 'cheap and nasty accommodation' with 'garish and tawdry coverings' good enough for these guests. This, Bevin argued, was a short-sighted attitude. In five or ten years this type of accommodation would simply not appeal to workers. In addition, industry, 'which will have to pay for the holidays, will demand the best possible results for its money and expect their workers to come back fit and well', not full of 'stodgey, unappetising food'. Further, Bevin asserted, resorts should pay more attention to the needs of working-class children and their mothers. 'After all', Bevin explained, 'the holiday is not just for the man, it is for the woman also.' The problem of suitable facilities for all the family was a 'very serious one indeed', Bevin claimed. Unless resorts adequately catered for children, with organised activities even in bad weather, 'the holiday will not have very beneficial results for the mother or the family'.[123] For members of the Committee, then, the provision of suitable sites of pleasure for workers and their families included inexpensive, but not cheap, accommodation, amusement for all ages, and nutritious food.

While the TUC and Committee members attempted to establish a solution to the problem of inadequate accommodation and inexpensive holidays, luxury holiday-camp entrepreneurs focused attention on the problems and the possibilities associated with millions of newly leisured workers and created a viable new industry with a vision of pleasure that competed with the traditional British holiday resorts. Unlike hoteliers who feared holidays with pay would bring resort chaos, entrepreneurs such as Henry 'Harry' Warner and William 'Billy' Butlin saw the potential in the emergent working-class market. They established their luxury holiday camps in opposition to small hotels and boarding houses, as sites of inexpensive mass pleasure that catered specifically to the needs of the housewife by providing childcare facilities and entertainment programmes for all ages in relatively luxurious surroundings with three hot, nutritious meals a day.

For the Amulree Committee, Butlin's and Warner's holiday camps proved to be the commercial answer to a difficult political problem. They were cheap, easily and quickly constructed, provided affordable mass accommodation and entertainment, and, perhaps most importantly, offered all family members a time to relax. The Committee could make the recommendation that all workers should receive one week's annual paid holiday only if there were sites at which that leisure could take place. Echoing the gendered language of the holidays with pay campaign, the Committee concluded in its report that facilities such as Warner's and Butlin's mass camps catered especially well to 'the [male] worker who wishes to take his family on an inexpensive holiday in which his wife can enjoy rest and recuperation and freedom so far as possible from arduous household duties'.[124] Thus, luxury holidays camps provided the physical sites at which the symbol of the campaign for paid holidays – the suffering housewife – could receive a break from her unpaid work without undermining the gender system that was believed to be central to the working-class household.

When the Committee published the report at the end of April 1938, it recommended that all full-time workers receive at least seven days' consecutive paid annual holiday, in addition to bank holidays. The report also recommended the immediate construction of large-scale holiday camps to accommodate the newly leisured workers and their families. The response of local governments, entrepreneurs, and unions was immediate. Municipal councils offered lower local tax rates for commercial holiday camps and even considered the construction of municipally funded and run holiday camps.[125] One week after the publication of the Committee's report, Butlin opened his second luxury holiday camp at Clacton-on-Sea, with accommodation for over 2,000, and announced plans to extend his camp at Skegness to provide accommodation for 4,500 guests each week.[126] Butlin then advertised his plans to open similar large-scale holiday camps at Ryde on the Isle of Wight in 1939 and Bournemouth in 1940.[127] His one-time partner, Harry Warner, opened his fourth holiday camp in 1938, with accommodation for a total of 40,000 visitors each season. In May 1939, the Derbyshire Miners' Union opened a holiday camp to accommodate a thousand people each week, based on the successful Butlin and Warner luxury camp models.[128] The LMS Railway and travel agent Thomas Cook & Son, Ltd. opened a large holiday camp in Prestatyn, North Wales, that accommodated 1,700 visitors, in July 1939, and the TUC proposed to build a large-scale holiday camp in Yarmouth for union members.[129] By the summer of 1939, Britain's new mass holiday industry stood poised to cater to millions of newly leisured workers and their families.

Conclusion

By the time the Holidays With Pay Act (1938) passed into law, luxury holiday camps had quickly become a feature of summer life in Britain.[130] They offered an enticing vision of leisure at a moment when British workers demanded paid holiday time and public policy sought to democratise leisure. Building on earlier ideas of all-inclusive camping holidays, Warner and Butlin developed more comfortable accommodation for the emerging working-class family market. Encouraged by the interwar debate that politicised leisure, Warner and Butlin seized the opportunity, even before the passage of the Holidays With Pay Act, to provide low-cost holiday destinations for those economically excluded from traditional resorts.[131] In response to a growing demand for inexpensive holidays and the popular campaign for paid leisure time, Warner and Butlin advertised their camps as 'A Week's Holiday for a Week's Pay', and targeted working-class families with the offer of one-price, pre-paid family holidays. Equipped with up-to-date facilities that catered for the perceived needs and desires of the worker's housewife – individual sleeping chalets, shops, hairdressing services, floodlit swimming pools, concerts, childcare services, ballroom dancing, tennis, boating, and bowling – the mass commercial holiday camps created by Warner and Butlin provided a new concept in modern leisure as package holidays under one roof.[132] The creation of this new form of mass pleasure both responded to and advanced the desire of the government to expand paid leisure time for workers and provide suitable accommodation for working-class families, especially the 'struggling' housewife.

As a central motif in the popular campaign for paid holidays in Britain, the plight of the working-class housewife appeared to garner support from workers because it shifted the image of the modern worker as emasculated by rationalisation and mass production to one that represented the British manual worker as the family breadwinner. While that image might not be an accurate depiction of the interwar household, it was one to which many working-class families aspired. At the same time that the image imagined the roles within the working-class household as divided along traditional gender lines, it also elevated the role of women's unwaged labour in the home as an important adjunct to waged labour and thus to the modern industrial economy. This appealed to feminists as well as to constituencies on the political left and right. Thus the success of the campaign rested on the rhetoric that appealed to a large cross-section of the population through gendered arguments that both imagined the British worker as the family breadwinner and used the image of the suffering housewife as a symbol of workers' needs.

The image also appealed to the new social sciences that focused on the family unit as the locus of workers' well-being. In their view, the role of the housewife gained significance as that of family budget-keeper and nutritionist. At the same time, the focus on the family meant that it was necessary to allow workers to holiday with their school-children during the six-weeks' summer break. This posed a significant logistical problem to those catering for workers and their families at the already overcrowded resorts. Yet, even as this vision of the wage-earner's family posed political problems, it also provided a discursive framework in which a new culture of mass leisure developed in the interwar years. The political and popular campaign for paid holidays and the image of the struggling housewife not only succeeded in bringing about the Holidays With Pay Act, it also provided the agenda for mass holidays that centred specifically on the needs of the housewife. The support of the Holidays With Pay Committee legitimised the holiday-camp industry and placed the provision of sites for mass leisure at the centre of debates over resort development in the mid-twentieth century.

Finally, the provisions of the Holidays With Pay Act, ostensibly passed as a milestone in social equity, reinforced the image of the British worker as male and maintained women's inequity in the labour market. While the popular campaign for paid leisure emphasised the plight of the 'poor British housewife', those workers who did not qualify for annual paid leisure time in 1938 included part-time and domestic service workers, those most likely to be female. Thus, while the Act recognised the right of all workers in a modern industrial nation to annual paid leisure time as an important signifier of social citizenship, it also defined who those workers were and, through exclusion, who they were not.[133] For many women, leisure came at a cost measured largely in terms of economic dependence. While the legislation embodied a shift in attitudes to working-class leisure, it also reinforced more conservative attitudes to women and work and the division of roles within the household on the basis of gender.

Other contemporary issues, such as the alleviation of hunger, the living wage debate, and the notion of social citizenship, fashioned the campaign rhetoric, predisposed the Committee, and finally shaped the Act itself. The campaign and the provisions of the Holidays With Pay Act are significant in a broad sense in that they exemplify some of the major debates and contradictions of the interwar years and serve as a prism through which to view the emergence of the welfare state. The campaign and the final legislation in many ways illustrate the multiple constituencies that influenced and made up the government of modernity. While the final provisions of the Act failed to provide *all* workers equally with annual paid holidays, the leisure industry that developed in response to the campaign for holidays with pay embodied some of the principles of the later welfare state that promised cradle-to-grave provisions for all Britons. Holiday camps provided the basic elements of welfare through accommodation, food, and childcare. Thus the vision for worker leisure that emerged in the interwar years was implicated in the development of one of the most comprehensive welfare systems in Europe.

Notes

1 'Mrs. Turner not buying joint today – her husband's pay is halved this week', *Daily Express*, 16 April 1938, p. 3.
2 The Holidays With Pay Committee, chaired by Lord Amulree, met for a year before publishing its recommendations. See The National Archives, Public Records Office, Kew (hereafter TNA: PRO), Holidays With Pay Committee Report, 28 April 1838, LAB 31/1, p. 1.
3 Holidays With Pay Act, November 1938, House of Commons Parliamentary Papers, (London: His Majesty's Stationery Office, 1938).
4 In 1922, 130 different industries or regions had paid holiday agreements that varied from three to twenty-one days per year. *Ministry of Labour Gazette*, Vol. XXX No. 12, December 1922, pp. 474–5. By the time the Committee met in April 1937, a quarter of a million workers received paid holidays. J. A. R. Pimlott, *The English-man's holiday: A social history* [1947] (Sussex: Harvester Press, 1976), p. 214.
5 Walton, *British seaside*, pp. 57–61.
6 For example, Pimlott, *Englishman's holiday*, pp. 211–37, L. C. B. Seaman, *Life in Britain between the wars* (London: B. T. Batsford Ltd., 1970), p. 164.
7 G. Cross, *Time and money: The making of consumer culture* (London: Routledge, 1993), pp. 99–127.
8 See S. Jones, 'Trade Union policy between the wars: The case of holidays with pay in Britain', *International Review of Social History*, 31 (1986), pp. 40–55.
9 A. Bingham, *Gender, modernity and the popular press in inter-war Britain* (Oxford: Oxford University Press, 2004), pp. 84–110. Together these five daily newspapers had a circulation of several million in interwar Britain.
10 Holidays With Pay Committee Report, 28 April 1938, TNA: PRO, LAB1/1, p. 38.
11 E. P. Thompson, *Customs in common: Studies in traditional popular culture* (New York: Norton, 1993), pp. 352–403.
12 Holidays With Pay Committee Report, 28 April 1938, TNA: PRO, LAB 1/1, pp. 11–12.
13 Walton, *British seaside*, p. 15.
14 T. Bennett, 'Ideology, hegemony, pleasure: Blackpool', in T. Bennett, C. Mercer and J. Woollacott, eds *Popular culture and social relations* (Milton Keynes: Open University Press, 1986), pp. 135–54, J. K. Walton, 'The demand for working-class seaside holidays in Victorian Britain', *Economic History Review*, new series, 34:2 (May 1981), pp. 249–65, and R. Poole, 'Oldham Wakes', in J. K. Walton and J. Walvin, eds *Leisure in Britain* (Manchester: Manchester University Press, 1983), pp. 71–98.
15 D. G. Green, 'The Friendly Societies and Adam-Smith Liberalism', in D. Gladstone, ed. *Before Beveridge: Welfare before the welfare state*, (London: IEA Health and Welfare Unit, 1999), pp. 18–25.

16 'First Co-operative Investment Trust, Limited', *Lansbury Labour Weekly*, 27 March 1926, p. 5. See also P. Gurney, *Co-operative culture and the politics of consumption in England, 1870–1930* (Manchester: Manchester University Press, 1996), and 'Labour's great arch: cooperation and cultural revolution in Britain, 1795–1926', in E. Furlough and C. Strikwerda, eds *Consumers against capitalism? Consumer cooperation in Europe, North America, and Japan, 1840–1990* (Lanham, MD: Rowman and Littlefield, 1999), pp. 135–72.

17 Gurney maintains that the Co-operative movement 'developed a transformative social and economic strategy based on the association of workers within the sphere of consumption'. Gurney, *Co-operative culture*, p. 22. Other scholars disagree and maintain that the Co-operative movement was simply another form of capitalism. See Hilton, *Consumerism*, pp. 35–41.

18 Barton, *Working-class organisations*, pp. 76–8.

19 Bailey, *Leisure and class*, pp. 47–115. For middle-class leisure activities see Rappaport, *Shopping for pleasure*, pp. 178–214.

20 Half-day excursion leaflets dated 1870s–1920s, John Johnson Collection Railways 10, Bodleian Library, Oxford (hereafter BL). See also Barton, *Working-class organisations*, pp. 73–106.

21 S. Dawson, 'The battle for Beachlands: Hayling Island and the development of coastal leisure in Britain, 1820–1960', *International Journal of Regional and Local Studies*, 3:1 (2007), 56–80.

22 London, Brighton and South Coast Railway, handbill, BL, John Johnson Travel Collection (hereafter JJTC). The Shop Act (1911) gave shop workers a paid half-day holiday on Wednesdays.

23 Elm Grove Free Church hosted a concert by members of the Band of Hope, *Hampshire Telegraph*, 30 September 1903. The Young Men's Institute winter programme began with a coffee evening at the Congregational church hall. *Hampshire Telegraph*, 10 November 1905.

24 Bailey, *Leisure and class*, pp. 47–90. While the theory of social control has recently been given less emphasis by scholars, Bailey's work remains important to an understanding of institutionalised working-class leisure in the nineteenth century.

25 Approximately 50 per cent of London's children belonged to organisations that went on camping trips. *The new survey of London life and labour: Life and leisure*, Vol. IX (London P. S. King & Son, 1935), pp. 78–88.

26 See Barton, *Working-class organisations*, pp. 107–32 for a discussion of collective bargaining for paid holidays.

27 Cross, *Time and money*, p. 81. George Lansbury (1859–1940), socialist and Christian pacifist, MP, editor of the *Daily Herald* and the leader of the Labour Party from 1932 to 1935.

28 *Lansbury Labour Weekly*, 17 April 1926, p. 5. This article claims that the Bill failed because of a lack of union support and agitation.

29 Jones, 'Trade Union Policy', p. 41.

30 P. Thane, 'The working class and state 'welfare' in Britain, 1880–1914', in D. Gladstone, ed. *Before Beveridge: Welfare before the welfare state*, (London: IEA

Health and Welfare Unit, 1999), pp. 86–112.

31 R. Rosenzweig, *Eight hours for what we will: Workers and leisure in an industrial city, 1870–1920* (Cambridge: Cambridge University Press, 1983), and C. Aron, *Working at play: A history of holidays in the United States* (Oxford: Oxford University Press, 1999).

32 D. Tanner, 'Restructuring postwar politics: Electing the governors', in K. Robbins, ed. *The British Isles, 1901–1951* (Oxford: Oxford University Press, 2002), pp. 50–4. The coalition government collapsed in 1922 and the general election returned a Conservative government to power.

33 See R. Graves and A. Lodge, *Long week-end: A social history of Great Britain, 1918–1939* [1940] (New York: Norton, 1963) and Pimlott, *Englishman's holiday*, pp. 211–68.

34 Holidays With Pay Committee Report, TNA: PRO, LAB 31/1, p. 12.

35 T. Veblen, *The theory of the leisure class* [1899] (London: Penguin, 1994), pp. 1–71.

36 See G. Braybon, *Women workers in the First World War* (London: Routledge, 1989), pp. 216–28, and Culleton, *Working-class culture*, pp. 169–76, R. McKibbin, *Classes and cultures: England 1918–1951* (Oxford: Oxford University Press, 1998), pp. 106–63.

37 The second Paid Holidays Bill failed to secure a second reading in the Conservative-led House of Commons.

38 'Holidays', Letter to the editor, *Lansbury Labour Weekly*, 17 April 1926, p. 5. The editor, George Lansbury, was a member of the Joint Committee on the Living Wage appointed by the government in 1927. See S. Pedersen, *Family, dependence, and the origins of the welfare state: Britain and France 1914–1945* (Cambridge: Cambridge University Press, 1993), pp. 192–208.

39 J. Vernon, *Hunger: A modern history* (Cambridge, MA: Belknap, 2007), pp. 81–117.

40 The TUC opposed family allowances because some felt that allowances paid to mothers emphasised the idea that working-class fathers were untrustworthy. Others saw family allowances as a way to force women out of the workplace, a reason to pay women less, prevent wage increases and discriminate against single workers. Pedersen, *Family dependence*, pp. 190–223.

41 Vernon, *Hunger*, pp. 118–58.

42 B. Drake, 'Starvation in the midst of plenty: A new plan for the state feeding of school children', *Fabian Tract* no. 240, December 1933.

43 A. Davin, 'Imperialism and motherhood', *History Workshop Journal*, 5 (Spring 1978), pp. 9–65. In the First World War the government recognised the importance of fried potatoes and fish to the working-class diet and fish fryers were exempt from conscription. J. Walton, *Fish and chips and the British working class, 1870–1940* (London: Leicester University Press, 1992), p. 19.

44 J. Vernon, 'The ethics of hunger and the assembly of society: the techno-politics of the school meal in Britain', *American Historical Review*, 110:3 (June 2005), pp. 693–725.

45 The Labour Party used similar rhetoric in its interwar campaign for price control. Hilton, *Consumerism*, pp. 108–36.

46 Aron, *Working at play*, pp. 197–8.

47 J. Greaves, *Industrial reorganisation and government policy in interwar Britain* (Aldershot: Ashgate, 2005).

48 A. Bullock, *The life and times of Ernest Bevin: Trade union leader 1881–1940* (London, Heinemann, 1960), chs 12–14. British industry lost a total of 356,340,000 work days due to strike action. Lloyd, *Empire, welfare state*, p. 146.

49 Taylorism deskilled labour, increased mechanization, and viewed labourers as merely cogs in the wheel of production. Cross, *Time and money*, pp. 28–33. The ILP expressed support for workers' holidays as a way to increase production in the 1920s. 'Labour: support for paid holidays', *The Times*, 9 January 1928, p. 1.

50 E. Winterton, MP (Labour) introduced the Annual Holiday Bill in 1929. Jones, 'Trade union policy', pp. 40–55.

51 J. Mensch, MD, 'The urban worker's need for holidays', *Labour Magazine*, Vol. X No. 11, March 1932, pp. 502–3.

52 Readers were offered a £2 prize for the article that exposed the worst working conditions in a factory, workshop or home industry. M. Philips, 'Where you work: £2 prize for the best exposure', *Lansbury Labour Weekly*, 3 April 1926, p. 2.

53 Aldous Huxley, *Brave new world* [1932] (New York, 1998).

54 Foreword, Huxley, ibid., p. xii.

55 See, for example, G. Cross, 'Holidays for all: The leisure question in the era of the Popular Front', *Journal of Contemporary History*, 24 (1989), pp. 599–621.

56 'Big holiday with pay drive: France and Belgium give fresh impetus to British workers', *Daily Herald*, 22 June 1936, p. 13.

57 'Meetings to be held at 200 Factories: Union hopes for thousands more members', *Daily Herald*, 22 June 1936, p. 13.

58 G. Rowson, 'Holidays with pay', *Fabian Quarterly* (London, 1937), p. 26.

59 For a discussion of middle-class family values see L. Davidoff and C. Hall, *Family fortunes: Men and women of the English middle class, 1780–1850* (London: University of Chicago Press, 1991), and J. Tosh, *A man's place: Masculinity and the middle-class home in Victorian England* (New Haven, CT: Yale University Press, 1999).

60 McKibbin, *Classes and cultures*, p. 109.

61 C. Steedman, *Childhood, culture and class in Britain: Margaret McMillan 1860–1931* (London: Virago, 1990), *Landscape for a good woman: A story of two lives* (New Brunswick, NJ: Rutgers University Press, 1994), and S. Rowbotham, *A century of women: The history of women in Britain and the United States in the twentieth century* (New York: Penguin, 1997), pp. 119–46.

62 Walton, 'Blackpool landlady revisited', pp. 23–30.

63 S. Todd, *Young women, work and family, 1918–1950* (Oxford: Oxford University Press, 2005), pp. 54–84.

64 W. Boyd and V. Ogilvie, eds *The challenge of leisure* (London: New Education Fellowship, 1936), p. 70.

65 J. Giles, *Women, identity and private life in Britain, 1900–50* (New York: St. Martin's Press, 1995), 27.

66 McKibbin, *Classes and cultures*, pp. 164–205.

67 E. Ross, *Love and toil: Motherhood in outcast London, 1870–1918* (New York: Oxford University Press, 1993), pp. 44–55.

68 Rowbotham, *Century of women*, p. 135.

69 'Malnutrition', Guy Rowson, MP, *House of Commons Parliamentary Debates* (hereafter *HCPD*) 13 April 1937, Vol. 322, pp. 853–99.

70 'Holidays with pay?' Letters to the Editor, *Daily Herald*, 22 June 1937, p. 8.

71 'Paid holidays go round the world', *Daily Express*, 13 April 1938, p. 9.

72 'Mrs. Turner not buying joint today', p. 3.

73 'Holidays with pay make Brighton brighter', *Daily Express*, 18 April 1938, p. 7.

74 'Holidays with pay', *Daily Herald*, 3 June 1937, p. 10.

75 'Fortnight's paid holiday at least', *Daily Herald*, 25 August 1937, p. 11.

76 'Hear this side at seaside', *Daily Herald*, 19 August 1937, p. 4.

77 'Labour women's drive went with a bang', *Daily Herald*, 5 July 1937, p. 13, and 'Crusade gives youth it's [*sic*] chance', *Daily Herald*, 19 July 1937, p. 11.

78 P. Thane, 'The women of the Labour Party and feminism, 1906–1945', in Harold L. Smith., ed. *British feminism in the twentieth century* (Amherst, MA: University of Massachusetts Press, 1990), pp. 124–43.

79 Hugh Dalton, MP, 'Labour's immediate programme', *Labour Woman*, May 1937, pp. 73–4.

80 '800 Labour women meet', *Daily Herald*, 18 May 1936, p. 13.

81 E. Ross, 'Not the sort that would sit on the doorstep: Respectability in pre-WWI London neighborhoods', *International Labor and Working Class History*, 27 (Spring 1985), pp. 39–59.

82 The coronation of George VI and Queen Elizabeth took place on 12 May 1937.

83 Hop-picking during the summer was a common type of family holiday where each member of the family earned a small wage from farmers who allowed the pickers to camp on their land. *Survey of London: Life and labour*, Vol. IX, p. 86.

84 S. E. R. Wynne, 'I knocked at six doors', *Daily Herald*, 23 July, 1937, p. 10.

85 Ibid.

86 Rowson, 'Holiday with pay', p. 26–31.

87 Holidays With Pay Committee Report, TNA: PRO, LAB 31/1, p. 1.

88 Holidays With Pay Committee Report, 28 April 1938, TNA: PRO, LAB 31/1, pp. 12–20.

89 Mr Ernest Brown, Minister of Labour, quoted in 'Spreadover holidays at last – principle accepted by Parliament', *Caterer and Hotel Keeper*, 8 April 1938, pp. 17–18.

90 The International Labour Organisation made the same argument at the 1935 conference in Geneva. Rowson, 'Holidays with pay', pp. 30–1.

91 British industry underwent rationalization in the 1920s and 1930s. See R. Church, *The rise and decline of the British motor industry* (Basingstoke: Macmillan, 1994), and D. Hebdige, 'Towards a cartography of taste, 1935–1962', *Hiding in the light: On images and things* [1989] (London: Routledge, 1994), pp. 45–76.

92 Holidays With Pay Committee Report, Part II, 28 April 1938, TNA: PRO, LAB 31/1, p. 25.

93 H. Land, 'Eleanor Rathbone and the economy of the family', *British feminism in the twentieth century*, pp. 104–23, and Thane, 'Women of the Labour Party', pp. 124–43.

94 Married women were ineligible for unemployment benefit unless they could prove that they had not left insurable employment and that they were actively seeking insurable employment. Pedersen, *Family dependence*, pp. 297–316.

95 Ibid., p. 130 and P. Thane, 'Population politics in post-war British culture', in B. Conekin, F. Mort and C. Waters, eds *Moments of modernity: Reconstructing Britain 1945–1964* (London: Rivers Oram Press, 1999), pp. 114–33.

96 Married and single women were often the first workers 'let go' in a slow period and thus often disqualified from holidays with pay because of the qualifying service time period clause in the collective agreements.

97 C. Langhamer, *Women's leisure in England, 1920–1960* (Manchester: Manchester University Press, 2000), pp. 133–86.

98 'Time off for Mother', *Daily Herald*, 30 April 1936, p. 5, and 'It's Mother's holiday too', *Daily Herald*, 9 July 1936, p. 5.

99 'Cooking away from home', *Daily Herald*, 31 July 1936, p. 5.

100 Holidays With Pay Committee Report, TNA: PRO, LAB 31/1, p. 26.

101 Ibid., pp. 29–30.

102 Ibid., p. 28.

103 Ibid.

104 'Holidays with Pay: TUC scheme', *Daily News Chronicle*, 9 June 1937, p. 7.

105 Ibid.

106 'Holidays with pay mean spread-over – or chaos', *Caterer and Hotel Keeper*, 10 September 1937, p. 3.

107 'Holidays for all', *The Economist*, 4 June 1938, Vol. CXXXI, no. 4945, pp. 527–8.

108 'Prepare for more holiday-makers', *Caterer and Hotel Keeper*, 4 February 1938, pp. 17–18.

109 D. Matless, *Landscape and Englishness* (London: Reaktion Books, 1998), p. 43.

110 J. Lowerson, 'Battles for the countryside', in *Class, culture and social change: A new view of the 1930s*, F. Gloversmith, ed. (Sussex: Harvester Press, 1980), pp. 258–80.

111 'Points from the British Health Resorts Association Conference at Skegness: TUC chief and holidays with pay', *Skegness News*, 28 April 1937, p. 7.

112 'Catering trade labour troubles', *Caterer and Hotelkeeper*, 12 April 1935, p. 31.

113 'Spreadover holidays at last – principle accepted by Parliament', *Caterer and Hotel Keeper*, 8 April 1938, pp. 17–18.

114 'Holidays with pay will force a spreadover: need for a national campaign', *Caterer and Hotel Keeper*, 8 October 1937, p. 19, 'Warning to seaside hoteliers – serious effect of holidays with pay Plan', *Caterer and Hotel Keeper*, 10 December 1937, p. 31.

115 'Mr. Brown tackles holiday chaos – plan for new school terms', *Daily Mail*, 7 April 1938, p. 16.

116 'MP to press for staggered holiday plan – backed by resorts and railways', *Daily Mail*, 2 April 1938, p. 11, 'MP has plan to spread holidays', *Daily Express*, 4 April 1938, p. 7.

117 'Stagger holidays with pay – Parliament backs plan for 11,000,000', *Daily Express*, 7 April 1938, p. 9 and 'Hotel's holiday problems reviewed', *Caterer and Hotel Keeper*, 20 May 1938, p. 26.

118 'School is family holiday bar', *Daily Express*, 19 April 1938, p. 7, 'But – beaches will be empty – stagger school holidays is seaside plea', *Daily Express*, 20 April 1938, p. 3.

119 'Staggering of holidays where Lancashire leads – Blackpool's gain', *Times*, 15 August 1938, p. 1.

120 'The timing of holidays proposed questionnaire to Divisional Controllers', Inter-Departmental Committee on Holidays with Pay, 30 September 1938, TNA: PRO, LAB 31/3, p. 92.

121 Holidays With Pay Committee Report, Part II, 28 April 1938, TNA: PRO, LAB 31/1, p. 37. For a discussion of the German and Italian models see S. Baranowski, 'Strength through joy: Tourism and national integration in the Third Reich', in E. Furlough and S. Baranowski, eds *Being elsewhere: Tourism, consumer culture, and identity in modern Europe and North America* (Ann Arbor, MI, 2001), pp. 213–36, and Victoria DeGrazia, *The culture of consent: Mass organisation of leisure in Fascist Italy* (Cambridge, 1981).

122 Holidays With Pay Committee Report, Part II, 28 April 1938, TNA: PRO, LAB 31/1, p. 37.

123 'Points from the British Health Resorts Association conference at Skegness – TUC chief and holidays with pay', *Skegness News*, 28 April 1937, p. 7.

124 Holidays With Pay Committee Report, Part II, 28 April 1938, TNA: PRO, LAB 31/1, p. 38.

125 'Low rating of holiday camps discussed by R.H.A. National Assembly', *Caterer and Hotel Keeper*, 7 July 1939, p. 16.

126 'Butlin's holiday camp wonderful progress and designs', *Clacton News and East Essex Advertiser*, 14 May 1938, p. 2.

127 'Butlin's plans more holiday camps at Ryde and Bournemouth', *Caterer and Hotel Keeper*, 8 June 1938, p. 11.

128 The Derbyshire Miner's Union holiday camp opened in May 1939 and accommodated 1,000 people each week. The Union organised weekly savings schemes for workers' holidays. G. Grafton, *The best summer of our lives: Derbyshire Miner's holiday camp* (Breedon Books, 2000).

129 'Giant holiday camp in North Wales', *Caterer and Hotel Keeper*, 7 July 1939, pp. 25, 26, 30, and 'Yarmouth protest at T.U.C. camps proposal', *Caterer and Hotel Keeper*, 25 August 1939, p. 10.

130 'Butlin's succeed with all-in tariff – holidays under one roof', *Caterer and Hotel Keeper*, 9 September 1938, p. 19.

131 N. Morgan and A. Pritchard, *Power and politics at the seaside: The development of Devon's resorts in the twentieth century* (Exeter: Exeter University Press, 1999).

132 'Butlin's succeed with all-in tariff – holidays under one roof', *Caterer and Hotel Keeper*, 9 September 1938, p. 19.

133 The Act also did not extend to Northern Ireland. Holidays with Pay Act, Parliamentary Papers (London: HMSO, 1938), p. 5.

2

'Holidays with pay, holidays with play!'[1] Building the luxury holiday-camp industry

Mr William Butlin's holiday camp at Skegness is a 'great experiment in cutting completely adrift from the standardised seaside resort', announced Gordon Beckles of the *Daily Express* in 1936. The camp, 'a cross between the Olympic Village in Berlin and a film studio', foregrounds 'a huge open-air swimming pool, set in the middle of lawns and rose-trees'. Behind the pool, Beckles continued, stand 'two immense dining halls capable of seating 800 people at once', two dance floors, two club bars, an open-air gymnasium and shops. The camp, he claimed, is a veritable village, complete with 'seven hundred one-room cottages in long rows' that stretch down to the boating lake and the campsite's own private beach. Butlin's great experiment offered all the essentials of a holiday resort – beautiful surroundings, accommodation, food, entertainment and healthy activities – for the all-inclusive price of approximately one week's pay.[2]

When the Amulree Committee recommended the creation of alternative and reasonably priced sites of family pleasure to accommodate the newly leisured workers, they referred in particular to holiday camps such as Butlin's in Skegness.[3] By the time the Committee published its findings in April 1938, an estimated 200 holiday camps existed in Britain and accommodated 30,000 people each week of the summer season.[4] As part of the interwar development of domestic coastal tourism, two mass camps owned by Butlin accommodated 100,000 guests, and four owned by Captain Harry Warner catered to almost 40,000 visitors each season. Other holiday camps varied in the degree of luxury and size, as well as political or religious affiliation. Some consisted of as little as tents in a field, while others included permanent buildings and barrack-style sleeping accommodation. Either way, the Amulree Committee saw holiday camps as inexpensive and healthy destinations where working families could inhale coastal air, eat regular meals, and participate in physical

The outdoor swimming pool at Butlin's Holiday Camp, Clacton, c. 1938   1

exercise not usually undertaken in the modern urban setting.[5]

Through its recommendation, the Amulree Committee gave legitimacy to the holiday-camp industry in Britain and Butlin's advertising slogan capitalised on this endorsement: 'Holidays With Pay, Holidays With Play at Butlin's'.[6] Warner and Butlin promoted their camps, purely commercial enterprises without any political or religious affiliation, in three popular newspapers that had supported the campaign for paid holidays – the *Daily Express*, the *Daily Herald*, and the *News Chronicle*. The papers, like the holiday camps, were an integral part of the development of mass culture and leisure between the wars.[7] These and other dailies' circulation increased dramatically between the wars.[8] All published holiday advice and advertisements in the summer months and some took a critical interest in Butlin's and Warner's holiday camps as a new social phenomenon, as the Gordon Beckles article illustrates.[9]

Yet the new mass holiday camps also drew criticism from those concerned about the seeming mindlessness of the regimented entertainment. Campers woke to the sound of a loudspeaker, ate meals at times announced by a bell, returned to chalets at the midnight curfew, and engaged in organised activities designed to enforce gaiety. Critics found the constant physical activities particularly irksome and indicative of an 'American-style' mass culture that many intellectuals abhorred for its seeming mindlessness. In the eyes of some critics, the camps contributed to an image of the working classes as dependent on organised holidays that required little or no individual imagination and limited personal privacy. Others saw the expansion of the holiday-camp industry as a threat to the development of Britain's coastal resorts. Hoteliers and caterers feared the camps as commercial competition and middle-class guests feared the incursion of the 'masses' into the midst of their pleasure resorts. In short, local and national opposition to the erection of holiday camps continued, despite the legitimacy provided by the recommendations of the Holidays With Pay Committee.

This chapter explores the way politics, class, and leisure intersected in the interwar period to legitimate and sustain the holiday-camp industry in Britain. The mass holiday camps that Butlin and Warner built emerged at a critical moment when paid holidays for workers were politicised and redefined as a right for all workers.[10] At the same time, the camps were part of the growth of mass culture and consumption that concerned social critics but that politicians and economists recognised as increasingly important to economic recovery.[11] For many working-class families, holiday camps remained too expensive. Nevertheless, holiday camps appeared to reconcile a vision of inexpensive pleasure with a new vision of working-class families as a significant market of consumers. As a variety of critics voiced a plethora of concerns about the new consumers and the type of mass holiday they were offered, Warner and Butlin built leisure empires, secure in the knowledge that they appeared to provide a commercial answer to a large political problem: the provision of a week's holiday for a week's pay.

Consuming the British seaside

The holiday-camp industry extended the development of Britain's coastline at the end of the nineteenth century and during the first half of the twentieth century. Popular belief in the efficacious nature of sea bathing and sea air encouraged the growth of coastal resorts and contributed to the demise of inland spa towns such as Bath and Leamington Spa from the mid-eighteenth century onwards.[12] As railway companies extended their services to connect urban centres to the coast, they capitalised on this penchant for the seaside. Cheap fares and day excursions gave many lower middle- and working-class customers access to the coastal areas.

Religious or temperance societies facilitated working-class access to rail travel by organising excursions for members and negotiating lower fares with the railways. Thomas Cook, secretary of the Leicester Temperance Society, planned his first excursion from Leicester to Loughborough in July 1841. Cook chartered a train and contracted a price with the Midland railway to fill the train with first, second, and third-class travellers. The success of this and other planned excursions for the Temperance society encouraged Cook to expand his idea into a commercial enterprise in 1845. 'Cook's Tours', as they were advertised, enabled many urban working-class consumers to venture to the coast for a day, often leaving the city at midnight to allow a maximum number of daylight hours at the seaside.[13]

By the 1870s, Blackpool had become the world's first working-class seaside resort, thanks to inexpensive train services, advertising, and the introduction of the secular August bank holiday in 1871 and annual holidays for some wage earners.[14] Located on the north-western coast of England, Blackpool catered for as many as four million visitors in July and August, largely due, as John Walton argues, to 'the availability of cheap, unpretentious accommodation' and convenient rail travel.[15] Although Blackpool was the first and largest such resort, the development of other resorts, such as Cleethorpes, Scarborough, and Bridlington, also benefited from northern industrial workers' day trips and longer holidays. Eastern resorts like Southend, Yarmouth, and Weston-Super-Mare attracted urban workers from the Midlands and London. Southsea and Brighton, short train rides from central London, provided sites for half-day excursions and day trips for London's shop workers and department store assistants.[16]

Sunday schools, temperance societies, and paternalistic employers embraced the seaside excursion as a healthier and more uplifting alternative to the fairgrounds, race meetings, and pubs that dominated popular holidays in the industrial towns in the early Victorian years. Coastal excursions offered urban workers the opportunity to inhale healthy air and to spend a few hours away from the debilitating atmosphere of Britain's industrial cities.[17] As the resorts grew to accommodate more visitors, entertainments and diversions based on popular working-class amusements developed as entrepreneurs began to view the lower middle and working classes as profitable and legitimate consumers. Much like New York's Coney Island, many British seaside resorts offered sites of gambling and sport, public houses, cheap theatres, pier shows, music halls, and fairground rides.[18] Unlike Coney Island, however, these resort areas did not necessarily become locations where middle- and working-class consumers mingled. In Britain, resort entertainments often served to segregate consumers along class lines.[19] In Blackpool, for example, the resort maintained two piers specifically to separate working-class customers from middle-class consumers. This social separation also reinforced an image of lower middle- and working-class pleasure as a particular kind of disordered mass sociability. The working-class pier contained large numbers of cheap amusements that encouraged high spirits, as well as heckling from crowds of often inebriated onlookers, adding to the perception of the lower classes as a disorderly and drunk swarm of pleasure seekers. These images, combined with the loud and high-spirited throngs of third-class excursionists pressed together in open-air rail carriages coming and going from the seaside, persuaded critics of the need for a more rational and organised recreation for the working-classes.

By the end of the nineteenth century, day excursions and short boarding-house stays at coastal areas increased, as did more organised camping holidays for young working men and boys. In order to counter the kind of disorganised mass sociability encouraged by train excursions and resort entertainments, Joseph Cunningham, a flour merchant and Sunday school teacher from Toxteth, Liverpool, established a camp on the Isle of Man in 1894.[20] Cunningham and his wife, Elizabeth, were Presbyterian teetotallers who worked for the Florence Institute for Boys in Liverpool.[21] In 1887 they planned the Institute's first annual summer camp for boys.[22] Despite the popularity of the camp, the meagre 10s tariff did not cover the cost of the week-long camping holiday. Facing lost revenues each year, the Institute dispensed with the services of the Cunninghams. In 1894, the Cunninghams opened their own campsite on the Isle of Man. The Cunninghams drew campers for their new venture, named the International Young Man's Holiday Camp, from the Florence Institute as well as from other Temperance Leagues and Harriers' Clubs.[23]

2   The Cunningham Camp tent accommodation and guests, c. 1910

The campers were single, lower middle-class tradesmen or shop workers capable of saving the weekly tariff of 17s. Guests slept in tents and shared the space with seven other young men, often complete strangers. Predicated on the principles of 'Muscular Christianity' that encouraged athletic activity with spiritual purity, the object of the Douglas camp, according to the illustrated *Camp Herald*, was to 'provide young men with a thoroughly delightful and health-giving holiday in the society of other happy young fellows of good moral character'.[24] Camp rules assisted in regulating the 'morality' of the young guests and included a strict curfew and regimented meal times. Most importantly, the campsite provided a venue 'where the greatest possible amount of health and enjoyment may be obtained with the least possible expenditure of cash'.[25] Health became a national concern after conscription for the Boer War discovered that two-thirds of the male British working-class were unfit for national service, and figured largely in the advertising of the camp.[26] The guests were encouraged to undertake sea-bathing, enter walking competitions, and compete in organised games. One camper wrote, 'I am very pleased to testify to the value of the camp as a health restorer on Nature's lines. I feel my blood has got enriched by the pure air and strengthened by the good food, and my spirits revived by the cheerful company.'[27] The cheerful company in this case was actually quite sober. Joseph Cunningham required each camper to sign a pledge of total abstinence from alcohol while at the camp. While this was true to Cunningham's own advocacy of temperance, it also reflected nineteenth-century middle-class anxieties surrounding working-

The Dining Pavilion at the Cunningham Camp, c. 1910   3

class alcohol consumption, especially in relation to leisure and amusements.[28]

The Cunningham camp also encouraged sexual abstinence, as it catered solely to single men.[29] Concern surrounding working-class sexuality permeated the camp organisation and the only woman present at the Douglas camp was Elizabeth Cunningham, the wife of the founder. The Cunninghams believed an all-male camp would prevent any potential heterosexual immorality. They strongly discouraged campers from fraternising with young women from the town and enforced a strict nightly curfew. The military-style bell tents and exercise regimen suggested that this was a camp determined to use physical activity and strict gender separation as a means to promote heterosexual purity.[30]

While the Cunningham camp catered solely to young men, political and religious groups saw the proselytising potential in the provision of cheap holiday destinations for couples and families.[31] New and organised forms of camping holidays built on older ideas but made provision for single and married women as well as children. One of the earliest opened near the Norfolk coast in 1906. Caister Socialist camp catered for urban workers, trade union leaders, and their families in tents on the outskirts of Yarmouth, a middle-class resort. Caister camp offered communal meals and games, political lectures and debates, as well as the opportunity to socialise with other workers and union leaders. Tents provided cheap accommodation and the camp directors ensured that all holiday makers contributed to the running of the camp by either making meals or organising games.[32]

4   Pillow fighting during Sports Day, Caister Camp, 1939

The camp was established by John Fletcher Dodd, a former grocer and a founder member of the Independent Labour Party. Like the Cunninghams, Fletcher Dodd was adamantly opposed to drinking and so the Caister camp rules forbade alcohol as well as gambling and bad language. Caister also enforced a noise curfew at 11 p.m. Although most of the first guests to the camp were Fletcher Dodd's socialist friends, the camp soon reached out to potential 'converts' and their families. Children were welcome too, although Fletcher Dodd drew the line at infants under 2 years of age.[33] Caister offered campers activities and entertainment. While some campers organised socials, dances, lectures, and debates, others shared in the day-to-day work of the camp. This work was divided along traditional gender lines. Women prepared and cooked the meals and cleaned dishes, men dug vegetables from the camp garden.[34] For married women especially, this type of self-catering holiday did not necessarily provide respite from daily routines. Although the mass camp setting made it different, at Caister, many women merely exchanged a familiar surrounding for an unfamiliar one. In terms of the nature and physical demands of their labour, not much changed.[35]

Despite the somewhat wholesome nature of the camp, it drew opposition from some residents in Yarmouth opposed to what they perceived as a 'socialist commune' in their midst. 'One might have supposed Caister Camp was an abode of savages from the violence of feeling stirred up against the camp and campers by certain interests in Great Yarmouth,' remembered one camper thirty years later. According to the account of this pioneer camper, large numbers of 'young nit-wits on their way to the [Norfolk] Broads used to pull up at the camp gate and demonstrate … dance and howl like dervishes'. The demonstrators came from a large Yarmouth boarding house for 'young gentlemen' who opposed the socialist camp, preferring the cheap commercial amusements of the Yarmouth resort. Fletcher Dodd attempted to calm the frenzied crowd and even invite them inside the camp. However, according to the memories of the Caister camper, his 'words were wasted, for the … young hooligans were not moved by reason'. Despite the local opposition to Caister and socialism, the campers accepted the disruptive behaviour as a 'bad joke' and continued to enjoy the various non-commercial activities afforded at the camp.[36]

Caister provided the model for inexpensive holiday camps organised by the Workers' Travel Association (WTA) and, later, other union holiday camps.[37] As a young man, William Brown (later general secretary to the Civil Service Clerical Association and a Labour MP) remembered going to Caister each year with his parents. According to Brown, the camp was somewhat 'bleak' for children and failed to provide much in the way of appropriate activities for younger campers, especially when it rained.[38] Children, even those of ardent socialists, found lectures and debates 'less than enthralling'.[39] The proximity of the camp to the amusements in Yarmouth provided some distraction for young campers but also added expense to the family's holiday. Later, as general secretary to the Civil Service Clerical Association, Brown formed the Civil Service Holiday Camp Company in 1924 and used Caister as his model – but addressed some of the earlier camp's shortcomings.[40] Brown wanted to build a more comfortable, yet still inexpensive, holiday camp exclusively for the use of members of his union and their families, with activities for all ages. Financed by union dues and contributions, the first camp proved hugely successful. Located at Corton near Lowestoft, Brown's camp offered more relaxing and permanent accommodation as well as ample entertainment for children. The Civil Service Holiday Camp provided 'perambulators and go-carts', a laundry for campers to wash nappies, and a 'baby patrol' in the evenings to allow parents to leave their children and enjoy the evening's entertainment.[41] During the day, tennis courts, bowling greens, organised sports, and dances occupied campers, and a dark room provided facilities for amateur photographers to develop their pictures. The popularity of the camp forced the company to look for a second site, which it found on Hayling Island.[42]

Hayling, a small island located off the south coast of Hampshire, became a popular resort for excursionists from urban areas such as Portsmouth and London in the late nineteenth century and, especially, after the First World War. The rural island with a population of less than 2,000 boasted a five-mile sandy southern shore, a fun fair, and an amusement area called 'The Grotto' owned by retired artillery captain Harry Warner. When the second Civil Service Union Camp opened in 1930, the nearby amusement park and fun fair provided the union camp with additional entertainment. These attractions were of course available only at an additional cost to campers. Yet the Union camp faced greater competition for workers' leisure time the following year when Warner opened what he described as the nation's first 'luxury' family holiday camp on Hayling Island.[43] Devoid of any political or religious affiliation, Warner's camp provided food, accommodation, activities organised by professional staff, excursions, and a variety of entertainment on site and at no extra charge to the campers. Unlike the earlier camps, Warner's guests were not expected to plan activities or assist in the running of the camp in any way.

While Warner's new camp built on the popularity of the older holiday-camp tradition – as a commercial venture without religious, moral, or political constraints, – Warner shifted the focus of workers' leisure consumption to one of pure pleasure. He recognised each member of the working-class family as an individual consumer and strove to offer facilities that provided for the needs and desires of each one. As such, the new-style holiday camps inaugurated by Warner helped to transform the nineteenth-century view of workers as a homogenous class and the idea that workers' pleasure should be 'rational' and dominated by politics, philanthropy, and religion. The new holiday camps of the 1930s emerged to meet the demands of the modern leisure consumer for affordable pleasure without the trappings of a nineteenth-century morality.

Harry Warner, Billy Butlin, and the luxury holiday-camp industry

Captain Henry James Warner bought the land around Norfolk Crescent on the southern shore of Hayling Island after the First World War and charged a penny for use of his tennis courts and twopence for a donkey ride.[44] Hayling resident Joan Harrison remembers the tennis courts on the beach and 'Captain Harry' taking her penny. Although money was 'hard to come by', there was no time limit and Joan and her brother 'played all afternoon for that penny'.[45] Sometime in the 1920s, Warner recognised the island's potential as a popular pleasure site for working people who already visited the island during the summer months. He opened a small seaside restaurant and amusement area called 'The Grotto', on the island's southern shore. Warner leased the land next to the Grotto to William 'Billy' Butlin who opened a fun fair in 1928.[46] Together the two men developed the site as an amusement park. They built beach huts, and dug a boating lake with a small island in the centre and populated it with monkeys.[47] Monkey Island, as it was known, proved a sensation to amusement park guests and an irritant to nearby residents, especially when the creatures escaped and created havoc in a neighbouring school for tubercular children.[48] As a result of the monkeys, and the noise from the fairground amusements, Warner and Butlin experienced considerable opposition from local residents, who actively conspired to rid Hayling of these elements of mass leisure.[49]

The amusement park was, however, extremely popular with excursionists and the growing number of holiday makers. In 1931 Warner used the profit from the Grotto to fund a new leisure scheme. Noting the popularity of the island as a family summer camping destination, Warner endeavoured to combine the desire for cheap holidays, a penchant for camping, and the popularity of the island in what was then an audacious business venture: a 'luxury' family holiday camp on the northern shore of the island.[50] In the midst of an economic depression, the development of luxury leisure for working people seemed somewhat incongruous. Yet that luxury was real to many guests and included private rooms, baby-sitting, a daily maid service, morning-to-night entertainment, and the provision of three hot meals a day served by uniformed waiters in a communal dining room. The camp provided visitors with an all-inclusive leisure site that showcased a private beach situated far away from the island's residential areas. Guests need not venture outside the campsite and incur further expenditure, although the camp management did plan trips to local places of interest on the mainland.[51] When the camp opened at Northney in 1931, families did not sleep under canvas as they did in other holiday camps. Instead, Warner's guests enjoyed wooden chalet accommodation with clean sheets daily, hot food, organised sports, concerts, competitions, and entertainment for all ages. None of the campers were expected to contribute to the running of the camp. Postcards advertising the camp showed groups of smiling campers relaxing on lawn chairs outside rows of identical small wooden chalets, with the northern beach in the background.[52] When it rained, guests moved indoors for amusements directed by camp staff, including beauty contests, knobbly-knee contests, treasure hunts, and 'topsy-turvy' parties, where men dressed as women and women dressed as men.

Warner's daughter-in-law Hazel later described the first camps as 'very basic' by modern standards. However, the provision of 'three cooked meals each day and activities such as swimming, archery, pony rides, and tennis', at no extra cost suggested a luxury with which most working families were not familiar.[53] The new holiday camp appealed to families on limited budgets.[54] The luxury, then, was tied in part to the financial security provided by the all-inclusiveness of the tariff and the provision of all activities for just two guineas per person. Families had no reason to fear that the cost of their holiday would unexpectedly exceed their budgets. Ensconced in comfortable accommodation, served with regular meals and entertained with constant activities, Warner's campers enjoyed a pleasurable and affordable luxury even on a limited income.

Perhaps even more importantly, the camps provided working families the freedom to enjoy a whole week away from home and everyday life. For families with limited resources in the interwar period, the Warner camp on Hayling Island offered a distraction from daily routines and the fantasy of middle-class extravagance as camp employees strove to 'serve' their guests with good food and non-stop entertainment. In this sense, pre-war holiday camps were at the forefront of a new leisure concept of distraction, fantasy, and desire.

5 Accommodation and activities available at Warner's Northney Camp   **5**

Unlike the post-Second World War Club Méditéranée, where the company chose to locate its 'villages' on small 'primitive' islands, without clocks, money, silverware, or western clothes for patrons who desired to *escape* civilisation, visitors to Warner's camp wanted the freedom to enjoy it.[55] Warner furnished the space in which the less-wealthy could enjoy the activities usually experienced on a daily basis by the affluent. For women and mothers, this included an escape from housework and child-rearing. At the Northney camp household chores and childcare were undertaken by camp employees who aimed to create a family-like environment. The special focus on the needs of women and children would later attract the attention of the Holidays With Pay Committee as it sought to find an inexpensive holiday site where the whole family could enjoy a break, including working housewives.

The Northney camp proved to be a financial success and prompted other entrepreneurs to open camps on Hayling, including the Sunshine Holiday Camp in 1936, and the Coronation Camp in 1938.[56] Other organisations chose sites along the south coast, close to Hayling Island, including the British Union of Fascists (BUF), which held summer family camps from 1933 to 1938. Unlike the at Warner camp, BUF members wore uniforms and slept under canvas at Pagham, West Wittering, and Selsey, although food and entertainment were provided.[57] Warner also expanded his leisure business and built three more camps before the outbreak of war in 1939, along the south and south eastern coasts of England at Seaton in Devon, Puckpool on the Isle of

Wight, and Dovercourt Bay in Essex. These camps not only enjoyed more sunshine hours during the summer months, but also were more easily accessible to urban centres, such as London and the Midlands.

Warner's success inspired his Hayling amusement park partner, Billy Butlin, to enter the luxury holiday-camp business. Butlin selected Skegness on the Lincolnshire coast as the site of his first holiday camp. When the Butlin camp opened in 1936, it was capable of accommodating a thousand guests each week, almost four times the size of Warner's camps. Butlin chose Skegness largely because it was already a popular resort town, but also because he had business interests there. He had opened his first permanent fun fair in Skegness in 1927 after several years as an itinerant showman.

Butlin's leisure empire had humble beginnings. Born William Heygate Butlin in South Africa in 1899 to the son of an English vicar and the daughter of a travelling showman, Butlin returned to England with his mother, Bertha, when her marriage failed. They joined her family as part of a travelling fair. Shortly after their return to England, Bertha met and married a Canadian and subsequently moved to Toronto. Billy followed his mother to Toronto in 1911 and quickly found a job with Eaton's department store in that city.[58] As an employee at Eaton's, Butlin first experienced a 'holiday camp' in Canada. Every year the managers and employees closed the store for a week and went camping. The campers played games together, rowed canoes, and enjoyed a week of organised fun.[59] Years later, Butlin claimed that the memory of this camping holiday in the Canadian wilderness stayed with him, and he had been determined to open his own holiday camp one day.[60]

In 1921, Butlin returned to his mother's family in England and the travelling fairground. By 1926, Butlin oversaw several stalls at the prestigious Bertram Mills Olympia Circus and Fair that ran annually for six weeks over the Christmas period. Butlin's stalls stood out for two reasons: he insisted that his stall-holders wear uniforms with a big 'B' (for Butlin) on the pocket, and he gave live budgerigars or puppies as prizes.[61] Butlin realised that he could make more money with a fun fair that was open year round and indoors, protected from the British weather. In 1927, Butlin rented warehouses in Skegness to keep his first permanent fun fair open all year round. He also introduced electric amusement rides that he saw in Canada after the First World War, including bumper cars. Butlin made a small fortune as the sole European distributor of the hugely successful American-made Dodgem bumper car.[62] With the profit from the Skegness and Dodgem ventures, Butlin opened another five permanent fun fairs, including the one on Hayling Island. By

1936, Butlin had sufficient business collateral to secure a loan to build his first luxury holiday camp just outside Skegness. By the time Butlin's camp opened, the luxury holiday-camp industry had already transformed the idea of camping under canvas into an all-inclusive mass package holiday.

Expansion, enthusiasm, and controversy

Warner and Butlin built on older ideas of successful holiday camps, yet their camps differed from their predecessors in significant ways. The size of the camps, the efficiency of their organisation, their comprehensiveness, luxury, and exceptional publicity greatly exceeded those of the earlier camps.[63] In addition, the new mass camps were stripped of the image of 'rational' recreation based on middle-class notions of sobriety and restraint because they did not have any political or religious affiliations, and because each camp had licensed bars that served alcohol to adult guests. While the Warner and Butlin camps provided organised activities, guests were free to create their own amusements without restrictions or preconceived ideas about the need to contain worker sociability within the bounds of middle-class notions of order. Warner and Butlin advertised nationally and locally, organised elaborate camp reunions out of season, created children's clubs that contacted members throughout the year, published newsletters and calendars, provided different camp pins each year for camp visitors, and, in so doing, created both product loyalty and an 'imagined community' of campers that was larger than the confines of their campsites.[64] At the same time, Warner and Butlin both distanced their new-style holidays from an older image of camps as providing rational recreation.

Warner's first camp on Hayling attracted guests largely through word of mouth and through his business contacts. The first sixteen-week season catered to approximately 700 guests. Many were middle- and lower middle-class individuals or couples, rather than working-class families who were unable to afford even the seemingly inexpensive rates. The following year, satisfied guests returned and brought friends, prompting Warner to expand the accommodation at Northney. In 1934, Warner advertised his camp in the left-leaning *News Chronicle*. By this time the Northney camp catered for 600 campers each week of the season, and holiday camps attracted national attention as a new and popular alternative to a hotel or boarding-house holiday.[65]

In gratitude for the rising number of regular paid advertisements in the paper, the *News Chronicle* ran an article in 1934 that announced holiday camps were 'Jolly Carefree Holidays', that offered a comparatively new alternative to the conventional holiday. The article claimed that holiday camps such as Warner's were 'a form of holiday that is attracting thousands of fresh holiday makers each year, and the extension of the camps made necessary by record bookings is proof of their tremendous popularity'. The author noted that it was 'no wonder this holiday-camp movement is growing – it offers all the usual amenities with good well-cooked food plus many extras' at no additional cost. Campers sleep in 'neat, well-equipped, chalet-type bungalows, lighted by electricity', and camps 'pride themselves on the fact that there is never a dull moment'. With conviviality the major concern at holiday camps, 'games, socials, etc are well organised for visitors' enjoyment'. A camp that offered 'invigorating air, good food, comfortable quarters and jolly companions', according to this enthusiastic author, was *the* holiday location for 1934.[66]

That same year, Warner opened a second camp at Seaton, in Devon. According to a relative, Butlin sent two of his trusted employees to help Warner and to take note of how the camp was run.[67] Two years later, the enthusiasm for holiday camps had not waned. Butlin opened his first camp at Skegness amid a fanfare of publicity. In a full-page advertisement in the *Daily Express*, Butlin claimed that his camp at the edge of the sea was the 'most modern and luxurious camp in the world'.[68] The amenities included 600 fireproof and waterproof chalets that contained the best beds available 'for the sole purpose of providing the weary with complete rest'. In addition, the camp kitchens contained modern equipment, capable of providing hundreds of guests with hot meals simultaneously.[69] Butlin also advertised locally in the *Skegness News*, where the camp amenities, including the black marble bathrooms and club lounges, were heralded as being 'as luxurious as the best London hotels'.[70]

Vernon Jenkins, Butlin's nephew, claims that Butlin wanted his venture to be 'bigger and better' than Warner's.[71] Yet despite the extravagant publicity, the camp was not actually completed when the first campers arrived. Guests, however, were encouraged to *imagine* the grounds with 12,000 rose bushes covering what was then mere rubble.[72] In addition to the unfinished site, the British weather proved more unseasonable than usual, as the April grand opening of the Skegness camp was met with sleet and snow. Despite this less than auspicious beginning, the local *Skegness News* interviewed several of the visitors, who complained about the weather but applauded the indoor activities available at the camp. The Grand Pavilion and Club Rooms housed a host of diversions, including billiards, snooker, table tennis, skittles, dancing, listening to music, reading, or joining in the physical culture classes. Two 'professionals' from London who expressed their disappointment with the weather also praised Butlin's camp. When asked if they had tried other holiday camps, the couple replied, 'Oh yes, several on the South Coast, but they are crude stone-age affairs compared with this one.'[73]

Despite the physical limitations of the unfinished campsite, Butlin succeeded in making his new camp different from all the others. Inspired by the memory of the 'happy camaraderie of that far off Canadian summer camp', Butlin worked to create an atmosphere where complete strangers would become life-long friends after a week at his camp.[74] To encourage campers to overcome the awkwardness of interacting with strangers, Butlin appointed a camp host and friendly assistants clad in red blazers and white flannel pants to mingle with the guests, see to their every need, and encourage the formation of friendships. Clearly identifiable, these 'Redcoats' quickly became the camp entertainers, physical fitness co-ordinators, dance instructors and partners, childcare providers, and mealtime comedians. They became visible symbols of the Butlin's holiday-camp motto, borrowed from Shakespeare and displayed on the outside of the dining room, 'Our true intent is all for your delight'.[75]

One of the Redcoats that summer was Cyril Reeve. He was also chief lifeguard. In his position as an entertainer, Reeve remembers that he was never 'short of a girlfriend'. In fact, Reeve met his future wife, Joan, while working. Joan was a schoolgirl of 14 at the time.[76] The holiday camp proved a success with guests like Joan as well as with employees like Cyril.

Local businesses, however, feared the competition and some residents objected to the erection of a mass camp outside the Skegness resort town. Butlin hoped to defuse local resistance by hosting dances and galas designed to give Skegness residents an opportunity to experience the type of entertainment available to camp guests. This also gave him another opportunity to make money. The 1s tickets included transport to and from the camp, as well as admission to the dance.[77] Every Sunday throughout the season the Skegness camp opened for public 'inspection'. Later, Butlin offered local residents a sixpenny day pass that included use of all the camp amenities. At the end of the first season Butlin promoted a Carnival at the park with free rides and entertainment for all those in fancy dress.[78] He also sponsored a local football team named 'Butlin's Athletic'.[79] To counter criticism, he contributed to charitable causes and organised events such as the Butlin's Skegness Hospital Carnival, held in and around the camp and town in aid of the local hospital fund.[80] To further garner local support, Butlin even adopted the image of the 'jolly fisherman', Skegness's town logo, in his camp advertisements.[81]

An article on the front page of the *Skegness News* in 1936 heralded the opening of the new camp, and also attempted to assuage the anxieties of other local businesses through an explanation of where the first week's camp visitors came from. The article pointed out that while the majority of visitors to Skegness in 1935, the year before the camp opened, came from the Midlands, over three-fifths of the 1936 campers came from the London boroughs. In addition, the local paper maintained, Mr Butlin had received enquiries about the camp from Scotland, Wales, Ireland, and almost every county in England. Despite what his detractors said to the contrary, Mr Butlin's holiday camp did not take visitors away from other hotels and boarding houses in Skegness, but rather expanded the clientele of the entire resort and put Skegness firmly on the holiday map.[82]

One chief appeal of the Skegness camp was its size and large-scale catering ability. In May 1938, the mayor of Boston Spa approached Butlin for help with a delicate situation: providing match-making services to the lonely-hearted. The mayor had received over a thousand letters from lonely single people aged 21 to 71, seeking help to find life partners. Apparently the avalanche of letters had arrived at the mayor's office after he had forwarded to the local press a letter that he had received from an Australian gentleman who wished to meet and marry an English woman. A Miss Bell answered the letter, corresponded with the Australian, and sent £15 to arrange for her passage to Australia. The correspondence ended abruptly, but the publicity surrounding the disappointed Miss Bell led to an avalanche of letters from lonely men wanting to meet her. After Miss Bell chose a suitor, more letters arrived at the mayor's office from lonely women wishing to have their letters sent on to the rejected men. 'The huge correspondence certainly reveals that there are hundreds and hundreds of lonely souls in this country', explained the mayor, 'each of whom is anxious to meet a member of the opposite sex who is ready to share both his or her joys and sorrows with a life companion.' In desperation, the mayor sought assistance from Butlin and the Rector of Skegness to deal with the huge number of singles requesting help. Both agreed. Butlin organised a 'Please-keep-it-a-Secret' weekend at the camp so that the lonely could meet. This would absolve the mayor from responsibility for any terrible matches. In a gesture that anticipated modern dating agencies, Butlin catered for the thousand lonely hearts free of charge and under the auspices of the Rector of Skegness, who agreed to perform any resulting nuptials.[83]

Butlin scored another public relations victory with locals when he invited over a thousand school children to the camp to celebrate his daughter Shirley's fifth birthday. The children enjoyed games and a gala performance in the

Grand Pavilion. Butlin engaged private buses to bring the children to the camp and celebrated the day with a five-foot-high cake.[84] The party and lavish scale of entertainment provided Butlin and his camp with a great deal of positive press.[85] In another effort to secure local support, Butlin organised a carnival to raise money for the local hospital.

Despite Butlin's apparent largesse, not all local businesses or residents relished the idea of the holiday camp in their midst. Some members of the Skegness resort community had worked hard to encourage the development of sea-front property designed to attract a 'certain class of visitor', that is, middle class. The camp, on the other hand, encouraged day trippers and a lower class of visitor to Skegness. Some local councillors wanted the camp renamed to more accurately reflect its geographical location outside the boundaries of Skegness in Ingoldmells. Others objected to Butlin's appropriation of the 'jolly fisherman' logo recently adopted by Skegness as the resort's advertising motif. This, for the five council members who opposed the holiday camp, was a misappropriation and, perhaps more seriously in their opinion, a misrepresentation of the town. Despite these very pointed objections, the majority of the council outvoted the five dissenters and argued that Butlin had actually put Skegness on the map. All the businesses in the resort, they asserted, benefited from Butlin's national advertising. With regard to the 'jolly fisherman' motif, Butlin's defenders pointed out that the logo actually belonged to the railway, not the town. Prior to adopting the image, Butlin had obtained permission from the railway company and, more importantly, from the creator of the logo, John Hassall.[86] To underscore the legitimacy of his use of the town logo, Butlin

Campers on the beach, Butlin's Holiday Camp, Skegness, c. 1936   **6**

invited Hassall to the Skegness camp and made sure that the local newspaper announced the visit.[87] Silenced for the time being, the irate council members continued to look for ways to discredit Butlin and his holiday-camp endeavour.

The following year, another councillor challenged the Sunday opening of

   Butlin's advert for an event in aid of the local hospital, 23 June 1937

Butlin's amusement park. As the park was incorporated into the holiday camp, the amusements and rides were open all day and evening. Protesting that the amusements were a temptation, Councillor Wheatley proposed that the park should not open until noon, so as to allow patrons to attend morning church services.[88] Butlin, conscious of a strong Sabbatarian following in Skegness, consented to the councillor's proposal with only one condition – that Wheatley also agree to close his billiard hall on Sunday mornings. Stunned by the counter-proposal, Wheatley argued that the Sunday opening of his billiard hall in Skegness gave employment to a disabled man who otherwise would be dependent on charity. Butlin, however, pointed out to Wheatley and the rest of the council that the disabled man in question had recently died. After an embarrassing silence, Wheatley withdrew his proposal and Butlin kept his amusement park open all day on Sundays.[89]

Despite his victory, Butlin was conscious of those concerned with the apparent drop in church attendance. To counter further criticism and under-score the idea of his camp holidays as wholesome family recreation, Butlin asked local ministers to conduct regular Sunday services in the holiday camp. In this way Butlin created a balance between Victorian Puritanism and twentieth-century libertinism. In July, the *Skegness News* reported that over 800 campers attended a religious service in the ballroom, led by the Reverend Canon A. H. Morris, Rector of Skegness. The newly installed cinema organ, played by a member of the camp staff, provided the music.[90] By September, the editor of *The Sunday Circle*, a Sabbatarian publication, had sent a corre-spondent to the camp to see what happened on a Sunday. The correspondent attended the service and noted that the camp management also catered to Roman Catholics. A bus left the camp on Sunday mornings and took them to the nearest Catholic Church, while Butlin and his staff set an example and all attended the open-air service conducted by Church of England clergy. The correspondent, suitably impressed by the service, stayed for the rest of the day and questioned those who accused holiday camps of immorality. 'Some people say that these camps are immoral', the reporter claimed, 'but I cannot see in a permanent camp organised as this one is how there can be the slightest loophole for anything wrong to take place.'[91]

Criticism of the Skegness camp continued, regardless of the endorsement of the Rector of Skegness and the correspondent from *The Sunday Circle*. Despite the local controversy in Skegness, the success of the camp encouraged Butlin and Warner to build a mass holiday camp at Dovercourt Bay, near Harwich, in a joint business venture a year after the opening of Butlin's first camp. A two-page spread about the new camp in the local *Harwich and Dovercourt Standard* emphasised the speed with which the camp was built and the number of local jobs it created. Additionally, the article noted the swiftness with which the plans had been agreed upon by the local council members, who, after the experience of Skegness, knew that the camp would bring publicity and visitors to their resort and 'put it on the map'. Not only did the camp provide a source of much-needed local employment in the economically depressed area, it was a £50,000 scheme that transformed sixty acres of grassland into a 'paradise for holidaymakers'. If ever there was a misnomer, the author claimed, 'it is to call this luxurious holiday centre a camp'. While the 'holiday camp vogue started with a collection of huts and tents', according to the article, 'the proprietors of the Dovercourt Camp were quick to see – after personal experience of some of the finest holiday camps that exist in various countries of the world – that this sort of thing was not good enough for the English holidaymaker'. Dovercourt was a new type of camp that 'improved and improved' on the old camps to produce 'the masterpiece … the ultra-modern conception of a luxury seaside hotel'.[92]

The *Standard* article focused on the generous meals (four a day), the fun-filled activities, and the comfort and cleanliness of the chalets. Holiday camps offered a varied daily programme and choices to the individual camper. The author claimed, 'Of course, you can be as active or as lazy as you like – that's the advantage of a holiday camp.' Holiday makers could choose to 'lounge in the sun and have a real rest', or join in 'one long round of games and sport entertainment without even going outside the camp'. For those so inclined, the 'beauties of the surrounding countryside' were close by, 'historic Harwich … only a mile away … Constable's country a few miles out', and 'coach trips through the district and to neighbouring towns', or simply 'wonderful spots for picnics and rambles' were available close to the camp.[93] In other words, a holiday at the camp could introduce guests to a world they did not know. Inside the camp itself, according to the article, 'there is never a dull moment. The staff makes it their job to see that things go with a swing.' For the athletic, the camp 'organised games and exercises for those who would seek fitness under the direction of an expert'. For the active holiday maker, the camp planned swimming galas, sports, and tennis tournaments. If the weather proved unseasonable, the camp provided indoor entertainment of all kinds, and every evening it furnished an orchestra for dancing, as well as the opportunity for campers to join in the fun and showcase their talents in the 'campers' own' concert.[94]

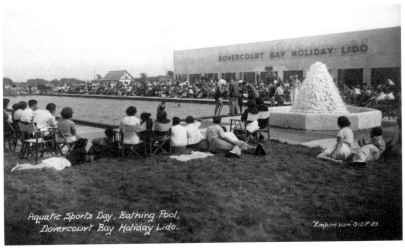

Aquatic Sports Day, Bathing Pool, Dovercourt Bay Holiday Lido.

Empire View 0108 23

Campers watching the Aquatic Sports Day at Dovercourt Bay, c. 1938   **8**

While the *Standard* article highlighted the modern aspects of consumption at Dovercourt Bay, it also pointed to the growing interest in 'historic' Britain that emerged with the heritage movement in the interwar years. The modern leisure consumer, the article implied, could enjoy the old and the new equally well either inside or outside the confines of the new campsite. While this versatility appealed to many holiday makers, it caused anxiety among others in the leisure industry who saw the flexibility of the new camps as a serious threat to their livelihoods. Indeed, while the camps attracted day trippers who could not afford to stay the entire week at the camp, week-long guests who could afford the weekly rate might otherwise have stayed at a local hotel. Local resistance to the growth of the commercial mass camps continued to increase, despite their popularity and the economic growth the camps brought to the local economy.

Child consumers and the problem of leisure

The *Standard* article paid particular attention to the entertainment and facilities for children at the Dovercourt camp. The provision of indoor entertainment during bad weather as well as the baby-sitting services made the camp attractive to families with children. The high-profile advertising and publicity alarmed others in the leisure industry, particularly the owners of small hotels and boarding houses, who saw the camps as competition for a new market of consumers – children. Hoteliers united to meet the growing competition. An association of boarding and apartment housekeepers, hoteliers, and caterers at Great Yarmouth, a popular middle-class seaside resort on the south-eastern coast of Britain, met to discuss an advertising campaign aimed to bring business to their facilities and divert profits from the growing number of holiday camps in the area.[95] Other hoteliers sought to provide facilities for children in order to lure patrons away from the holiday camps.

In a series of articles in the *Caterer and Hotel Keeper*, the industry tried to promote new initiatives to tempt holiday makers with children to seek accommodation in hotels rather than holiday camps. To that end, the journal aimed to supply practical ideas for hotels with a large holiday clientele. The unpredictable nature of the weather forced a particular 'British' type of indoor amusement culture to emerge. A. E. Nickolds, the organiser of entertainments at a leading seaside hotel, wrote, 'It is hardly necessary to stress the fact that it is commercially sound to do everything to make visitors happy when they are confined to the hotel' because of bad weather. He continued, guests will 'quickly realise that efforts are being made in this direction and will respond and so help to entertain themselves'. Nickolds suggested card games and table tennis tournaments, organised at short notice. Another amusing game, he suggested, is 'blow football'. Here the players divide into two teams and kneel or sit round a table and endeavour to blow the ball into the goal area which has been previously chalked out at each end of the table. Children and adults, Nickolds claimed, 'can mix happily in these games'.[96]

The following month, Anne Sheraton wrote an article for the *Caterer and Hotel Keeper* titled 'Catering for Children in Holiday Hotels'. Sheraton maintained that 'Children often present a difficult problem in the "grown-up" atmosphere of an [sic] hotel, and it is a good plan to provide them with a room of their own.' She continued, 'A play room and a dining room for the special use of small guests are profitable and rather unusual attractions that should well repay for space and upkeep, particularly in seaside and country hotels.' Furnished with bright, modern nursery toys and small, low furniture, these rooms promised to please the children and their parents alike. There was no mention, however, of supervision for the children, who presumably would be cared for by either parents or nannies in separate rooms from other adults.[97]

Later that year, A. E. Nickolds once again offered practical advice to hoteliers catering for children. He began, 'It is a well known axiom that by amusing the child you please the parent. The hotelier who sets out to cater for children will reap his reward' in increased bookings and a loyal clientele. Nickolds suggested setting aside one day of the week as a 'special children's day ... with special entertainment for the kiddies'. For the special day, children, according to Nickolds, loved nothing better than a picnic, 'and it is never difficult to arrange to hire a suitable *charabanc* [motorised bus] and take a party to some of the adjacent woods' for games and a picnic. In the case of a rainy day, 'a fancy dress tea party is a great favourite', or an egg-and-spoon race using ping-pong balls in a small indoor space. Most importantly, 'at the conclusion of the party or sports', each child should receive a prize, and, Nickolds explained, 'the organiser can be sure that everyone will go away quite happy and satisfied'.[98]

Despite the effort to provide amusements for their guests, hoteliers saw holiday camps, especially the large-scale Warner and Butlin camps, as a serious threat to their business. The large camps benefited from economies of scale and were able to provide a vast array of amenities and services. Luxury holiday camps solved the problem of the British weather and incorporated indoor facilities, including age-appropriate clubrooms, snooker and billiard halls, table tennis and skittles, concerts, fancy-dress competitions, beauty pageants, plays, and physical culture classes that small hoteliers simply could not compete with.[99]

To a certain extent, the hotel industry's attention to children mirrored contemporary efforts in related industries, like department stores that developed specialised children's clothes and toy departments and featured toy exhibitions and circus acts to attract the child consumer.[100] In addition, manufacturers marketed directly to child consumers through advertisements in national publications such as the *Boys'* or *Girls' Weekly* or *Hobbies* as well as in more specialist and local magazines such as the fortnightly Manchester *Motor Cycle Book for Boys*.[101] As scholars point out, by the 1930s there was a plethora of hobbies magazines that targeted Britain's youthful consumers, as well as organisations like the Boy Scouts and Girl Guides that required uniforms and thus competed with the cinema and dance halls for disposable income.[102] Daily papers increasingly featured weekly children's supplements – stories, puzzles, advice, cartons, and fiction – in an effort to redefine themselves as 'family newspapers'.[103] Indeed, as one sales trainer put it, the years after the First World War were 'the children's age'.[104] The efforts to target Britain's youth were part of a growing awareness of children as consumers in their own right. As Warner and Butlin catered for the leisure needs and desires of the child consumer in their holiday camps they facilitated the shift in consumer ideology that was taking place during the interwar years.

Local critics

While some hoteliers tried to imitate the camp facilities, others obstructed the construction of more camps at public meetings and council hearings. When Butlin planned to open a second mass camp in Clacton-on-Sea in 1937, opposition from residents and local hoteliers increased. The *Caterer and Hotelkeeper* claimed, 'Anxiety throughout the country among seaside hotel proprietors over the growth of holiday camps came to a head in Clacton-on-Sea this week.' Hoteliers in Clacton opposed a scheme for the construction of Butlin's holiday camp, ostensibly because he planned to include a fun fair. The hoteliers alleged that the fun fair already operating in the town lowered 'the tone of the resort' and caused 'annoyance to hotel visitors' because of the noise and the 'class' of patron it served. In addition, Butlin's plans proposed to build 948 chalets on twenty acres of land zoned for nine homes per acre. The proposed population density of the campsite therefore threatened to seriously impact the aesthetics of the present resort. George Pollock, a spokesman for the Clacton Hotel and Boarding House Association, went further. He complained that the speed of construction meant that the 'jerry-built' chalets had 'two-inch thick walls, with no adequate sewerage'. The camp, in his view, threatened to contaminate Clacton's air with noise and create a hygiene hazard for the rest of the resort community through overflowing waste products. Pollock's argument gained more vocal support when one local resident at the hearing shouted that Britain contained 'too many holiday camps' and Clacton 'does not want Butlins!'[105]

In addition to the potential sanitary pollution, critics of holiday camps charged proprietors with colluding in immoral behaviour. Critics perceived holiday camps as a venue for illicit sexual activity because of the inexpensive accommodation and the entertainment contained within the confines of the campsites. In particular, detractors saw fun fairs with new electric rides that were noisy, fast, exciting, and dangerous as morally suspect.[106] This was amplified by the itinerant nature of fairgrounds and the travelling showmen associated with them. Although the fun fair at Butlin's Skegness camp was a permanent fairground, it did not escape this suspicion. The clientele most closely associated with fun fairs were day trippers or excursionists, largely working-class people whose public behaviour and perceived 'loose' sexual morality gave critics cause for concern. These were also the guests most likely to go to the relatively inexpensive holiday camps or pay sixpence to enter the holiday campsite for a day. Hoteliers and residents who opposed Butlin's scheme to build a luxury holiday camp in Clacton preferred to keep this type of visitor away from their resort.

Opponents in Clacton gained the support of at least one vocal member at the annual meeting of the British Hotel Association, who claimed in a speech that holiday-camp owners invited prostitutes to the camp to service guests. This was possible because, the association member contended, unlike hotels that vetted their clientele through the registration process and the relatively high price of a room to prevent such 'immoral' activities as prostitution, adultery, or homosexual liaisons, holiday camps offered cheap accommodation, and organised activities that encouraged physical closeness between guests, to anyone willing and able to pay.[107] In addition, opponents argued, the sheer size of the new mass holiday camps encouraged individual anonymity and potential immoral activities. Indeed, holiday camps promoted an atmosphere of physically close friendliness between complete strangers through competitions such pillow fights, tugs-of-war, knobbly-knee contests (where men and women stood side by side behind a barrier showing only their bare legs to the judges), or bathing-beauty competitions where women paraded in skimpy bathing suits before other guests. Holiday camps, in the view of their critics, both promoted and colluded in potentially immoral behaviour on a mass scale.

Vernon Jenkins claims that the first early-morning loud-speaker message accidently contributed to the idea of immorality at Butlin's camp. The early-morning message told campers it was 'time to get up', time for breakfast, and 'by the way' it was also 'time to go back to your own chalets'.[108] It was meant as a joke, although there was an element of truth to it, Jenkins claims. Detractors picked up on the 'joke' and used it as evidence of sexual misconduct.

Butlin nevertheless heatedly denied the allegations. According to Butlin, every guest applied in writing to his camp, providing a name and address, plus a deposit in advance. Butlin explained that the average patron of the holiday camp is a 'clean-minded family man who would make unpleasant people so uncomfortable that they would clear out of their own accord'. In addition, the camp management reserved the right to 'expel any person who is found guilty of misbehaviour'. And, Butlin explained, this right 'would be immediately used if it became necessary'. It was therefore 'ridiculous to lay sweeping charges of immorality against holiday campers', he claimed. 'You have only to see one of the open-air church services at our camp to realise the absurdity of any such charge.' Butlin argued that two weeks earlier the Bishop of Grimsby had conducted the service at the Skegness camp, followed by the Bishop of Lincoln the succeeding week, and both these 'eminent ecclesiastics expressed their wholehearted approval of the camp. Is there any hotel in the country', Butlin asked, 'that can say the same?' As to the suggestion that the

BUTLIN'S LUXURY HOLIDAY CAMP, CLACTON-ON-SEA.

9   Butlin's Luxury Holiday Camp, Clacton-on-Sea, c. 1939

management invited prostitutes to service guests, Butlin argued the charge was 'so absurd as to be ludicrous'. The Skegness enterprise represented an investment of £120,000, therefore any 'sane person will realise that people who have invested very considerable sums in an enterprise of this character will not risk the disfavour of the masses by encouraging loose conduct'. His camp offered affordable and respectable holidays that kept guests 'so busily occupied with wholesome and health-giving activities that they [had] ... neither the time nor the inclination for mischief'.[109]

While critics continued to malign the holiday-camp industry, local resistance to Butlin's new camp in Clacton persisted. By way of compromise and in an effort to defuse the resistance to his new business venture, Butlin offered hoteliers and town boosters an unprecedented opportunity to advertise Clacton as a whole rather than simply his new camp. Butlin had engaged ten canvassers to go to businesses that employed 500 to 1,000 workers to explain the amenities available at the new camp later in the season. Many of those canvassed expressed an interest in Clacton, but not in the new holiday camp, as a potential venue for their summer holiday. This response suggested that either the idea of an organised, all-inclusive holiday-camp holiday did not appeal to everyone, or the cost remained outside the range of many workers. Butlin suggested that, in the interest of marketing the resort as a whole, the canvassers offer a list of the names and addresses and tariffs of hotels and boarding houses to potential guests not interested in the holiday camp. While not permitted to take hotel bookings, the canvassers could pass the information

'Elizabethan style' chalet accommodation at Butlin's Clacton Holiday Camp **10**

back to the hoteliers. This co-operation, according to Butlin, 'would materially assist the hotels and boarding houses and also prove a benefit to Clacton as a whole'.[110] It would also smooth the way for the grand opening of Butlin's second camp in Clacton in 1938 with accommodation for 2,000 guests each week of the season.[111] While this solution did not completely appease holiday-camp detractors, it did at least defuse the potentially damaging antagonism in Clacton.

In his memoir, Butlin jokingly remembers the opposition to his business ventures. Local antagonism accompanied any plans for the erection of a holiday camp, largely, he claimed, because of their mass appeal and success.[112] Undeterred by the very public hostility to his camps, Butlin used even negative press to promote what he described as a holiday 'revolution'.[113] Warner also faced some local opposition to the development of his holiday camps, but it was the size of the Butlin camps that appeared to pose a greater threat to opponents. Although Warner catered for a maximum of 600 guests per camp each week, Butlin accommodated over 1,000 at Skegness and 2,000 at Clacton, with plans to extend to as many as 10,000 campers per week at other sites.[114] Both Warner and Butlin claimed to revolutionise the holiday-camp industry through the all-inclusiveness of their tariff, and through the quality of their entertainments and accommodation. Yet Butlin in particular utilised economies of scale to provide them and, in doing so, took the idea of standardised mass leisure to a new level.

'Enforced gaiety': political support and national critics

In 1938 Butlin asked Lord Strabolgi, Labour MP for Hull, to open his new camp at Clacton. Butlin's aim was twofold. Strabolgi, as an MP, lent political legitimacy to the endeavour. One of the pioneers of the camping movement, a former amateur boxer and naval officer, Strabolgi was also well known as a strong supporter of the new industry. Holiday camps like the one at Clacton, argued Strabolgi in his speech, were endeavours that provided people with a truly British experience within their own country. Commenting on the accommodation, the meals, and the entertainment, Strabolgi claimed that Britons need not travel abroad to experience 'a democratic movement', where 'everyone was treated alike'.[115] The recent successful campaign for holidays with pay was indicative of the social equality in Britain. In Butlin's camp, Strabolgi maintained, that equality continued. 'There [is] no first, second, or third class … Everyone [is] treated alike. Rich people and people of modest means [can] come' to the camp and receive 'the same treatment, same meals, same games and same pleasures'.[116] According to Strabolgi, holiday camps like the one at Clacton embodied all the elements of social equality that British democracy envisaged.

Despite Strabolgi's enthusiastic support, Butlin's new camp, like Skegness two years earlier, however, was barely finished. While construction and landscaping continued to occupy Butlin, opposition to his Skegness camp took on another and more ominous form.[117] The campsite experienced two large fires in five

II   Butlin's Luxury Holiday Camp, Clacton-on-Sea, advert, 29 April 1938

days in February 1939, just before the beginning of the third season. Police attributed both fires to arson. The first blaze destroyed the largest building on the campsite, the Viennese Ballroom and concert hall, complete with a brand-new Hammond Organ and the linen for 2,000 guests.[118] Butlin received an anonymous letter after this first fire that claimed it was a deliberate attempt to destroy the holiday camp. The evening before the second fire, a man 'advanced in his cups' in a local pub predicted there would be another fire at the camp. The second blaze, accompanied by three explosions, consumed the dining hall and the American cocktail bar.[119] Exasperated at what he saw as the second malicious attempt to destroy the camp at Skegness, Butlin used the publicity from the fires to advertise improvements to the camp as he rebuilt Skegness in time for the Easter opening of the 1939 season.[120]

Butlin countered opposition to his camps and used any publicity to promote the facilities and wide choice of activities and entertainment available to his guests. The large number of guests and the provision of activities on a mass scale meant that, unlike at other resorts, every camper could enjoy all activities free of charge. National critics, however, pointed to the standardisation of the mass holiday industry as indicative of *less* choice and a sign of more incipient changes in British culture and society. In their history of interwar Britain, Robert Graves and Alan Hodge argue that the 'American-style' holiday camps of the 1930s catered largely for the lower middle-class 'shop-girls and salesmen' happy to have everything organised for them by camp staff.[121]

The modern cocktail bar at Butlin's Skegness Camp, c. 1936   **12**

Others saw the camps as ceaseless activity and obligatory fun. Guy Ramsay of the *News Chronicle* claimed in 1937 that holiday camps represented 'A major social phenomenon' that altered the 'age-old manner of the English holiday'. As a nation, Ramsay claimed, the English 'have always been accused of taking … pleasures sadly'. Now, however, holiday camps compel the English to take holidays 'in enforced gaiety'. The camps cost approximately £3 per week, roughly equivalent to the weekly wage of a manual worker (and still too expensive for most wage-earners). For the same £3, Ramsay continued, guests 'have partners or opponents for every game' played. Despite the plethora of choice, Ramsay concluded, surrounded by hundreds of other guests, the option for solitude or meditation was not available.[122]

While the holiday camps provided each guest with the material aspects of a holiday, according to Ramsay, the camps were spiritually bereft, with no time for real rest, solitude, or thought. The 'completely communal life … the unflagging striving for gaiety – even the bathrooms are labelled "lads" and "lasses" rather than "Ladies" and "Gentlemen" – the eternal music, incessantly blaring; the radio-control', and, most importantly, 'the organisation of pleasure as a business', ultimately led to a hollow and spiritually bankrupt experience. After one day at Butlin's Skegness, Ramsay concluded, 'The camp is unquestionably a move in the direction of the Brave New World so bitterly satirised by Aldous Huxley.'[123]

Ramsay's reference to Huxley's dystopia, in which Fordist principles of mass production are applied to every aspect of daily life in an attempt to maintain social stability, resonated strongly with a larger group of intellectual critics.[124] Opposed to what they perceived as the 'Americanisation' of British popular culture and the growth of mass leisure, contemporary social critics such as F. R. Leavis and George Orwell abhorred the standardised entertainments and incessant group activities of the holiday camps.[125] The American 'cocktail' and 'milk bars' in the camps and the perpetual striving for gaiety signalled, for these critics, the insipid spread of American popular culture.[126] The consumption of mass-produced goods and amusements, they claimed, dulled the intellect and diluted the character of British culture. For these British intellectuals, America served as 'the image of industrial barbarism; a country with no past and therefore no culture', and a very real threat to British society.[127] Echoing the critique of modernity and consumer capitalism in the work of Theodor Adorno and Max Horkheimer in Germany and of novelists like Sinclair Lewis in the United States, Leavis and Orwell expressed anxiety about the apparent ability of the new and powerful culture industry to create passivity and political conformity among consumers.[128] For the British critics, 'Americanisation' was not so much a process as the invocation of a number of 'ideological themes' such as the breakdown of patriarchy and the 'feminisation' of British culture.[129] In his novel *Coming up for Air*, Orwell wrote about the youth who worked in the 'slick and shiny and streamlined' milk bars and adopted a disinterested rudeness toward older customers who ventured in.[130] The standardised cocktails and the food and drink sold at the milk bars replaced older English drinks like stout and cider or tea with a sort of 'phantom stuff' that came out of 'a carton or a tin … or squirted out of a tap or squeezed out of a tube' and was 'tasteless'.[131] For Orwell, Americanisation was the process that stimulated a desire for more standardisation – a desire that not only standardised taste but dulled the senses to the extent that it was impossible to distinguish between flavour and appearance.[132] Thus, for Orwell, the consumption of the unvarying products of American industrialisation and the influence of an ever-expanding mass culture signified a critical loss of an older and more masculine culture.

Later cultural theorists like Andreas Huyssen claim that the universalising attribution of femininity to mass culture began in the nineteenth century and coincided with the age of burgeoning socialism and the first major women's movement.[133] The threat that both these movements posed to the dominant culture was expressed as the feminisation of the 'masses' in general and 'mass culture' in particular. Huyssen argues that the 'political, psychological, and aesthetic discourse around the turn of the century consistently and obsessively' gendered mass culture and the masses as feminine and 'high culture' as male, because not only were the masses 'knocking at the gate', so were women knocking at the gate of a male-dominated high culture.[134] When social critics perceived a lack of personality and choice in the emerging mass culture of the 1920s and 1930s, implicit in their criticism was the gendered notion of the 'mass' as somehow 'feminised' by the consumption of American-style entertainment.

For British intellectual elites, the consumption of standardised goods and entertainments available in holiday camps, as well as the influence of mass media, changed the lives and values of an older and more 'authentic' British working-class culture and, as a result, maintained sharp class divisions. According to authors like Orwell and Leavis, authentic culture centred on a more creative type of leisure requiring an interactive response, or an activity that promoted thoughtful contemplation. Leisure should stimulate intellectual growth in some way, and not act merely as a distraction. Americanisation in this sense supported a culture industry that created inexpensive, standardised entertainments such as those that were available at Butlin's and Warner's camps and that were passive and required no intellectual response.[135] Yet, as British historian Matthew Hilton points out, the perceived threat of Americanisation and the consumption of standardised leisure and entertainment seemed to cause anxiety only among the middle-class elites with resources to consume in alternate ways.[136] For many working- and lower middle-class consumers, the relatively inexpensive American-style entertainment and goods made available by standardisation and mass production offered a degree of choice hitherto unknown.[137]

While intellectuals feared that the working classes were subdued and made politically inactive by the consumption of mass pleasure, others feared that resorts would be overrun by the 'unwashed' masses. At the annual dinner of the Hastings and St Leonard's Hotels and Caterers' Association in December 1937, the mayor of Hastings, Councillor E. M. Ford, voiced alarm about the effect of holidays with pay on resort clientele. The mayor predicted an increased 'patronage of seaside resorts by *the masses*', and a decrease in the patronage '*of the classes*', and warned that holidays with pay would see 'the teeming millions in London and the Midlands … descend like locusts' on southern seaside resorts (his emphasis).[138] For this particular hotelier, the predicament that the hotel industry faced included insufficient facilities, but more pressingly, a fear of what the 'teeming millions' of excursionists would do to middle-class resorts. Not only would an increased working-class clientele lead to a loss of middle-class customers and reduce the prestige of the resort, but Mayor Ford feared that the 'teeming millions' would consume the resort like a plague of biblical proportions.

In his speech, the mayor of Hastings voiced an anxiety highlighted by the economic and political instability of the interwar years – an unease about the activities of the working classes when massed. The identification of the crowd with the lower instincts, emotions, and sensations emanated from ancient times. The extension of the franchise, the rise of mass retailing, the growth of socialism, and the emergence of mass entertainment all contributed to a fear of the 'masses'. The development of social psychology in France and England in the late nineteenth and early twentieth centuries supplied a scientific foundation for the idea of collective behaviour. The ideas propounded by French social psychologist Gustave Le Bon, who studied the thinking and emotions of crowds, which he regarded as essentially irrational in behaviour and tending towards hysteria, gained currency in early twentieth-century Britain.[139] The English translation of Le Bon's *The Crowd* went through twelve editions by

1920 and augmented Wilfred Trotter's 1916 portrayal of the masses in *Instinct of the Herd in Peace and War*.[140] These ideas, combined with the belief that the working classes preferred crowds, created an image of workers as individuals with base instincts, drawn to excesses, unpredictability, and transgressive behaviours when massed.

Public events gave force to these psychological theories. Perceptions of working-class hooliganism and petty crime became enshrined in popular memory of the Blackpool Carnivals of 1923 and 1924. In an attempt to extend the holiday season after the First World War, Blackpool organised a week-long carnival in 1923 to encourage business and enhance the reputation of the town. The success of the 1923 carnival encouraged promoters to plan one the following year. However, the second carnival was beset with reports of unruly behaviour, public displays of sexuality, crime, and hooliganism. In addition, inebriated day-trippers returned to inland towns in no fit state to return to work the following day and so promoters relinquished the idea of a third annual carnival.[141] The 'carnivals promoted hedonism and irresponsibility', historian John Walton points out, and also encouraged workers to enjoy pleasure 'outside the agreed holiday periods'.[142] The result was disapproval and an unintended reputation for the town. While Blackpool was safely in the north of England, Brighton was uncomfortably close to Hastings, and when Graham Greene's novel *Brighton Rock* uncovered a fictional underworld of crime and disorder mingling with the masses on the beaches and under the pier, anxieties among resort promoters, like the mayor of St Leonard's, increased.[143]

Greene's novel about protection rackets and gang warfare in Brighton exposed a seamier side of the town inundated with mass amusements, entertainments, and mindless, fun-loving crowds. Pinkie, a youth who has overreached himself in his criminal ambitions, is caught up in a life of gang violence and racketeering around the Brighton races. Greene based his novel and characters in *Brighton Rock* on newspaper accounts of a 1936 court case that involved a gang of sixteen men, armed with hatchets, hammers, and iron bars which attacked a bookmaker and his clerk.[144] The court found all the accused guilty of aggravated assault and claimed their incarceration as the end of the race gangs in Brighton. The publicity resulting from the trial brought unusually large crowds of working-class youths to Brighton the following week, presenting the town with an orgy of potential criminal activity.[145]

Greene, a frequent visitor to Brighton, found the newspaper accounts of the trial and its aftermath intriguing. Yet he also wrote his novel as a scathing critique of Brighton in the 1930s, with its mass amusements and hordes of day trippers who acted as a cover for Pinkie's fictitious underworld. The novel opens with Hale, a newspaperman lost among the 'fifty thousand people down for the day' who 'came in by train from Victoria every five minutes'. Despite the anonymity of the swarming crowds, Hale fears for his life as he anticipates that Colleoni's gang will find and kill him for his part in exposing their rackets.[146] At first the crowds make Hale fear for his life, but as he continues to drink, the soulless masses become a protective force. Ultimately Hale is found and murdered. Just as the real-life story of Brighton's underworld captured the attention of the novelist, so Greene's dramatisation of the seedier side of Brighton in the 1930s captured the imagination of working-class youths, drawing them to the seaside resort. Crowds of urban holiday makers filled the beaches once frequented by royalty, while many hoteliers, such as the mayor of St. Leonard's, feared that holidays with pay and the promotion of mass leisure, such as holiday camps, would simply drive even more holiday makers away from their middle-class resorts for fear of the masses.

While the mayor of St Leonard's expressed anxiety about overcrowding and the potential destruction of the coastal resorts by working-class crowds, entrepreneurs like Butlin openly welcomed holiday makers of any class and intended to meet their needs. Although the 'unwashed masses' so feared by the mayor of St Leonard's most often entered the camps as day trippers, the perception remained that holiday camps attracted workers and their families. In an interview with a correspondent for the *Caterer and Hotel Keeper*, Butlin discussed his plans to extend the Skegness camp to accommodate 4,500 guests each week, and build more holiday camps on the same scale. 'I hope to open a new [camp] each year', declared Butlin, to cater for the burgeoning market. The first season for his new camp at Clacton was fully booked in the first week, maintained Butlin. As a result of the desire for a holiday-camp holiday, Butlin was forced to refuse almost 75 per cent of all applications in 1938. The demand for his type of holiday existed, claimed Butlin, and he intended to build camps to accommodate that demand. Unlike the hoteliers who sought to dispel the crowds, the holiday-camp industry and men like Butlin planned for crowds and catered enthusiastically to any class of guest.[147]

Conclusion

The holiday camps built by Warner and Butlin in the 1930s were part of a larger development of Britain's coastal areas and the expansion of mass leisure in the interwar years. Despite the economic depression of the 1930s, Warner and

Butlin built on older forms of leisure that incorporated nineteenth-century ideas of coastal air as health giving and a twentieth-century penchant for physical fitness and mass entertainment. At the same time, Warner and Butlin distanced themselves from the political and religious morality of the earlier camps through commercialism. The holidays-with-pay campaign helped to legitimise the industry, both directly as more workers received annual paid holidays, and indirectly by focusing attention on the working family as a valuable consumer market. Although a camp holiday was still too expensive for most working-class families, holiday camps did provide family holidays for those who could afford them and shifted the focus of attention to catering for children and teenagers. Entrepreneurs like Warner and Butlin recognised the shift in consumer ideology that politicised leisure. Claiming to provide luxury at an affordable price, they helped to transform class politics from one that maintained luxury as the exclusive privilege of the rich into one that included working people and their children. Additionally, as economists on all sides of the political spectrum came to recognise domestic consumption as the key to economic recovery, inexpensive British holiday-camp holidays potentially served to attract the newly leisured workers to spend their leisure time and money in Britain.

Reaction to the camps at local and national levels suggests how, despite government support, mass consumption was a site of contest over the meaning of leisure and the nature of the consumer. As an experiment in mass enjoyment, the camps threatened to intrude into a formally middle- and upper-class terrain of pleasure. Supporters recognised the potential of the camps for the promotion of their towns; detractors decried the class of consumer attracted by the camps. While holiday-camp entrepreneurs welcomed children and teenagers, local residents feared being overwhelmed by youthful delinquents. On a national level, intellectual critics saw holiday camps as an attempt to maintain social stability in a time of political and economic uncertainty. Their critique centred on the regimentation and group activities in the camps, which appeared to deprive individuals of the need to think for themselves. For some critics, the new holiday camps appeared to usher in Huxley's *Brave New World*. For others the mass, standardised pleasure signalled the Americanisation of British culture and simply disengaged the leisure consumer from reality. Mirroring international concern about the growth of totalitarianism and the role of the culture industry in promoting apparent political apathy, for these critics, mass pleasure represented a form of political repression rather than the opportunity to consume inexpensive entertainment otherwise unattainable to many with limited resources.

Men like Warner and Butlin, however, saw the provision of inexpensive annual leisure and distraction from the monotony of modern life as a basic right of every working family as well as the foundation of a potentially lucrative industry. Warner and Butlin responded to what they perceived as the desire of working families by offering frivolous entertainment, constant activity, childcare, activities for teenagers, and regular food at an affordable price. Their leisure empires gained considerable legitimacy and support from the Holidays With Pay Committee, yet it was wartime preparations and policies that significantly aided the growth and expansion of the post-Second World War holiday-camp industry. Significantly, the holidays and the camp culture developed in the 1930s survived the war years and emerged as a uniquely British institution that expanded during post-Second World War austerity. The next chapter explores the way Warner and Butlin constructed a camp culture that survived the war and austerity and helped to make Warner and Butlin household names in post-Second World War Britain.

Notes

1 'Skegness camp opened – W. E. Butlin's faith in advertising', *World's Fair*, 18 April 1936, p. 1.

2 'National newspaper gives Skegness valuable publicity', *Skegness News*, 26 August 1936, p. 1. A week at Butlin's Skegness holiday camp cost between £2 2s. and £3 per person per week, depending on the week selected.

3 Holiday with Pay Committee Report, Part II, 28 April 1938, TNA: PRO, LAB 31/1, p. 38.

4 The 'season' traditionally began in May and continued until September, but also included Easter.

5 Report of the Holidays with Pay Committee, TNA: PRO, LAB 31/1, p. 50.

6 'Skegness holiday camp opened – W. E. Butlin's faith in advertising', *World's Fair*, 18 April 1936, p. 1.

7 T. R. Nevett, *Advertising in Britain: A history* (London, 1982), p. 156.

8 The *Daily Herald* and the *Daily Express* increased their circulation to over two million each by the mid-1930s. The *Express* used aggressive marketing and set new records for newspaper sales throughout the 1930s. See Bingham, *Gender, modernity and popular press*, pp. 22–46 and D. L. LeMahieu, *A culture for democracy: Mass communication and the cultivated mind between the wars* (Oxford: Clarendon Press, 1988), p. 257.

9 'Where to spend your summer holidays', *Daily Herald*, 25 April 1936, pp. 6–7.

10 Cross, *Time and Money*, pp. 99–100.

11 Hilton, *Consumerism*, pp. 108–36.

12 J. Walvin, *Beside the seaside: A social history of the popular seaside holiday* (London: Penguin, 1978), p. 67 and J. Hassan, *The seaside, health and the environment in*

England and Wales since 1800 (Aldershot: Ashgate Publishing, 2003), pp. 6–7.

13 E. Swinglehurst, *Cook's Tours: The story of popular travel* (Poole: Blandford Press, 1982), pp. 7–33.

14 J. Walton, 'The world's first working-class seaside resort? Blackpool revisited, 1840–1974', *Lancashire and Cheshire Antiquarian Society* (1994), pp. 23–30.

15 Walton, 'Blackpool landlady revisited', pp. 23–30. Thomas Cook also established cheap hostels for his excursion customers. See Swinglehurst, *Cook's Tours*, p. 32.

16 Walton, 'Demand for working-class seaside holidays', pp. 249–65.

17 D. Prynn, 'The Clarion Clubs, rambling and the holiday associations in Britain since the 1890s', *Journal of Contemporary History*, 11:2/3 (1976), pp. 65–77.

18 J. Kasson, *Amusing the million: Coney Island at the turn of the century* (New York: Hill & Wang, 1978), p. 73 and W. Register, *The kid of Coney Island: Fred Thompson and the rise of American amusements* (Oxford: Oxford University Press, 2001), pp. 3–22.

19 Bennett, 'Hegemony, ideology, pleasure', pp. 135–54.

20 Ward and Hardy, *Goodnight campers!* pp. 18–22.

21 The Florence Institute for Boys provided training in basic skills for future employment for poor and orphaned boys. Beaven, *Leisure, citizenship*, pp. 25–43.

22 Ward and Hardy, *Goodnight campers!* pp. 18–22.

23 J. Drower, *Good clean fun: The story of Britain's first holiday camp* (London: Arcadia Books, 1982), p. 21.

24 *The Camp Herald: For Season 1904 – March till October, The International Young Man's Holiday Camp, Douglas, Isle of Man, 1904*, p. 2 and D. E. Hall, ed. *Muscular Christianity: Embodying the Victorian age* (Cambridge: Cambridge University Press, 1994), introduction.

25 *Camp Herald*: 1904, p. 2.

26 Davin, 'Imperialism and motherhood', p. 10.

27 Letter from 'Stockton-on-Tees', *The Camp Herald: The International Young Man's Holiday Camp, Douglas, Isle of Man*, 1904, p. 10.

28 For a discussion of nineteenth-century anxieties about working-class alcohol consumption see C. G. Brown, *The death of Christian Britain* (London: Routledge, 2001), pp. 118–120 and Ross, *Love and toil*, pp. 42–44.

29 Cross, *Time and money*, pp. 101–5.

30 Homo-social environments existed in education and work. See Deslandes, *Oxbridge men* and A. Gilbert, 'Buggery and the British Navy, 1700–1861', *Journal of Social History*, 10 (1976), pp. 72–98.

31 See C. Waters, *British Socialists and the politics of popular culture* (Manchester: Manchester University Press, 1990) for a discussion of the political uses of holiday camps before the Second World War.

32 Barton, *Working-class organisations*, pp. 146–7.

33 Ward and Hardy, *Goodnight campers!* pp. 12–17.

34 Ibid., p. 16.

35 Langhamer, *Women's leisure*, p. 39.

36 F. T., '1066 and all that', *Holiday Camp Review*, 1:2 (May 1938), pp. 3–4, British Library (hereafter BL) PP.1832.HK.

37 E. W. Wimble, 'New free service for our readers: Holiday hints and suggestion bureau – watch for coupon', *Lansbury Labour Weekly*, 17 April 1926, p. 2.

38 W. J. Brown, *So far* ... (London: George Allen & Unwin, 1943), pp. 113–14.

39 Ibid., p. 113.

40 Ward and Hardy, *Goodnight campers!* pp. 44–55. Other unions followed and the National Association of Local Government Officers opened a holiday camp at Croyde Bay in Devon in 1930, and two years later a second camp at Coyton Bay, near Scarborough. See 'Holiday camp developments', *Caterer and Hotel Keeper*, 11 February 1933, p. 252.

41 Brown, *So far* ..., pp. 114–16.

42 Ibid., p. 115.

43 Hayling Island is approximately five miles in length, shaped like an upside-down 'T'. The southern shore that makes up the widest portion of the island is approximately five miles across. Warner chose to locate his first camp on the north shore, as far away from the fun fair and the union camp as was geographically possible.

44 Norfolk Crescent was an attempt to replicate the Royal Crescents at Brighton and Bath. William Padwick began building in 1825, but work was never completed. When he died in 1864, bankruptcy forced his son to auction the Crescent. See 'Particulars and Conditions of Sale', 23 September 1864, Hampshire Record Office (hereafter HRO) 114M90/2/1–8.

45 J. Harrison, interview with author, 14 September 2001.

46 H. Warner, interview by P. Baxter, 1998, Wessex Sound and Film Archive (hereafter WSFA) AV632/16/S1.

47 Agreement between the Rural District Council of Havant and H .J. Warner of the Grotto, Hayling Island, 14 March 1932, HRO 15M75 DDC/446.

48 Letter from L. Cannon, Superintendent of St Patrick's Open Air School, Hayling Island, to W. G. Madgewick, Clerk to Havant and Waterloo Urban District Council, 7 July 1933; letters from W. G. Madgewick to L. Cannon, 10 July 1933, W. G. Madgewick to H. Warner, 4 August 1933, and H. Warner to W. G. Madge-wick, 11 August 1933, HRO 15M74/DDC46.

49 The removal of the amusements featured in the 1932 local election campaign. See election letter from P. H. Cockayne of Gable Head, Hayling Island, addressed to the electors of Hayling Island; and A. E. Jones, Red House, Beach Road, Hayling Island, letter to the electors of Hayling Island, March 1932, Portsmouth Central Library, Local Studies Collection (PCL LSC).

50 Hayling was a rural island but in the summer months many farmers rented fields to visitors in tents, caravans, and converted railway carriages. Patricia Ross, *Hayling Island voices* (Stroud: Tempus, 2000), ch. 8.

51 The Northney camp was approximately one mile from the closest railway station, at Langstone, and three miles from the closest mainland town of Havant.

52 Ward and Hardy, *Goodnight campers!* p. 55.

53 H. Warner, WSFA AV 623/36/1–51.

54 'Holiday attractions and accommodation', Northney holiday-camp advert, *News Chronicle*, 30 June 1933, p. 16.

55 E. Furlough, 'Packaging pleasures: Club Méditéranée and French consumer culture, 1950–1968', *French Historical Studies*, 18:1 (Spring 1993), pp. 65–81.

56 Sunshine holiday-camp advert, *Daily Herald*, 19 May 1936, p. 14.

57 J. A. Booker, *Blackshirts-on-Sea: A pictorial history of the Mosley summer camps 1933–1938* (London: Brockingday Publications, 1999), p. 112.

58 R. McQueen, *The Eatons: The rise and fall of Canada's Royal family* (Toronto: Stoddart, 1999), p. 4.

59 The summer camp for men was established in 1917, with tents, a swimming pool and sports programmes. Employees could spend a week or just a day at Work-a-day camp. McQueen, *The Eatons*, p. 40. A similar type of company holiday existed in France and Britain in the early twentieth century. Cross, *Time and money*, pp. 99–127.

60 W. Butlin with P. Dacre, *The Billy Butlin story: A showman to the end* (London: Robeson, 1982), p. 114.

61 Ibid., pp. 29–81.

62 C. Mills, *The Bertram Mills Circus story* (London: Hutchinson, 1965), p. 36.

63 'Skegness holiday camp opened: W. E. Butlin's faith in advertising', *World's Fair*, 18 April 1936, p. 1.

64 I borrow the term 'imagined community' from Benedict Anderson, who explores the processes of community creation in *Imagined communities: Reflections on the origin and spread of nationalism* (London: Verso, 1991).

65 Northney holiday-camp advertisement, *Daily News Chronicle*, 9 June 1934, p. 15.

66 'News Chronicle sunshine inset', *News Chronicle*, 14 June 1934, p. 10.

67 C. Pithey in *Secret lives: Billy Butlin*, 52 mins, dir. Nick Goodwin, Praxis Films Ltd. (1997).

68 Butlin claims the advert cost an extraordinary £500 and was a gamble that paid off. R. North, *The Butlin story* (London, 1962), pp. 50–1.

69 'Holidays are jollydays at Butlin's Skegness holiday camp', *Daily Express*, 11 April 1936, p. 3.

70 'Easter opening of Mr. W. E. Butlin's new £50,000 holiday camp at Skegness', *Skegness News*, 15 April 1936, p. 1.

71 V. Jenkins in *Secret lives*.

72 One key missing amenity was water, although builders and plumbers worked through the night before the grand opening and successfully established a water supply. Butlin with Dacre, *Butlin story*, pp. 106–8.

73 'Easter opening of Mr. W. E. Butlin's new £50,000 holiday camp at Skegness', *Skegness News*, 15 April 1936, p. 1. Butlin increased the accommodation at Skegness from 1,400 to 1,800 guests in the second season. 'Extensions at Skegness holiday camp', *Skegness News*, 17 February 1937, p. 3.

74 Butlin with Dacre, *Butlin story*, p. 114.

75 Butlin claimed that he chose the motto but had no idea the quote was from Shakespeare. See ibid., pp. 109–10.

76 C. Reeve in *Secret lives*.

77 'Gala dance at Butlin's super holiday camp', *Skegness News*, 6 May 1936, p. 4.

78 Butlin's advert, *Skegness News*, 22 September 1937, p. 7.

79 'Butlin's avenge previous defeat – decisive home win', *Clacton News and East Essex Advertiser*, 29 January 1938, p. 10.

80 Butlin's Skegness Hospital Carnival advert, *Skegness News*, 23 June 1937, p. 5.

81 The Jolly Fisherman logo was designed by artist John Hassall before the First World War, and adopted as the Skegness resort symbol after the war.

82 'Easter opening of Mr. W. E. Butlin's new £50,000 holiday camp at Skegness', *Skegness News*, 15 April 1936, p. 1.

83 'Mayor of Boston comes for help to Skegness', *Skegness News*, 4 May 1938, p. 3.

84 'Over a thousand local children entertained at Shirley Butlin's birthday party', *Skegness News*, 30 September 1936, p. 3.

85 'Shirley Butlin's birthday party', *World's Fair*, 3 October 1936, p. 3.

86 'Mr. Butlin attacked: amazing resolutions moved at monthly Council meeting', *Skegness News*, 3 June 1936, p. 1.

87 'Famous poster artists meet at holiday camp', *Skegness News*, 15 September 1937, p. 4.

88 For a history of Sabbatarian opposition to leisure on Sundays see Pimlott, *Englishman's holiday*, ch. 9.

89 'Minutes of the Joint Advisory Commission quote: Mr. W. E. Butlin's challenge', *Skegness News*, 3 March 1937, p. 8.

90 'Skegness Rector conducts holiday-camp service', *Skegness News*, 28 July 1937, p. 6.

91 *The Sunday Circle* editorial was also reported in the local Skegness paper. See 'Free Churches and the holiday camp', *Skegness News*, 8 September 1937, p. 7.

92 'Opening of Dovercourt Bay holiday camp: really a modern seaside hotel', *Harwich and Dovercourt Standard*, 12 June 1937, pp. 2–3. Warner and Butlin collaborated on the design of the Dovercourt Bay holiday camp. Butlin served on Warner's company board for many years.

93 For a discussion of interwar pastoralism see J. Esty, *A shrinking island: Modernism and national culture in England* (Princeton: Princeton University Press, 2004), chs. 1, 4 and A. Howkins, *The death of rural England: A social history of the countryside since 1900* (London, 2003), Part II.

94 'Opening of Dovercourt Bay holiday camp – really a modern seaside hotel', *Harwich and Dovercourt Standard*, 12 June 1937, pp. 2–3.

95 'Yarmouth hotel-keepers unite – new Association formed – will meet holiday-camp competition', *Caterer and Hotel Keeper*, 10 June 1933, p. 10.

96 A. E. Nickolds, 'Keeping your guests amused: how to avoid boredom of wet days', *Caterer and Hotel Keeper*, 3 April 1936, pp. 35–6.

97 A. Sheraton, 'Catering for children in holiday hotels', *Caterer and Hotel Keeper*, 8 May 1936, pp. 24–5.

98 A. E. Nickolds, 'You will please the parents if you cater for the children', *Caterer and Hotel Keeper*, 11 September 1936, pp. 24–5.

99 'Easter opening of Mr. W. E. Butlin's New £50,000 holiday camp at Skegness', *Skegness News*, 15 April 1936, p. 1.

100 See L. Jacobson, *Raising consumers: Children and the American mass market in the early twentieth century* (New York: Columbia University Press, 2004), pp. 93–126.

101 See P. Tinkler, *Constructing girlhood: Popular magazines for girls growing up in England, 1920–1950* (London: Taylor & Francis, 1995).

102 D. Fowler, 'Teenage consumers? Young wage-earners and leisure in Manchester, 1919–1939', in A. Davies, S. Fielding and T. Wyke, eds *Worker's worlds: Cultures and communities in Manchester and Salford 1880–1939* (Manchester: Manchester University Press, 1992), pp. 145–6.

103 Bingham, *Gender, modernity and the popular press*, pp. 104–5.

104 A. J. Greenly, *Psychology as a sales factor* (London: Pitman, 1927) p. 196.

105 'Hoteliers oppose holiday-camp scheme: Strong protests at Clacton enquiry', *Caterer and Hotel Keeper*, 23 July 1937, p. 12.

106 McKibben, *Classes and cultures*, pp. 164–205, L. Rabbinovitz, 'Temptations of pleasure: Nickleodeons, amusement parks, and the sights of female sexuality', *Camera Obscura*, 23 May 1990, pp. 71–88, and J. Flanders, *Consuming passions: Leisure and pleasure in Victorian Britain* (London: HarperPress, 2006).

107 'Mr. William Butlin writes on holiday camps: Holiday-camp magnate reveals the truth', *Skegness News*, 14 July 1937, p. 3.

108 Jenkins in *Secret Lives*.

109 'Mr. William Butlin writes on holiday camps: Holiday-camp magnate reveals the truth', *Skegness News*, 14 July 1937, p. 3.

110 'Butlin's offer to Clacton hoteliers: Campaign for boosting Clacton', *Clacton News and East Essex Advertiser*, 15 January 1938, p. 1.

111 'Opening of Butlin's holiday camp: Best thing in Clacton's history', *Clacton News and East Essex Advertiser*, 18 June, 1938, p. 9, 'Butlin super celebration week', *Clacton News and East Essex Advertiser*, 2 July 1938, p. 11, and 'Another £100,000 luxury holiday camp opened at Clacton-on-Sea', *Skegness News*, 22 June 1938, p. 2, 'Clacton holiday camp visited – accommodation for two thousand', *Skegness News*, 27 July 1938, p. 7.

112 Butlin with Dacre, *Butlin story*, chs. 5–6.

113 'Holidays with play – the holiday revolution Butlin's luxury camps', *Daily Mirror*, 28 April 1939, p. 10.

114 'Butlin's two new schemes – holiday camp at Filey: hotel in Ostend', *Caterer and Hotel Keeper*, 28 July 1939, p. 9.

115 'Opening of Butlin's luxury holiday camp', *Clacton News*, 18 June 1938, p. 9.

116 The Skegness press noted, 'Another £100,000 luxury holiday camp opened at Clacton-on-Sea', *Skegness News*, 22 June 1938, p. 2.

117 Road construction and landscaping was unfinished at the camp. Building continued behind ten-foot-high screens. 'Butlin's holiday camp preparing for opening', *Clacton News*, 11 June 1938, p. 5.

118 'Big blaze at holiday camp: Main concert hall destroyed', *Skegness News*, 8 February 1939, p. 5.

119 'Mystery of second big fire at Butlin's holiday camp: Second malicious attempt allegation', *Skegness News*, 15 February 1939, p. 1.

120 'Million in great forget crisis holiday', *Daily Herald*, pp. 7 April 1939, p. 9, Holidays with play, Butlin's advert, *Daily Herald*, 15 April 1939, p. 9, and Luxury holiday camping, Butlin's advert, *Daily Mirror*, 15 April 1939, p. 10.

121 Other camps met the needs of specific guests such as musicians or actors. Graves and Lodge, *Long weekend*, p. 381.

122 G. Ramsey, 'Thousands of people are having a new kind of holiday', *News Chronicle*, 24 June 1937, p. 10.

123 Ibid.

124 A. Huxley, *Brave new world* [1932] (New York: HarperCollins, 1998).

125 R. Hoggart, *The uses of literacy* (New Brunswick: Transaction Publishers, 1998), p. 180.

126 See F. R. Leavis, *Mass civilization and minority culture* (London: Folcourt, 1930), *Culture and environment* (London: Chatto & Windus, 1933), and G. Orwell, *Coming up for air* (London: Pitman, 1962), for a critique of Americanisation.

127 Hebdige, 'Cartography of taste', p. 58.

128 T. W. Adorno and M. Horkheimer, 'The culture industry: Enlightenment as mass deception', in M. G. Durham and D. M. Keller, eds *Media and cultural studies: Keyworks* (Malden MA: Blackwell Publishers Inc, 2001), pp. 71–101 and S. Lewis, *Main street* (New York: Signet, 1920) and *Babbitt* [1922] (New York: Signet, 1961).

129 Hebdige, 'Cartography of taste', p. 58 and Victoria de Grazia, *Irresistible empire: America's advance through twentieth century Europe* (Cambridge, MA: Belknap, 2005), pp. 552–6.

130 Orwell, *Coming up*, p. 26.

131 Ibid.

132 G. Orwell, *The road to Wigan pier* (San Diego: Harcourt 1958), p. 204.

133 A. Huyssen, *After the great divide: Modernism, mass culture, postmodernism* (Bloomington: Indiana University Press, 1986), pp. 44–62. Also S. Barrows, *Distorting mirrors: Visions of the crowd in late nineteenth century France* (New Haven, CT: Yale University Press 1981), ch. 7, and J. Carey, *The intellectuals and the masses: Pride and prejudice among the literary intelligentsia, 1880–1939* (London: Faber and Faber, 1993), Part I.

134 Huyssen, *After the great divide*, p. 47.

135 Leavis, *Mass civilization*, pp. 6–8.

136 Hilton, *Consumerism*, pp. 79–107.

137 B. Newman, 'Holidays and social class', in M. Smith, S. Parker and C. Smith, eds *Leisure and society in Britain* (London: Allen Lane, 1973), pp. 230–40.

138 'Warning to seaside hoteliers serious effect of holidays with pay plan: "masses" to drive away "classes"', *Caterer and Hotel Keeper*, 10 December 1937, p. 31.

139 G. Le Bon, *The crowd: A study of the popular mind* (London: Unwin, 1896), p. 15. On Le Bon see R. Nye, *The origins of crowd psychology: Gustave Le Bon and the crisis of mass democracy in the Third Republic* (London: Sage Publications, 1975).

140 LeMahieu, *Culture for democracy*, pp. 103–37 and R. Soffer, *Ethics and society in England: The revolution in the social sciences, 1870–1914* (Berkeley: University of California Press, 1978), pp. 217–51 for a discussion of Trotter.

141 J. Walton, 'Popular entertainment and public order: The Blackpool carnivals of 1923–4', *Northern History*, 34 (1998), pp. 170–88.

142 Ibid., p. 187.

143 G. Greene, *Brighton rock* [1938] (New York: Alfred A. Knopf, 1996).

144 'Sixteen sentenced behind locked doors', *Daily Herald*, 30 July 1936, p. 1.

145 J. Carey, 'Introduction', in Greene, *Brighton rock*, p. ix and N. Sherry, *The life of Graham Greene, 1904–1939* Vol. I (New York, 1989), ch. 39. Greene spent some time at the Brighton races in an attempt to write a more realistic novel.

146 Greene, *Brighton rock*, p. 9.

147 'Butlin plans more holiday camps', *Caterer and Hotel Keeper*, 8 July 1938, p. 11.

3

Advertising holiday-camp culture and inventing social harmony

On the last day of May 1936, British aviators Amy and Jim Mollison, newly returned from their record-setting transatlantic flight, landed at Butlin's Skegness holiday camp.[1] Blown off course by the blustery weather, the tiny plane and its two occupants finally touched down in a field just outside the campsite, much to the delight of thousands of onlookers. Following the celebrated couple's ecstatic welcome by Butlin, local Skegness dignitaries and over 15,000 campers and visitors looked on as they oversaw the opening of the camp's new bathing pool. A short while later Butlin asked Amy if she would like to stay for a few days. 'Oh yes', she replied, because the camp was 'an ideal holiday' with everything on hand. The Skegness camp was, Amy said, 'especially suitable for people who have only a week' for an annual summer holiday. Indeed, the famous aviatrix claimed, 'it would be a good thing to have a holiday camp like this at every seaside place … in England'.[2] Butlin was delighted with her response.

The decision to ask the famous couple to open the new bathing pool at the Skegness camp was part of Butlin's effort to publicise his new commercial venture. Yet the use of national celebrities like the Mollisons for publicity also marked a significant shift in the nature of holiday-camp advertising. Although the use of personal endorsement to sell products has a long history, the notion of celebrity testimonies increased in the interwar years as the range of those who gained celebrity status expanded to include common people with uncommon abilities. The professionalisation of the advertising industry, in combination with new and improved printing technologies, meant that larger sections of the British public saw quality images of celebrities in a greater number of media. Furthermore, the possibility of who could become a celebrity also changed. Prior to the First World War, celebrity was often reserved for royalty or those with high social status. After the war, the expansion of daily newspapers, weekly magazines, cinema, and radio appeared to democratise celebrity by opening up new opportunities for consumer-product endorsement by members of different class groups. Thus, the intersection of two emergent interwar industries – advertising and luxury holiday camps – challenged traditional ideas of celebrity and, at the same time, helped to create brand-name recognition and consumer loyalty for the holiday camps.[3]

Advertisements in the 1930s highlighted the unique nature of the holiday camps as well as the celebrity-style entertainment that campers could expect. In addition to the well-publicised performances by a number of famous entertainers, 'surprise' celebrity appearances at the camps created an atmosphere of anticipation that promised to make each camp holiday distinctive. The ploy worked, and satisfied customers returned each year.

For Warner and Butlin, the trick was to ensure that holiday goers returned to *their* camps and not those of their competitors. To do so, the two entrepreneurs carefully packaged their camps and created a brand consciousness through specific advertising strategies that made their names familiar to as many consumers as possible. They also created an appealing holiday-camp culture.[4] As we have seen, this camp culture grew around the physical structures and amenities of the campsites. But there was more to holiday-camp culture than modern buildings and comfortable quarters. Camp culture also depended upon the unique activities and entertainment that promoted friendliness and familiarity between camp hosts and guests. Butlin's and Warner's camps both reinvented and borrowed from older working-class traditions and ultimately transformed and nationalised working-class culture by their marketing strategies. Even as critics saw the mass camps as part of the 'Americanisation' of popular culture, Butlin and Warner promoted their camp culture as essentially British. To sell this camp culture to potential holiday makers, Warner and Butlin paid for large advertisements in national newspapers and magazines.[5] They also encouraged reporters to write about their camps and persuaded entertainers and overnight British celebrities, like the Mollisons, to visit them.

This chapter explores the creation of this unique holiday-camp culture, paying careful attention to the way Butlin and Warner used advertising to market that culture to the British public. The camp culture fostered by Butlin and Warner countered the voices of cultural critics who condemned interwar mass culture as 'alienating'. Instead, Butlin and Warner promoted the camps as sites of community building that would extend beyond the individual camp experience into broader national culture. In many ways, the language of mutuality and class togetherness that Butlin and Warner used to promote their camps foreshadowed efforts of the wartime government to maintain civilian morale during the Second World War. When the hostilities ended, this aspect of camp culture re-emerged intact and energised in the postwar period. By considering the vision of holiday-camp culture marketed by Butlin and Warner, this chapter also explores holiday camps as part of the larger commercialisation of leisure in interwar Britain.

Advertising interwar leisure

During the economic uncertainties of the 1930s, leisure industries in Britain grew in a way that defied, and may even have profited from, the constraints of the world market system. Commercial passenger aircraft attracted wealthier customers with comfortable international flights and refrigerated meals that enticed consumers to travel to the far reaches of the world. Britain's Imperial Airlines was one of the first commercial airlines to successfully meet the needs of passengers in this way, in 1936.[6] Cruise ships like the *Queen Mary*, launched by the Cunard-White Star Line in 1936, advertised the luxurious amenities onboard their floating cities in national newspapers and trade journals such as the *Caterer and Hotel Keeper*.[7] The ship contained gymnasiums, *jardinières*, libraries, cinemas, smoking rooms, cocktail bars, swimming pools, and children's playrooms, designed for the comfort of all guests. Air-conditioned rooms with lavish maple, sycamore, ash, and gilt décor, offered a spectacular holiday at sea surrounded by opulence, extravagance, comfort, and an unrivalled quality of service.[8]

Travel magazines and travel agencies also flourished in interwar Britain. *Holiday Travel*, a quarterly magazine devoted to 'every phase of travel at home and abroad' selected and wrote about exclusive new holiday sites throughout Europe and the world, and gave advice to travellers concerning appropriate clothing and fashion accessories.[9] Travel companies like Frame's Tours, Dean and Dawson, as well as Cook's Travel published brochures and advertised in national newspapers and magazines to appeal to travellers searching for a specialised holiday. They offered cycling tours of Denmark, angling holidays in New Zealand, the opportunity to experience a typical Hungarian Christmas in Budapest, or an exotic holiday in Africa, Asia, or South America.[10] Even the socialist-inspired WTA encouraged members to plan ahead for short, cheap holidays in France and Luxembourg.[11] Commenting on a century of tourism, an article in *The Times* declared that the pioneers of the travel industry 'made journeys all over the world possible and easy for anyone' – with, of course, adequate resources to pay.[12]

State-sponsored foreign travel agencies targeted British holiday makers with brochures, leaflets, and travel magazines advertising unusual and 'exotic' destinations. Intourist in the USSR offered guided historic tours of Soviet Central Asia, complete with camel rides and unusual culinary experiences.[13] The Third Reich reduced fares for foreigners travelling in Germany in the 1930s, and the Berlin Olympics in 1936 afforded the opportunity to showcase the Nazi regime and offered official travel discounts of up to 60 per cent for overseas visitors.[14] Thus the interwar leisure industry sold new destinations and new technologies for travel and enjoyment.[15]

The vast majority of Britons, however, never travelled outside of Britain. By 1931, national politics supported the domestic tourist industry and consumption through a 'Buy British campaign'.[16] The earlier Health Resorts and Watering Places Act (1921) had removed some advertising restrictions and encouraged coastal towns to promote their resorts through the appropriation of catchy phrases and illustrations.[17] Blackpool took advantage of the new advertising laws and in 1931 used an image of a scantily clad woman sunbathing, with four male figures, equally scantily clad, watching her from afar, to illustrate the town's claim to be 'the place in the sun', where visitors presumably had little need for warm clothes. Clacton chose the image of a full champagne glass with the caption, 'Clacton's Champagne Air is Just the Tonic for Your Holiday', to illustrate the health-giving effects of the Essex seashore. Sidmouth and Seaton in Devon highlighted their coastal attractions with a cliff and beach view, while Brighton and Hove promoted the activities available in their resort by images of figures engaged in playing tennis, cricket, golf, bathing, speed boating, hiking, fishing, yachting, dancing, bowling, attending greyhound and horse races, and listening to music. A caption claimed that the advertisement illustrated only a 'few of the delights' of Brighton and Hove, where the air was like 'wine' and visitors could imbibe to their heart's content.[18]

Resorts took advantage of new media to develop images and slogans aimed to attract the patronage of a desired class. Resorts self-identified as either 'select' or 'popular' through their advertising campaigns. For example, Scarborough adroitly promoted selectivity through a guide-book filled with images of stylish visitors in blazers and boaters, reinforced by slogans such as 'The Queen of Watering Places', or 'The Eden by the Sea'. At the other end of the social scale, Ramsgate identified itself as a popular resort and 'produced guide books that were unashamedly brash and vulgar, with bathing belles seen through keyholes on the cover and texts introduced by "Sunny Spot, the Boy who brings the right places into the limelight"'.[19]

Postcards were also important as a way to portray a particular image of resorts and their desired or anticipated clientele. For example, cards featuring the 'delights' of Bournemouth portrayed images of the newly built Winter Garden and the luscious foliage of the pleasure park to attract a middle-class tourist. Blackpool postcards, on the other hand, showed images of the mass amusements available along the Golden Mile and saucy cartoons of buxom bathing beauties in compromising positions. Whereas the Bournemouth postcards depicted scenes of decorum and polish, the Blackpool postcards demonstrated the imagined delights of wild abandon and sexual consumption that one might encounter while on holiday.[20] Both worked to attract consumers by emphasising the type of entertainment and distractions available at each resort. Skilful advertising developed a relationship between the language and the imagery with understood notions of who was and who was not welcome at the resorts. Advertisements and the resort promoters behind them imagined leisure consumers in terms of separate social classes with specific cultural desires and preferences.[21] The presumed class-based taste often determined the language and imagery of the advert as well as the type of entertainment and facilities available at resorts.[22] While there is no way to assess whether the advertising appealed to the target audience, historians agree that an increase in domestic tourism aided the development of Britain's coastal resorts in the 1920s and 1930s.[23]

Holiday camps and advertising

Coastal towns advertised the varieties of experience and accommodation available in their resorts; holiday camps promoted theirs more succinctly. Often simply a small description nestled among advertisements for boarding houses and other inexpensive holiday accommodation, the camps relied on functional, rather than flashy, copy. In 1933, the *News Chronicle* ran an advertisement for the Caister camp that stated simply:

> Caister Holiday Camp, Caister-on-Sea, Norfolk. Near Gt. Yarmouth and Broads; Tennis and bathing free, fine Dance Hall, first-class band, good catering, 40 acres, huts fitted elec. Light, mod. Sanitation, Apply booklet.[24]

An advert the same year for a holiday camp in Abergele, North Wales was even more concise:

North Wales Holiday Camp (Dept. N) Abergele-Rhyl: ladies, gents, families: hall, huts, tents: £2. 2 shillings Weekly. Booklet free.[25]

The simplicity of the adverts reflected the budgetary constraints of the holiday-camp industry that strove to limit costs (newspapers charged by the word for advertisements) and also the nature of the holiday itself. Caister and Abergele were low-cost destinations for those who enjoyed communal living accommodation in huts or tents, outdoor activities, and simple entertainment.

By comparison, Captain Harry Warner promoted his 'luxury' camp (opened two years earlier) in the same section of the *News Chronicle* with an advertisement that was eight times the size of the others. Surrounded by an attractive border, Warner's promotion included more description of the camp locale. Warner's Northney Holiday Camp, according to the advert, provided an 'ideal holiday' in a 'charming sheltered spot facing Chichester Harbour, amidst rural surroundings'. The camp on Hayling boasted 'perfect bathing and boating', and the opportunity to play tennis and miniature golf. Unlike the camps at Caister and Rhyl that provided communal wooden huts for accommodation, Warner's camp on Hayling offered individual and 'delightful bungalows', each with running water and electric lights, suggesting the type of luxury available at Northney. For the same price as other holiday camps (two guineas per person per week), Warner included all meals, entertainment, and activities, with no hidden extra cost to guests.[26]

The all-inclusiveness of the weekly rate, and the flexibility of holiday-camp entertainment and amenities that did not depend on good weather for success, were an advantage even for early holidays. The most popular weeks of the season fell in August, especially the first week of the month, when many people chose to lengthen the Bank holiday weekend into their annual holiday.[27] At the beginning of Warner's fourth season, he promoted Hayling as ideal choice for earlier June holidays. The mild island climate made the island especially suitable for spring as well as summer holidays, according to advertisements, and ensured that Warner filled his camp to capacity each week of the season.[28] 'Hayling's wonderful warm spring sunshine' was, a 1934 advert claimed, an added attraction for those contemplating an early holiday.[29]

Others took note of Warner's success on Hayling and opened more camps on the island. The Sunshine Holiday Camp opened in 1936 a few miles away from Northney. Accommodation at the Sunshine included 'Snug beds' and plenty of good food. The camp, claimed an advert, acted like a club introducing members to dozens of 'jolly friends' for the affordable price of two guineas per week.[30] Indeed, holiday camps resembled sports clubs or associations in

Sunshine Holiday Camp advertisement, c. 1939

the way they were structured and in the way the management encouraged the involvement of campers in the entertainment and activities. Replicating older Working Men's Clubs and popular interwar sports organisations, holiday camps promoted their holidays as a joint venture with their guests.[31] By 1937, the Coronation Bungalow Camp opened at the eastern end of Hayling to celebrate the forthcoming coronation of Edward VIII.[32] With William Brown's Civil Service Union camp, the small island now boasted four holiday camps.[33] When the *Daily Express* featured a half-page map of Britain marking the location of holiday camps, the map focused the attention of potential campers on the small island as home to a choice of four different camps.[34]

As Warner contemplated expanding the number of his camps he asked his guests for feedback to ensure that his holiday camps met the needs of all tastes. Each camper was encouraged to talk to the manager or to the entertainment staff and to offer a critique of activities and suggestions aimed to improve the experience of all campers. Based on these suggestions, when Warner opened his second camp he wanted to satisfy the desires of those who wished to enjoy an activity-packed holiday as well as those who wished for a quieter experience. Seaton in Devon was a small and fairly quiet resort. Warner's second camp there provided activities and entertainment, while the local environment provided a degree of repose.[35] The camp at Seaton thus suited those who felt energetic as well as those who preferred to rest quietly.[36]

By 1937, Warner added Dovercourt Bay in Essex to his chain of holiday camps. This time, Warner used his name and the reputation of his other two camps to advertise the new enterprise. An advertisement claiming Warner's 'Long-established reputation for good food, good service and exceptional comfort' now offered three locations for a holiday-camp holiday.[37] In early June of the camp's opening year the *News Chronicle* promoted Warner and his new camp. 'Mr. H. J. Warner, of Northney and Seaton, now presents DOVERCOURT BAY, HOLIDAY CAMP, ESSEX, on the Sunny Suffolk Border.' The newly opened camp was 'ultra modern', and offered the 'perfect change of holiday for which' many looked, according to the advert. Accommodation consisted of 'Beautifully appointed brick chalets overlooking the sea', with hot baths and all the comforts of a hotel. The campsite boasted 'a lovely sandy beach', organised sports, bathing and tennis, dancing, music, and mirth, all for 45s a week.[38] A camp brochure boasted 'A holiday at Dovercourt Bay Holiday Camp is never to be forgotten.'[39] Beautifully planned and with 'the most up-to-date' equipment, the jolly crowd of camp guests ensured a happy holiday even without friend or family.[40] In fact, holiday camps were the perfect destination for individuals and camp culture the perfect way to make friends.

The local press took the opportunity to promote both Warner's new camp and his pioneering entrepreneurship in the luxury holiday-camp business. The *Harwich and Dovercourt Standard* maintained that while the holiday-camp vogue had started with a collection of huts and tents, 'the proprietors of the Dovercourt Camp were quick to see – after personal experience of some of the finest holiday camps that exist in various countries of the world – that this sort of thing was not good enough for the English holidaymaker'. As a result, Warner started a 'new type of camp', and 'improved and improved' them; Dovercourt Bay is the 'masterpiece'.[41] This enterprise, the author claimed, will put the whole town very definitely 'on the map'. The nationwide publicity for the camp promised future prosperity for the whole resort.[42] Warner's enterprises on Hayling, in Seaton, and Dovercourt Bay were important because they advertised more than simply the camps. Warner's marketing promoted the entire resort, thus benefiting the local economy.[43] Warner used local building merchants and suppliers for his camps and incorporated the names of the local businesses in the adverts. The other businesses contributed to the cost and the advert was made physically larger and more prominent, benefiting all concerned. The adverts thus served several purposes. They promoted the camp to potential guests, they advertised allied industries as well as their collaboration with domestic tourism, and they alerted interested parties to the economic benefits of leisure. This type of advertising helped to quell criticism by promoting the product, the production, and the potential profits for a variety of industries. It also established the holiday-camp industry as fundamentally British – from the bricks to the beds, from the electrical wiring to the roses. As more camps opened, local economies benefited not only from the larger numbers of visitors but also from the business generated by supplying

14   Campers at Dovercourt Bay Holiday Camp, c. 1937

the camps with food and equipment. For small rural resorts like Hayling, Warner's holiday camp gave many local inhabitants much-needed alternative employment.

By 1938 national and local government were alerted to the economic potential of tourism by the publication of an economic study of international and domestic tourism.[44] Later in the year a state-aided bureau opened in London to help publicise holidays in Britain. Funded by the government, the bureau promoted Britain as a holiday destination as part of the larger campaign to 'buy British' and help boost the economy. Holiday-camp proprietors were eligible

Butlin's Skegness and Clacton holiday camps, advert, 1 May 1939

15

for membership for an annual fee and that membership gave the right to have camp brochures displayed in the London location. Staff at the bureau would also assist with enquiries and help to promote British holiday camps.[45] The bureau was particularly interested in the promotion of camps that met a certain 'standard' of accommodation. These facilities came under the jurisdiction of the National Federation of Permanent Holiday Camps (NFPHC), an organisation formed in 1935. Founded and chaired by Warner, the NFPHC established standards for food, accommodation, comfort, conduct, and amenities of holiday camps. Eligibility for membership depended on meeting Federation standards, as well as on adequate water supply and sanitation. The NFPHC gave prestige to the holiday-camp industry as a monitoring organisation, and also served to advertise the high standards of members. Each year the organisation published *The Holiday Camp Book*, which advertised its members and included competitions and useful information for those planning a holiday-camp holiday.[46] The London bureau and the Federation worked in concert to market and promote British holidays and holiday destinations, linking the state directly with the promotion of the industry.

A few months after the establishment of the London bureau, Warner opened a camp at Puckpool on the Isle of Wight, expanding his leisure empire to include four luxury holiday camps in the south of England. 'All Warner's experience in catering for holiday happiness has gone to the planning of this new super-camp', a 1939 brochure claimed, and the camp's 'beautiful situation and manifold features are expected to make it, though opened only this year, an instant success'. Puckpool, the brochure asserted, has a magic of its own 'for it is a beauty spot even among the many beautiful places in this enchanted isle'.[47] The Puckpool camp promised to entice more tourists, stimulate the local economy, and create more profits for Warner.

Capturing a national market

By the time Butlin opened his first holiday camp at Skegness in 1936, he had spent five years watching his business partner, Warner, develop his camp on Hayling Island. While the camp transformed the island into a popular holiday destination, Warner had to start virtually from scratch marketing Hayling as an attractive holiday site. Skegness, on the other hand, was already a well-known resort. Although Butlin would not have to convince people that Skegness was an ideal locale for rest and relaxation, he would have to persuade them to choose his all-inclusive holiday camp as an alternative to the more familiar hotels and boarding houses in the resort. The key to his success was to market his camps as a more personal, more enjoyable, and more 'British' experience.

Butlin had to convince the public that his camp was better and different from the others. As Butlin paid for larger newspaper adverts and made more extravagant claims, an article in the local Skegness newspaper agreed with him. The paper celebrated the opening of Butlin's new enterprise and the anonymous author explained the difference between the older-style holiday camps and the luxury camps of 1936. 'The Holiday Camp of a few years ago concentrated largely on providing cheap sleeping accommodations in the vicinity of a popular resort which its patrons visited to enjoy the usual round of attractions.' Unlike other types of holiday, the camps of 1936 are 'absolutely self-contained', providing guests with a 'never ceasing round of indoor and outdoor recreations, sports, and pastimes', without 'involving its patrons in any additional expense'.[48]

As daily newspapers dedicated separate holiday sections to camp advertising, entrepreneurs used more sophisticated techniques. A 1936 advert in the *Daily Herald* expanded the earlier succinct message about the Abergele camp by describing the facilities and accommodation available to singles and families. The Abergele camp, according to the advert, was the 'most popular place on the Welsh coast'. Potter's Cliff camp, close to Great Yarmouth, described a holiday at this camp as 'luxury … on the ocean edge'.[49] Faced with such competition, Butlin claimed that his camp had 'more amenities and more attractions than any other'.[50] With accommodation for a thousand guests a week, a holiday at Butlin's Skegness was simply 'one large jolly party'.[51] Indeed, boasted Butlin, his camp was the 'last word in holiday ideas'.[52]

To bolster these claims, Butlin focused on creating unforgettable experiences for his guests. In 1936, Butlin negotiated the broadcast of a national radio show from his Skegness camp. Information about Butlin's holiday camp reached millions of homes in Britain, courtesy of the British Broadcasting Corporation (BBC), free of charge.[53] Advertisements for Butlin's camp were interspersed with community singing and music conducted by Eric Weston, a nationally renowned band leader, and a popular comedy duo, Jimmy Loft and Ted Cartwright.[54]

The BBC broadcast was a personal coup for Butlin and the experience of a lifetime for his guests. The BBC limited dance-band music to fifteen hours a week and usually broadcast live from the big London hotels to the provinces. A broadcast from Skegness inverted the traditional relationship between provinces and metropolis. Despite the assertion that broadcasting was the 'final step in the true democratisation of Music', the BBC tightly controlled the source and type of music to be democratised.[55] In addition, the BBC carefully monitored the content of 'popular' variety programmes that included comedy acts and songs sung 'casually'.[56] Indeed, despite their popularity with listeners, vaudeville and variety radio programmes were rare.[57] The broadcast from Skegness then represented a distinct shift in programming policy and a rare opportunity for radio listeners. A triumph for Butlin, the radio show established holiday-camp entertainment firmly in the popular musical and comedy tradition appreciated by the working and lower middle classes but treated with disdain by the cultural elites.

The *Skegness News* enthusiastically reported the event and described the scene of the broadcast. 'The ballroom, with its illumination scheme of over a thousand coloured lights, and full of animation radiating from a thousand eager young people, presented an unforgettable picture to those taking part in the thrill of a mass broadcast.' For those campers and local residents taking part, it was indeed a unique experience to be part of a national radio show, alongside a famous orchestra and comedians, if only for one evening.[58] The broadcast ended with the audience giving a rousing rendition of the holiday-camp chorus, 'Goodnight Campers' sung to the popular tune 'Goodnight Sweetheart',[59]

> Good night, campers, I can see you yawning
> Good night, campers, see you in the morning.
> You must cheer up or else you will be dead
> For I've heard it said – folks die in bed,
> So I'll say good night campers
> Don't sleep on your braces.
> Good night, campers, put your teeth in Jeyes's
> Drown your sorrows, bring your bottles back tomorrow,
> Good night campers, GOOD NIGHT![60]

The words of the song illustrate one of the appeals of camp culture – the successful commercialisation of an older working-class culture. 'Goodnight Sweetheart' was one of the most popular and well-known songs of the 1930s. By altering the words, Butlin appropriated the tune and associated his camp with the popularity of the melody. The new words replicated other working-class songs that combined the cheerful, the morbid, and the absurd. Butlin also utilised earlier religious formats that engaged audiences and encouraged an emotional sense of community. Group singing was an important aspect of the evangelical tradition as well as a central aspect of working-class culture. Just as earlier religious groups like the Methodists and the Salvation Army recognised

Campers pose with Miss Nottinghamshire and Miss Warwickshire, Skegness,   **16**
1937

the importance of popular music as they altered the words of popular songs to convey a message of salvation to their working-class audiences, so Butlin changed the words of this song to signal the end of the entertainment and the close of the evening.[61]

While Butlin harnessed older traditions, he also promoted his camp as a venue for modern national competitions. In 1937, the Skegness camp hosted the annual *Daily Mail* beauty contest held in August. A popular contest, the publicity surrounding the competition provided Butlin's camp with additional national advertising. The presence of one of Britain's leading film stars, Miss Rene Ray, as the chief judge for the competition ensured national press coverage of the event, the campers, and the facilities.[62] Ray, a popular star of a number of recent British films, graciously judged the competition, posed for the camera and signed autographs for hundreds of enraptured guests and visitors at the camp.[63]

The success of the *Daily Mail* beauty contest encouraged Butlin to organise his own competition and, a fortnight later, persuade British-born Hollywood actress Elizabeth Allan to judge the 'Perfect Figure Competition' at the camp.[64] Allan, who was born in Skegness, drew a huge crowd at the camp and brought an element of glamour to the competition. Known for her beauty and quick wit, Allan bantered with the camp comic after the competition, much to the delight of the crowd and the reporter from the *Skegness News*.[65]

Through his promotion of beauty contests and perfect-figure competitions, Butlin tapped into the cult of glamour that emerged largely as the result of cultural shifts after the First World War and which altered the way women's bodies were displayed and perceived.[66] The achievements of female aviators like Amy Johnson, as well as of female athletes, received a lot of media interest that focused readers' awareness on women's bodies in a new way that highlighted physical prowess and muscular development. This attention to the body was further accentuated by shifts in fashion that revealed more of women's bodies, as well as by the commercialisation of cosmetics.[67] New technologies in printing and film production promoted photographs and images of fashion and glamour in a more uniform way for mass consumption. Indeed, commercial photography was a booming business in 1930s Britain.[68] The circulation of women's magazines increased as the quality of the images and the expansion of distribution networks grew.[69] Additionally, the film industry provided cultural representations of glamour as actresses portrayed characters that illustrated and modelled how beautiful women should look and dress. Magazine articles and photographs of Hollywood and British film stars like Ray and Allan enabled consumers to retain these images at home. Tapping into the cult of glamour and modern consumption patterns, Butlin offered his guests the opportunity to meet stars in the flesh. This moved celebrity from the realm of fantasy to reality.

Ray and Allan were not the only actresses to entertain and interact with campers. The increasing celebrity attached to stage and screen performers was due, in large part, to the fact that in the interwar years the British public went to the cinema as many as three times each week.[70] In his autobiography, Butlin remembered that in the early years of the camp, 'all kinds of VIPS accepted invitations to visit us as the camps became more widely known'. The most famous, according to Butlin, was Gracie Fields, one of Britain's brightest theatrical (and film) stars, who gave up working in a cotton mill for a life on the stage. Earning a phenomenal £1,200 a week at the London Palladium in 1938, Fields was an interwar music-hall and cinema phenomenon.[71] Known to most of the British public simply as 'Our Gracie', Fields, according to one historian, 'combined an extraordinary singing voice, a natural comic talent and an inexhaustible vitality' to become a national symbol of working-class high spirits and good nature.[72] Fields entertained guests at the Skegness Sunday evening camp concert in 1938 and thrilled campers with her songs, her comedy, and her stage presence.[73] For the campers that evening, she truly was 'our Gracie'.

Butlin made celebrity accessible to everyman or everywoman. By his bringing together of guests and popular public figures like Fields, the distance between the stage and screen personas and reality grew closer. The presence of celebrities like Fields, born above a fish-and-chip shop in Rochdale, greatly enhanced the holiday experience for Butlin's guests, as they served as examples of the way ordinary working-class people could transform into stars. At the same time, the interaction between the performers and the guests also transformed the camps into a space that both personalised celebrity and promoted the idea of its accessibility to anyone.

Another popular comic actress and impersonator, Florence Desmond, also came to Skegness in August 1938.[74] Desmond had starred with Fields in *Sally in Our Alley* and arrived at the camp with Yorkshire cricket batsman Len Hutton. The day before, 22–year-old Hutton had scored a record-breaking 364 runs for England in a test match against Australia at the Oval cricket ground.[75] In less than twenty-four hours, Butlin persuaded the overnight celebrity to act as judge for the weekly camp beauty contest, while Desmond presented the prizes. After the contest the campers urged Desmond to 'do a turn'. She obliged with an impromptu rendition of popular songs, including

Gracie Fields's 'Sally'. Hutton thrilled Butlin and the rest of the staff when he booked a week's holiday at the camp for the following month.[76]

Butlin claimed that he never had a specific advertising or entertainment plan for his camps. Rather, the businessman preferred spur-of-the-moment decisions that enabled him to harness the publicity value of the overnight

17   Carnival Night at Butlin's Skegness Camp, advert, 22 September 1937

celebrities as well as the more established stars of the screen and stage.[77] The star quality of the impromptu entertainment signalled Butlin's holiday camp as a unique place to see Gracie Fields or Florence Desmond, or to meet the man who almost single-handedly enabled the England eleven to keep some national cricket pride. Yet Butlin was also suggesting that his camp was a place where celebrities could be made. The publicity surrounding the famous guests promoted Butlin's camp and the Skegness resort on a national level but also kept those celebrities in the public eye.

Holidays, health and happiness

During the interwar years a health and fitness culture emerged in Britain.[78] When Butlin opened a second camp at Clacton in 1938, he took out a half page advertisement in the *Daily Mail* incorporating a personal message thanking all the local businesses involved in the project for making the camp and the forthcoming 'Festival of Health and Happiness' possible. The festival and the camp were the result of months of intensive planning and the 'splendid co-operation' of an immense number of people.[79] Flanked by pictures of happy campers enjoying the services and amenities provided by the camp, the advertisement captured the frenetic activity Butlin offered his guests. The local paper featured

Butlin's Festival of Health and Happiness advert, 2 July 1938   **18**

photographs of the two themed bars – a 'Smuggler's Cave' and a 'Spanish Galleon' – as well as the fully equipped gymnasium, and billiard hall 'furnished in oak', ready to host the festival that would focus on health and happiness at the new camp.[80]

Butlin's festival capitalised on recent national and international competitions as well as the penchant of the British public for spectator sports. The businessman hosted a week of world-famous athletic attractions that included daily boxing exhibitions by Len Harvey, the British light-weight champion, and tennis matches between the British Professional Lawn Tennis champion, Dan Maskell and the 1937 tournament runner-up, H. Paulsen.[81] The festival continued with exhibition table tennis from former Swaythling Cup championship players J. K. Hyde and R. D. Jones; exhibition swimming from E. H. Temme, the celebrated British Channel swimmer, and diving from Briscoe Ray, the winner of the three-metre springboard-diving gold medal for Britain at the 1934 British Empire Games.[82] In addition to the athletic and swimming displays, Butlin organised a celebrity snooker match between Joe Davis and H. Lindrum, with a prize of 100 guineas. Butlin charged 1s for daily admission to the camp festival and 2s 6d for admission to the evening dances, which included music by Lew Stone and his swing band, and the BBC radio favourite, Mantovani and his orchestra.[83]

The festival gave guests the opportunity to witness athletic exhibitions, which, alongside spectator sports, were increasingly popular in interwar Britain. Radio programmes provided listeners with commentaries on national and international competitions and newspapers gave detailed descriptions of football matches and horse races. Newsreels, screened before films at the cinema, appealed to a wider audience than even the popular dailies and increased the public's appreciation and knowledge of sporting events and linked a nation of cinema goers with the world of athletics.[84] The decision to invite nationally known athletes as part of the entertainment at Butlin's camp capitalised on the popularity of sport and provided unique experiences for guests, who might find an athlete sitting beside them at dinner time.

Festival music by popular bands and orchestras accommodated the interwar dance craze at a reasonable price. Dancing, especially ballroom dancing, was one of the most popular pastimes for all social classes in Britain. Many fashionable dances, like the Black-Bottom, Varsity Drag, and the Charleston, were influenced by jazz and came from the United States. Some British dance professionals believed that the dances were anti-social because of the alarming side-kicks, so much so that in 1920 dance teachers met informally in London to devise a way to regulate and reform the dances.[85] As a result of the informal regulation and the innovative techniques of Victor Silvester and Phyllis Clarke, the winners of the 1922 World Dancing Championship, British ballroom dancing emerged as a distinct form in the 1920s and 1930s. Silvester promoted a 'natural style', a 'fluid and unfussy type of dancing' and taught many of the stars of the interwar years.[86] Butlin invited Silvester and his wife to come to the festival at Skegness and give lessons and exhibitions to the campers. Their presence at the camp meant that guests could learn or improve their dance techniques, as each evening the camp hosted dances in the new ballroom with music provided by Lew Stone and his band, winners of the *News Chronicle* international dance band competition, the popular BBC radio performers Mantovani and his orchestra, and Harry Botham and his 'boys'.[87] Perhaps as a reflection of the extraordinary costs involved in the provision of this type of quality entertainment, admission to the dances in the evening increased to 5s.[88]

The festivals were successful money makers for Butlin. At the same time, they were also part of the interwar democratisation of leisure. Butlin maintained that his camps were devoid of class distinctions and built on the idea that people of all classes needed to have fun on holiday. The entertainment at the camps tapped into the increasing commercialisation of popular pleasure and sports in the interwar years. What was unique about the entertainment at Butlin's camps was the closer connection to the entertainers and sports personalities, which made class boundaries less distinct. When some celebrity performers returned to the camp as guests, as did Len Hutton, the England cricketer, for example, the distance between class and celebrity status blurred even further as Hutton sat alongside other guests at meal times and joined in the organised activities.

After the festivals, Butlin continued to seek celebrity publicity for his two camps. At the end of July 1938, Mr Jimmy Forsyth, director of the Gaumont British Film Corporation and the Elstree and Pinewood Film Studios, came to the Skegness camp to judge 'Butlin's Bathing Belle for 1938'.[89] Forsythe was also the producer of the 'Miss Great Britain' and 'Golden Voice Girl' competitions and the following month he judged a beauty contest at the Clacton camp. The famous producer chose and crowned Miss Sylvia Thompson of Cardiff 'Miss Butlin 1938'.[90] The presence of such a renowned judge allowed young female campers to imagine competing at the national level or even appearing as an actress on the big screen.[91] Forsythe, the organiser of the national beauty competition and director of one of the largest movie companies in Britain, was a celebrity in his own right and this enhanced the experience for many competitors.[92] His presence also suggested that campers might have the chance to be 'discovered' as a future film star or nationally recognised beauty. Celebrity status then appeared accessible to anyone at the camp.

Butlin thus made celebrities of the campers themselves. Photographers took pictures of campers as they participated in the activities or as they watched, and used the photos in brochures and as postcards. Guests could send these pictures of themselves to friends and family or keep them as a souvenir of their stay at the camp. Each week, individual campers saw their names in the local paper if they won competitions.[93] Butlin even made short daily movies of campers enjoying the activities of the camp and screened the films in the evenings. These evening films were much like the interwar newsreels that captured soccer matches on film, often featuring far more footage of the spectators than of the game.[94] Campers had the novel experience and opportunity of seeing each other, involved in the games or as spectators, on the big screen.[95]

Butlin created a distinctive culture and a community within the camp itself. Like Warner, Butlin gave pins to guests each week as they registered. Unlike Warner, Butlin changed the designs frequently so that a camper who chose to take two separate weeks of holiday in one year received two different pins as an emblem of loyalty and readmission. Campers bearing a large number of pins that displayed their allegiance to Butlin's were treated as celebrities and as old friends by managers and staff. At the same time, guests new to the camp received a warm welcome too. One of the greatest appeals of holiday camps lay in this culture of informal 'friendliness'. The *News Chronicle*, for example, claimed, 'Your [camping] companions will be your friends from the first day at the camp, all aiming at having a jolly good holiday.'[96] The *Skegness News* similarly noted that 'even the loneliest camper arriving on Saturday makes dozens of new friends in the cheery atmosphere before the end of the week', creating a 'spirit of tolerance and broadmindedness' that makes 'the whole world a happier place'.[97]

Indeed, a letter from Miss E. Moss of Kingstanley, Birmingham to the *Skegness News* underscored the friendliness of the camp. Miss Moss was initially apprehensive when she arrived at Butlin's holiday camp alone, but was soon put at ease by the friendliness of the camp staff and their relationship with the guests. She wrote, 'I met Sydney at dinner. Sydney was the waiter at my table. He welcomed me with a smile, he served me with a smile, he introduced me to the other table guests with a smile, in fact', claimed Miss Moss, 'he did everything with a smile.' As a result, Miss Moss soon made friends and spent two weeks at the camp, hiking, dancing, playing games, and joining in the physical culture classes.[98]

It was the friendliness of camp culture that prompted a group of Fleet Street journalists in 1938 to publish the *Holiday Camp Review*, a monthly magazine, to act as a link between camps and campers throughout the year. The first volume, published in April 1938, coincided with the publication of the Holidays With Pay Committee recommendations. All the editors of the new magazine were 'enthusiastic holiday camper[s]' who had 'tasted the joys of camp holidays' and wanted others to do the same.[99] The journalists hoped the publication would help 'campers … keep in touch with the life and activities of the camps, long after the trace[s] of sunburn h[ave] faded away'. The magazine, they maintained, belonged to campers not content to allow the good 'fellowship and camaraderie of the camps [to] lie dormant' throughout the year. 'Don't stand on ceremony in addressing yourselves to us', the authors urged. 'Think of us … as … Jimmy, Harry, or Bill, Peggy, Dorothy or Grace of Hut 16, 60 or 90.'[100]

A 23–year-old clerk wrote to *Holiday Camp Review* about his experience as a camper. Although the clerk wanted to go abroad during his holiday, 'quite frankly', he wrote, 'I could not afford it … so I went to a holiday camp'. The clerk offered his story as an encouragement to others in a similar situation. 'I arrived on Saturday evening after a sticky and crowded train journey,' he claimed, and although the camp management did not bring 'out the red carpet and brass band', he was met immediately by a 'very pleasant manager chap who saw that [I] got a good meal right away'. Shown to his 'roomy' accommodation with running water, the new guest quickly dressed for the evening dance that was already under way. Before long the reluctant camper joined in without any formal introductions. At breakfast the next morning he made friends and spent the day swimming and sunbathing on the beach. 'There is nothing like a holiday camp for good companionship,' he claimed. 'It's easy to get to know people, everybody's friendly and there is plenty of social life', planned by a very helpful management staff. In fact, the clerk maintained, 'there was something doing every minute of the day and the beauty of it was that if you wanted to be alone there was plenty of room to do it in'. Best of all, claimed the clerk, the price was inclusive and there were 'absolutely no extras' to budget for. After two weeks the clerk returned reluctantly to work but planned to return to the same camp for his next holiday.[101]

The all-inclusiveness of holiday camps appealed to those with limited budgets. Yet the idea of including accommodation, meals, activities, and entertainment in one price was part of an older holiday-camp tradition. Indeed, Warner and Butlin built their commercial camps on a pre-existing and popular culture. The daily activities at Butlin's camp replicated those of the earlier camps – the football matches, the evening sing-alongs, the informality, and the communal meals. Yet despite the fact that many of the camp activities were part of this older culture, men like Butlin and Warner were able to market their camps as completely modern and new. What differentiated their enterprises from the more established camps in Britain was the extent of the advertising, the exceptional quality of the entertainment, and the organisation and sheer size of the camps. When Butlin opened the Skegness camp, the local paper claimed that it provided a really new and modern popular holiday experience. Other holiday resorts, the paper argued, were being fast left behind and were in danger of being considered 'old fashioned' by the young people who were at the forefront of the new vogue in holidays where 'physical and mental improvement accompanied recreation and pleasure' inexpensively.[102]

A typical week's programme at the Skegness camp included daily 'physical culture' classes, children's play classes, swimming classes for beginners and the advanced, as well as an opportunity to learn to ride a horse. On Monday, the staff organised a bathing-beauty contest and a men's knobbly-knee competition. In the afternoon, professional dancers organised a tea dance for campers, and in the evening a 'Music Hall and Gipsy Camp Fire'. Tuesday included an opportunity to hike with a group to local historic sites, play cricket structured around geographical affinity in a North v. South competition; the afternoon included a table tennis tournament, and the evening entertainment consisted of a camp dance with music by a double-handed orchestra of seven performers. On Wednesday, a putting competition entertained campers, as well as a 'Midlands v. the Rest' soccer match. For those wishing for more intellectual stimulation, camp staff organised a treasure hunt based on a 'Mental Intelligence Test', and in the evening a carnival dance completed the day's entertainment, with prizes given to the best 'Fancy, Humorous and Original Costumes'. On Thursday, campers could play 'Crazy Cricket', with women attired as men and vice versa, or could watch or compete in the camp swimming gala and water polo matches. The afternoon activities included a lawn tennis tournament, and in the evening the camp Talent Concert entertained guests, as well as the opportunity to join in a midnight hike. On Friday, the final day of the camp week, activities included a motor trip to Sandringham, an inter-county mixed tug-of-war, and field sports on the beach. Special entertainment for children consisted of a fancy-dress tea party, and the evening ended with a grand farewell night and rendering of the 'Camper's Chorus' and 'Auld Lang Syne', before saying goodbye to the camp the following morning.[103]

Butlin claimed that the activities in the camp were designed to give 'guests plenty of healthy exercise and good honest amusements'. In an attempt to strike a balance between purity and indulgence, he employed professional exercise instructors 'willing and ready to show them [campers] the way to exercise'. The camp also employed instructors for ordinary recreation, dance hostesses for those interested in learning and practising the latest dances, and two permanent orchestras that played during meal times. Guests, asserted Butlin, ranged from the office worker to the professional classes. 'It is quite common', he claimed, for the camp to entertain 'the chief constable and the chief engineer of the town', in the same week. 'I know of any number of people of the £1,000 a year class who are regular patrons,' maintained Butlin. As a result of the atmosphere of comradeship fostered among guests, the camp promoted an 'absence of class distinction which makes the permanent holiday camper go home feeling that he has really had a wonderful holiday'. Compared to other types of holidays, the unique spirit of the camp gave ample opportunity for guests to form friendships with others from different social backgrounds, as camp hosts worked to introduce campers to each other without any 'stuffy' formality.[104] Indeed, every camper began their holiday at Butlin's secure in the knowledge that all other guests had paid the same amount for the same service, accommodation, food, and entertainment.

Butlin and Warner claimed that camp activities created an atmosphere of endless fun. They played with and overturned Victorian forms of sport and entertainment. Both men promoted comedy and self-parody exercises that simultaneously mocked and valorised working-class bodies. These experiences were the hallmark of many of the camp activities. Knobbly Knees and Ugly Faces competitions filled the camps' entertainment timetables and provided a 'low-brow' alternative to the more glamorous and 'high-brow' beauty contests of mainstream culture, while Topsy-Turvey competitions, sports, and dances (where men dressed in women's clothes and women dressed in men's clothes) made a charade of established gender rules. Although the programme retained traditional class-based sports like cricket, Butlin and his staff undermined the established rules that insisted on eleven players each side. Like the annual Shrovetide street or 'mob' soccer games captured on newsreel, where the populations of entire towns came together to play in the riotous matches, cricket in Butlin's camp resembled an unruly and boisterous farce.[105] As one observer noted, 'Camp cricket has rules of its own and is nothing like the serious game played on county grounds.' As a result, the game 'is very much more entertaining for both players and spectators ....' Instead of the standard eleven-a-side, teams numbered anything from 'eleven to one hundred and eleven, according to the number of enthusiasts who register' to play. Solid rubber replaced the leather ball, and thus team members at Butlin's camp did not need to wear pads and gloves. 'The only penalty for serious cricketers who demonstrate their prowess by hitting the ball into a chalet three or four blocks away', according to the same observer, 'is that they are required to lend assistance in locating the ball if the fielder gets into the wrong chalet, and is so captivated by a charming young lady he finds there that he fails to return.'[106] The players' role in the subversion of rules was the highlight of the game and brought total disorder to the traditional and established conventions of cricket.

For some campers, however, the endless and rowdy group activities were a problem. One reader of the *Holiday Camp Review* claimed, 'I'll tell you what I *don't* want. I don't want to spend my holiday in a constant uproar. I don't want to be organised every minute of the day.' The camper continued, 'I hate camps which have an elaborate time-table of activities from sunrise to sunset and after.' Indeed, the reader exclaimed, 'I hate the type of person who is never happy unless he is organising a crowd of people to do something they don't really want to do but haven't the nerve to refuse.' Despite this litany of dislikes, however, the reader claimed to enjoy holiday camps very much – as long as the campers were allowed to desist from constant organised activity. The individual camper should be free to 'kick around on his own in peace and quiet if he wants to, without the risk of being seized by a crowd of yelling maniacs and pitch-forked into some game that gives him a pain in the neck'. While many campers enjoyed 'letting off steam', another type of camper also existed 'who wants peace and quiet'. The perfect holiday camp, according to this reader, should be able to satisfy the needs of all.[107]

In many ways the *Holiday Camp Review* acted as a feedback loop for holiday-camp entrepreneurs like Warner and Butlin. They saw the publication as an important aspect of consumer desire. Understanding that a small minority of their guests desired 'peace and quiet', both men provided reading rooms and libraries for these guests. Warner and Butlin also understood that campers wanted to continue to enjoy camp culture throughout the year. The campers' monthly magazine helped do this, as did winter reunions. Like many of the other 200 holiday camps in Britain, Butlin and Warner organised winter reunions for guests. Reunions were part of older camp culture and took place all over the country, often within the campsites themselves. Warner used his all of four camps for reunions, but Butlin chose alternate venues. Nearly a thousand people who had spent their summer holiday at Butlin's Skegness camp in 1937 attended a 'Campers' Reunion Ball' at the Nottingham Palais de Danse in November the same year.[108] The evening was organised at a location close to the railway station for ease of travelling. The following winter, requests from campers prompted Butlin to open his new Clacton-on-Sea camp to summer guests for a Christmas and a New Year party. The parties included an 'organised programme of entertainments', the 'usual incidental amusements' of camp culture, and impromptu games and dances.[109]

The following year, on 19 January 1939, and in keeping with his penchant for national advertising, Butlin organised a mass reunion in London at the Empress Hall in Earl's Court for all his former guests. This extravagant reunion in London attracted national attention. Advertised as the 'Greatest Carnival Dance Ever', Butlin's reunion featured music led by four nationally renowned band leaders – Lew Stone, Mantovani, Jack Hylton and Ambrose – and continuous dancing from 8 p.m. until 2 a.m. Tickets, bought in advance, cost 3s 6d, on the day, 5s. Although the reunion was primarily for campers, a small number of tickets were made available to those who had not been guests at either Skegness or Clacton in the previous year, in the hope that they would consider a holiday at one of Butlin's camps.[110]

Family camps and friendly faces

Butlin's reunions and the publicity he and other holiday-camp entrepreneurs used were part of the expansion of the domestic leisure industry in Britain in the interwar years. Critics, however, saw the new mass leisure facilities like the camps and the cinemas as emblematic of an increasingly fragmented society. Modern production techniques isolated workers and new technologies of mass pleasure, they argued, added to the process of political alienation. Modern pleasure, for these critics, subverted social unrest and pacified the worker. Yet holiday-camp culture suggested an alternate vision; one of social harmony and togetherness through informal fun and games. According to Harry Warner's daughter-in-law Hazel, his early camps focused on the idea of family and friendship as the key selling points. Unlike Butlin's camps that expanded each year to accommodate thousands of guests, Warner chose to keep his camps relatively small (approximately 600 guests) 'so everyone would know each other at the end of the week'. By re-working popular nineteenth-century forms of leisure, the entertainment at the camps was designed to bring guests physically together and encourage interaction between performers and the audience. Music-hall variety acts, popular comedians, singers and big bands played to an audience that would ordinarily be excluded by the prohibitive cost of quality entertainment. Parents were able to relax completely, as the camps 'always had somebody for the children', including 'night patrols' to enable adults to dance in the ballroom every evening. Indeed, ballroom dancing was an integral part of the holiday-camp experience and daytime lessons enhanced evening pleasure. Warner 'wanted to build a business where people could really have a holiday', maintains his daughter-in-law, and the camps were quite 'remarkable' and 'like a big family' for staff and guests alike.[111]

The idea of holiday camps as 'family' was important not only to allow campers to give feedback and retain a sense of ownership of their holiday experience; it also suggested a more intimate relationship among campers and staff. As more people chose to holiday at the camps, Warner promoted his role as the 'fatherly' patriarch, overseeing the enjoyment of his family. A typical prewar camp brochure featured a short letter from Warner to potential guests promising the experience of a lifetime at one of his camps. Inside the brochure, a picture of the smiling Captain watching a group of cheerful

19   *Warner's Holiday Camp* brochure, 1938

guests is accompanied by the caption, 'Everybody is having such a grand time I cannot help feeling happy'.[112]

Advertising the family-centred camps and promoting them as a destination for extended families, Warner claimed that grandparents enjoyed the 'exuberance of their younger companions' and that, like the Captain himself, older guests were thrilled and delighted with the 'happy scenes around them'. Parents with small children, secure in the knowledge that the 'household and all home worries were behind, that meals, hot baths and all the attendant anxieties were not their troubles', relaxed and enjoyed their holiday. The young people, 'bursting with excess energy ... commanded everyone's attention' through their athleticism, claimed Warner. In fact, the campsite was not only a place where extended families could regenerate; new communities and families of friends could also be made because, at the end of a long day of activity, campers happily bade goodnight to hundreds of new friends.[113]

Warner could not organise sunshine all the time, but he assured his guests that, whatever the weather, campers 'can always be sure of a really good holiday and plenty to occupy' all age groups and every member of the family. Indeed, Warner declared, 'if there is anything you can think of that we have forgotten, please let us know'. This was an essential aspect of Warner's camps – the opportunity for all holiday makers to contribute to their own experience by requesting something new or simply a change. Warner, as the father figure, invited the rest of the camp 'family' to make their wishes known so that everyone enjoyed their holiday experience.[114]

Warner claimed that the physical fitness classes always astonished newcomers to camp holidays. 'Indeed', Warner claimed, 'a very great person, when visiting [a camp] last year, remarked on the total absence of that holiday reserve which is supposed to be the trait of the English character.' The 'very great person' made the comment when he was shown 500 campers 'of all ages and of both sexes, joyfully and with gay abandon being put through their physical jerks by our experts'.[115] Indeed, the holiday-camp experience helped to create a new 'English' identity and a community of healthy members.

Even those without the energy could enjoy the vitality of others. Warner described himself as middle-aged, with a tendency to 'corpulence'. This prevented him from joining in the games but it did not stop him from enjoying camp sports as a spectator. The Captain, like a parent at a school sports day, never ceased 'to get a thrill out of the scenes on ... [the camp] ... sports fields'. He enjoyed the excitement of inter-camp matches, organised among the local holiday camps.[116] In a subversion of mainstream culture that segregated women's soccer from the more popular men's games, the highlight of each week at Warner's was the Girls versus Boys football match, when the 'whole camp turns out to cheer on ... favourite[s]' and watch the prizes being presented at the end of the day.[117] Warner's enthusiasm for the sports, he claimed, was 'eclipsed' only by the 'spirit' of the players themselves.[118]

Despite all the sunshine, sport, and happy companionship in the world, a healthy holiday required good food. Interwar concerns about hunger and malnutrition amongst the lower classes prompted Warner to act like a concerned parent to his guests.[119] The majority of guests came from the lower middle classes and Warner claimed to pay 'particular attention' to the menus and food preparation, as well as the dining room facilities. Campers, the brochure claimed, sit in sun-drenched dining rooms at 'separate tables' with 'spotless napery, glistening silver, and vases of flowers fresh daily from the camp's own garden'. Capable, efficient, and hygienically minded staff under 'qualified chefs' provide 'constantly varied and tempting menus', because only the 'best food is good enough' for Warner's guests.[120]

As Warner personally advertised his camps in brochures he used images of himself to familiarise new guests with the activities and amenities of his camps, like a family member or a family friend. He used photography to present readers with a visual commentary alongside his written remarks. This visual literacy in advertising mirrored a new journalism style epitomised by *Picture Post*, a popular weekly modelled on the American magazine *Life*, launched in 1938. The journal 'simultaneously addressed escapist fantasy, mundane practicality and hope for the future', and included many leisure articles.[121] A 1939 *Picture Post* article by Tom Wintringham focused on Butlin's Skegness camp, which accommodated 4,000 guests per week, a number that included many returning campers. The 'mass-produced semi-luxury' of the camp, the journalist claimed, provided the 'private refuge' of individual chalets that contrasted sharply with the intrusions of boarding-house landladies. 'But added to this privacy, and not conflicting with it', claimed Wintringham, the camp provided 'as much social life and as much play as ... [campers] ... desire and can endure.' Wintringham claimed that Butlin's Skegness, contemptuously called 'regimented enjoyment' by critics, provided guests with the means to enjoyment and leisure, physical exercise and pleasure. For those detractors who criticised the crowds at the camp, Wintringham pointed out that four-fifths of all British holiday makers spent their holiday in crowded seaside resorts because they want to 'see and do things, laugh at and with people, be "in" things'. For those who wanted solitude, deckchairs and reading lounges sufficed at the camp. 'But if you don't

want to be lonely', Wintringham continued, 'there are about eighty young
men and girls in red jackets whose business is not to be busy, but to talk to
people and introduce them to others.' For some observers like Wintringham,
the rapid success of holiday camps like Skegness appeared likely to spread as
swiftly 'and become as big a thing … as the cinema or the tea-shop'.[122]

Despite this optimistic prediction, less than a month after Wintringham's
article in *Picture Post* magazine, the 1939 holiday season ended abruptly with
the declaration of war. Butlin and Warner both closed their camps immediately
because of their proximity to the south-eastern coast, and because the British
government planned to use the camps for military personnel. Other holiday
camps throughout Britain were requisitioned and used to house prisoners of
war, German and Italian aliens, troops, and civilian workers. Nevertheless, the
holiday-camp industry established in the interwar years, and the unique camp
culture developed within the camps, re-emerged largely intact after the cessation of hostilities in 1945.

Conclusion

The camps built by Butlin and Warner in the 1930s rapidly became known
as value-for-money package holidays. Butlin and Warner took advantage of
developments in advertising techniques to promote their camps in popular
national and local newspapers. The widespread advertising, along with the
elaborate entertainment and mass organisation of the camps, helped to make
their interwar leisure enterprises successful. In addition, the publicity created by
surprise guests created an atmosphere of suspense and expectation that a holiday
would involve the appearance of a national celebrity to entertain campers.

The entrepreneurs also used advertising to counter criticism and to illustrate the value of the camps to the local economy. By graphically illustrating
their collaboration with other British industries and local businesses, Butlin
and Warner successfully presented their camps as beneficial to local economies. The holiday-camp industry both benefited from and was part of the
immense growth of leisure in interwar Britain. As the government recognised
the economic benefits of domestic tourism, official support for the camps
increased, implicating the state directly in the promotion of mass pleasure.

The next chapter explores the nexus of war and leisure in mid twentieth-
century Britain. The camp culture forged in the interwar years gained a
prominent place in the national consciousness, in a way that belies the number
of people who actually holidayed at camps. The manner in which Warner and

Butlin marketed their camps ensured that, even if a person had never visited a camp, he or she understood the camps as a uniquely British industry. In the years following the Second World War, Warner and Butlin would continue to market their holiday camps as a British enterprise that was predicated upon and that perpetuated a collective wartime experience.

Notes

1 '"Amy", landing at Skegness, spends two hours in the resort on Whit Sunday', *Skegness News*, 3 June 1936, p. 1. Amy Mollison (nee Johnson) established several long-distance records with her solo flights to Australia in 1930, to Tokyo in 1932, and to the Cape of Good Hope and back in 1936. In 1932 she married Jim Mollison. Together Johnson and Mollison flew the Atlantic in 1936. See B. Rieger, 'Fast couples: technology, gender, and modernity in Britain and Germany during the 1930s', *Historical Research*, 76: 193 (August 2003), pp. 364–88.

2 'Skegness is great! Amy's reply to Mr. W. E. Butlin, the ideal holiday', *Skegness News*, 3 June 1936, p. 1.

3 Nevett, *Advertising in Britain*, pp. 138–48.

4 See S. Strasser, *Satisfaction guaranteed: The making of the American mass market* (New York: Pantheon, 1989) for a discussion of the development of brand consciousness.

5 See, for example, *Warner Calendar 1936*, Portsmouth Central Library, Local Studies Collection (hereafter PCLLSC).

6 'Stewards of the air – how meals are served to air passengers', *Caterer and Hotel Keeper*, 27 November 1936, p. 26.

7 'R.M.S. "Queen Mary"', Queen Mary supplement, *Caterer and Hotel Keeper*, 22 May 1936, pp. iii–xx.

8 'R.M.S. Queen Mary: Greatest floating hotel', ibid.

9 M. Kyle, 'Eve packs her suitcase: Fashion and beauty aids for a sunshine holiday', *Holiday Travel*, May 1934, pp. 97–9. BL, JJTC, Travel Agencies, 2.

10 *Holiday abroad: Summer 1939* (London: Frame's Tours Ltd., Southampton Row, 1939).

11 *The travel log: A monthly magazine of travel and holidays at home and abroad and the journal of the Worker's Travel Association*, Vol. XIII No. 1 November 1938, pp. 2, 29. Holidays in France became less expensive after the devaluation of the franc in 1936 and again in May 1938.

12 'Rise of travel agencies – a century of tourism', *The Times*, 26 October 1937, pp. xxxiv–xxxv.

13 *The golden road to Turkestan: Tours to Soviet Central Asia* (Moscow: 1933), JJTC, Travel Booklets, 4, BL (hereafter JJTC/TB4).

14 *Travel in Germany* (Berlin: 1936), pp. 6, JJTC/TB4, BL.

15 Not all tour operators flourished in the 1930s. George Lunn's Tours Ltd filed for bankruptcy in 1933. 'George Lunn's Tours, Ltd – many hotel creditors', *Caterer and Hotel Keeper*, 21 January 1933, p. 118.

16 S. Constantine, 'The buy British campaign of 1931', *European Journal of Marketing* (1987), 21: 4, pp. 44–59.

17 Until the 1921 Act, most leaflets and tourist guides were written by private individuals or businesses, rather than by the resorts being promoted by the local council or corporation.

18 'For health and happiness', *News Chronicle*, 18 June 1931, p. 6. In 1932, Blackpool was promoted as the 'perfect tonic' for 'good health', Blackpool advert, *News Chronicle*, 2 June 1932, p. 7. Hastings and St Leonard's followed Blackpool's lead and became 'Britain's best tonic', illustrated by a smartly dressed woman walking a large dog along the sea shore. Hastings and St Leonard's advert, *News Chronicle*, 2 June 1932, p. 7. Eastbourne promoted the south-coast weather and claimed to be 'The sunshine record resort', illustrated by a sunbathing beauty on the beach attended by an attentive male in shirt and tie. Eastbourne advert, *News Chronicle*, 2 June 1932, p. 7.

19 N. Yates, 'Selling the seaside', *History Today*, 38:8 (1988), p. 24.

20 R. Roberts, 'The Corporation as impresario: The municipal provision of entertainment in Victorian and Edwardian Bournemouth', in J. Walton and J. Walvin, eds. *Leisure in Britain, 1780–1939* (Manchester: Manchester University Press, 1983), pp. 136–57, and J. Walton, 'Municipal government and the holiday industry in Blackpool', in ibid., pp. 159–86.

21 See Barton, *Working-class organisations*, pp. 133–78.

22 M. Hilton, 'Advertising the modernist aesthetic of the marketplace? The cultural relationship between the tobacco manufacturer and the "mass" of consumers in Britain, 1870–1940', in M. Daunton and B. Rieger, eds *Meanings of modernity: Britain from the late-Victorian era to World War II*, (Oxford: Berg, 2001), pp. 45–70.

23 S. Farrant, 'London by the sea: Resort development on the south coast of England, 1880–1939', *Journal of Contemporary History*, 22 (1987), pp. 137–62.

24 'Caister holiday camp', holiday accommodation advert, *News Chronicle*, 15 June 1933, p. 19.

25 'North Wales holiday camp', holiday accommodation advert, *News Chronicle*, 15 June 1933, p. 19.

26 'Holiday attractions and accommodation', Northney holiday-camp advert, *Daily News Chronicle*, 30 June 1933, p. 16.

27 The August Bank Holiday was the first Monday of August until 1965, when it was changed to the last Monday in August.

28 Northney holiday-camp advert, *Daily Herald*, 8 May 1936, p. 14, and Northney holiday-camp advert, *Daily Herald*, 19 May 1936, p. 14.

29 'Holiday accommodation', Northney holiday-camp advert, *News Chronicle*, 9 June 1934, p. 15.

30 Sunshine holiday-camp advert, *Daily Herald*, 19 May 1936, p. 14.

31 J. Hill, 'League cricket in the north and Midlands, 1900–1940', in R. Holt, ed. *Sport and the working class in modern Britain* (Manchester: Manchester University Press, 1990), pp. 121–41, S. Jones, 'Working class sport in Manchester between the wars', in ibid., pp. 67–83, and R. Wheeler, 'Organized sport and organized labour: The worker's sport's movement', *Journal of Contemporary History*, 13: 2 (1978) pp. 191–210.

32 The Coronation camp opened in July 1937.

33 'Holiday camps and chalets – this is the holiday!' *News Chronicle*, 10 June 1937, p. 19.

34 Holiday camps advert, *Daily Express*, 23 April 1938, p. 18.

35 Holiday camps and chalets advert, *Daily Herald*, 8 June 1937, p. 14.

36 *Warner's Seaton holiday camp, Devon*, Warner brochure (Essex, 1938).

37 Holiday camps and chalets adverts, *Daily Herald*, 8 June 1937, p. 14.

38 Holiday accommodation adverts, *News Chronicle*, 2 June 1937, p. 14. Butlin helped Warner to design the new Dovercourt Bay camp. 'Daily newspaper describes a new kind of holiday: remarkable tribute to the genius of Mr. W. E. Butlin', *Skegness News*, 30 June 1937, p. 7.

39 *Warner's Dovercourt Bay holiday camp*, Warner brochure (Essex, 1938).

40 Ibid.

41 'Opening of Dovercourt Bay holiday camp: really a modern seaside hotel', *Harwich and Dovercourt Standard*, 12 June 1937, pp. 2–3.

42 'Some interesting facts and figures: kitchens can serve 1,500 meals at once', *Harwich and Dovercourt Standard*, 12 June 1937, p. 3.

43 'Another holiday camp opened – Dovercourt Bay benefits from Butlin enterprise', *Skegness News*, 16 June 1937, p. 5.

44 F. W. Ogilvie, *The tourist movement: An economic study* (London: Staples Press Limited, 1938).

45 'State-aided bureau to help publicise holiday camps', *Holiday Camp Review*, 1:2 (May 1938), p. 4.

46 *The Holiday camp book: The official book of the National Federation of Permanent Holiday Camps* (London: Clerke and Cockeran, 1949).

47 'Warner's Puckpool holiday camp, Ryde', Warner brochure insert (Essex, 1939).

48 'How Skegness is catering for the new holiday vogue: recreation must be provided as well as amusement', *Skegness News*, 19 August 1936, p. 3.

49 Holiday-camp adverts, *Daily Herald*, 19 May 1936, p. 14.

50 Butlin's Skegness holiday-camp advert, *Daily Herald*, 8 May 1936, p. 14.

51 Ibid.

52 Ibid.

53 LeMahieu, *Culture for democracy*, pp. 148–9.

54 Butlin again advertised his camp on the radio when he held a Brass Band Festival at the Skegness camp in April 1939. 'Butlin's Brass Band Festival to be broadcast', *World's Fair*, 22 April 1939, p. 13.

55 P. Scannell and D. Cardiff, *A social history of British broadcasting, Volume One 1922–1939: Serving the Nation* (Oxford: Basil Blackwell, 1991), p. 195.

56 Songs sung casually were the popular songs of the day that were tuneful and easy to sing by amateurs without a microphone, ibid. p. 192.

57 Rarely broadcast vaudeville and variety radio shows were extremely popular, ibid., pp. 190–6.

58 'Features of the Skegness broadcast', *Skegness News*, 29 July 1936, p. 3.

59 'Goodnight sweetheart', by Ray Noble, was one of the most popular songs of the interwar years in Britain and the US. McKibbin, *Classes and cultures*, p. 413.

60 'Radio history made by latest Skegness broadcast – first programme ever relayed from a British holiday camp', *Skegness News*, 19 July 1936, pp. 1, 3.

61 Brown, *Death of Christian Britain*, pp. 145–69. See also P. Walker, *Pulling the devil's kingdom down: The Salvation Army in Victorian Britain* (Berkeley: University of California Press, 2001).

62 'Film star picks beauty contest winner', *Skegness News*, 25 August 1937, p. 3.

63 Rene Ray (or Renee Ray), born in 1911, appeared in five films in 1935 and three in 1936.

64 Elizabeth Allan was born in Skegness in 1908 (or 1910). She appeared in forty-six films, including *David Copperfield* (1935), *A Tale of Two Cities* (1935) and *Camille* (1936) with Greta Garbo.

65 'Elizabeth Allan judges Perfect Figure competition at Butlin's holiday camp', *Skegness News*, 8 September 1937, p. 5.

66 See B. Melman, *Women and the popular imagination in the twenties: Flappers and nymphs* (London: Macmillan, 1988), S. Jeffreys, 'Women and sexuality', in *Women's history: Britain 1850–1945* (New York: Routledge, 1995), pp. 193–216, and S. Alexander, 'Becoming a woman: Growing up in the 1920s and 1930s', in *Becoming a Woman and other essays in 19th and 20th century feminist history* (London: New York University Press, 1994).

67 K. Peiss, 'Making up, making over: Cosmetics, consumer culture, and women's identity', in V. de Grazia and E. Furlough, eds *The sex of things: Gender and consumption in historical perspective* (Berkeley: University of California Press, 1996), pp. 311–36.

68 H. Wilkinson, 'The new heraldry: Stock photography, visual literacy, and advertising in 1930s Britain', *Journal of Design History*, 10:1 (1997), pp. 23–38.

69 Langhamer, *Women's leisure*, 175–6.

70 Many Hollywood films succeeded because of their popularity among British audiences. McKibben, *Classes and culture*, pp. 419–56.

71 Gracie Fields was born in Rochdale, Lancashire and starred in films including *Sally in Our Alley* (1931), *Looking on the Bright Side* (1932), *This Week of Grace* (1933), *Sing as We Go* (1934), *Look Up and Laugh* (1935), *The Show Goes On* (1937), and *Shipyard Sally* (1939). Most of Field's films depicted working-class life with a message of cheerfulness and courage in the face of unemployment and adversity. Richards, *Films and British national identity*, pp. 262–7.

72 Ibid., pp. 262–3.

73 Butlin with Dacre, *Butlin story*, p. 113.

74 Florence Desmond (Florence Dawson), born in 1905, was a popular actress, comedienne, and impersonator. She appeared in numerous films, including *The Road to Fortune* (1930), *Sally in Our Alley* (1931), *The Marriage Bond* (1932), *Mr. Skitch* (1933), *Gay Love* (1934), and *Accused* (1936).

75 Len Hutton began playing for Yorkshire in 1934 at the age of 17. The 364 runs took a staggering thirteen hours to achieve and broke Don Bradman's record for the highest individual score in test matches. Derek Birley, *Playing the game: Sport and British society, 1910–45* (Manchester: Manchester University Press, 1995), p. 313.

76 'Len Hutton comes to Skegness', *Skegness News*, 31 August 1938, p. 6.

77 Butlin with Dacre, *Butlin story*, p. 113.

78 F. Le Gros Clark, *National fitness: A brief essay on contemporary Britain* (London: Macmillan and Co., Limited, 1938).

79 Butlin's holiday-camp advert, *Daily Mail*, 29 April 1938, p. 10.

80 'Butlin's holiday camp – wonderful designs and progress', *Clacton News and East Essex Advertiser*, 14 May 1938, p. 8.

81 Len Harvey was British Middleweight Champion 1929–33, British Light Heavy-weight Champion in 1933, and World Light Heavyweight Champion 1939–42. S. Shipley, 'Boxing', in Tony Mason, ed. *Sport in Britain: A social history* (Cambridge: Cambridge University Press, 1989), pp. 78–115. Harvey also starred in two films, *Excuse My Glove* (1936), and *The Bermondsey Kid* (1933). See 'Len Harvey, boxer, dead at 69; fought in every weight class', *New York Times*, 29 November, 1976, p. 30. Dan Maskell (1908–92) was the first teaching coach at the All England Lawn Tennis and Croquet Club, Wimbledon, and Britain's professional champion for sixteen years. H. Walker, 'Lawn Tennis', in *Sport in Britain*, pp. 245–75.

82 E. H. Temme was the first man to swim the English Channel in 1927, and again in 1934.

83 Butlin's luxury holiday-camp advert, *Clacton News*, 2 July 1938, p. 7.

84 M. Huggins, 'Projecting the visual: British newsreels, soccer and popular culture 1918–39', *International Journal of the History of Sport*, 24:1 (2007), pp. 80–102.

85 McKibbin, *Classes and cultures*, pp. 386–418.

86 Victor Silvester (1900–78) is credited with developing British Ballroom dancing, ibid.

87 In February 1933, the *Daily News Chronicle* held a competition between British and US dance bands. The British public chose Lew Stone and Jack Hylton, beating the American rivals and winning the £1,500 prize. '£1,500 dance record contest', *Daily News Chronicle*, 28 April 1933, p. 1.

88 Butlin's Skegness holiday-camp advert, *Skegness News*, 6 July 1938, p. 3.

89 Butlin's holiday-camp advert, *Skegness News*, 20 July 1938, p. 5.

90 'Around the holiday camp: Bathing beauty contest', *Clacton News*, 20 August 1938, p. 10.

91 Forsythe regularly used his position as beauty contest organiser to select potential movie stars.

92 Richards, *Films and British national identity*, p. 74.

93 The local newspaper featured weekly articles about the holiday camps and published the names of competition winners. See 'Holiday-camp paragraphs', *Skegness News*, 2 September 1936, p. 4. The Clacton camp received similar attention from the local paper, especially when football was played. See 'Butlin's avenge previous defeat', *Clacton News and East Essex Advertiser*, 29 January 1938, p. 10.

94 Huggins, 'Projecting the visual', p. 81.

95 'Holiday-camp paragraphs', *Skegness News*, 2 September 1936, p. 4.

96 'Holiday camps and chalets – this is the holiday!' *News Chronicle*, 10 June 1937, p. 19.

97 'How Skegness is catering for the new holiday vogue – recreation must be provided as well as amusement', *Skegness News*, 19 August 1936, p. 3.

98 'Holiday camp impressions – Birmingham young lady's happy May holiday', *Skegness News*, 13 May 1936, p. 3.

99 *Holiday Camp Review*, 1:1 (April 1938), p. 1. BL PP. 1832.HK.

100 Editorial, 'To introduce ourselves', ibid.

101 T. S. 'First time at a camp but going back for more', *Holiday Camp Review*, 1:2 (May 1938), p. 2, BL PP. 1832.HK.

102 'How Skegness is catering for the new holiday vogue: recreation must be provided as well as amusement', *Skegness News*, 19 August 1936, p. 3.

103 Ibid.

104 'Mr. William Butlin writes on holiday camps', *Skegness News*, 14 July 1937, p. 3.

105 Huggins, 'Projecting the visual', p. 90.

106 'How holiday camp appetites are created and satisfied', *Skegness News*, 26 August 1936, p. 6.

107 'What we want from camps', *Holiday Camp Review*, 1:3 (June 1938), pp. 3–4, BL PP. 1832.HK.

108 'Butlin campers at Nottingham dance', *World's Fair*, 13 November 1937, p. 47.

109 'Butlin's holiday camp to open for Christmas and New Year', *World's Fair*, 5 November 1938, p. 15.

110 'Butlin's reunion', advert, *Daily Mail*, 3 January 1939, p. 4.

111 H. Warner, WSFA AV 623/36/1–51.

112 *Make this year's holiday your best holiday at Warner's holiday camp*, Warner brochure (Essex, 1938), pp. 2–3.

113 Ibid.

114 Ibid., p. 4.

115 Ibid.

116 Ibid.

117 Interwar women's soccer teams increased, but the English Football Association banned women's teams from using grounds of affiliated clubs in 1921. Huggins, 'Projecting the visual', p. 95.

118 *Make this year's holiday*, pp. 5–6.

119 Vernon, *Hunger*, pp. 118–58.

120 *Make this year's holiday*, pp. 5–6.

121 Leisure articles were often written by J. B. Priestly. See A. Sargeant, *British cinema: A critical history* (London: British Film Institute, 2005), p. 175.

122 T. Wintringham, 'Holiday camp', *Picture Post*, 5 August 1939, pp. 43–9.

4

War and the business of leisure

In August 1939, Mrs A. S. Heath, manager of the Manor Hotel in Hindhead, wrote a letter of protest to her local council. Heath strenuously objected to a government proposal to build a holiday camp close to the famous Surrey beauty spot and adjacent to her hotel. Hindhead had been developed as an inland resort in the nineteenth century and frequented by Arthur Conan Doyle and George Bernard Shaw, and the air of the locality was considered to have the same health-giving qualities as that in Switzerland.[1] The planned camp was part of a scheme to provide low-cost holiday centres for working people in peacetime and for use as evacuation camps in case of war. The proposal met with a multitude of objections from local residents and hoteliers like Heath. The idea of the camp, she wrote, 'is most alarming. Our [Manor Hotel] visitors are almost entirely quiet elderly people or invalids' and, Heath continued, 'a large camp of this type would certainly drive them away for good'.[2] As a result of dozens of letters of protest, the Haslemere Urban Council held a special meeting to discuss the government proposals. After a heated discussion the council decided to oppose the camp on the grounds that it would be 'prejudicial to the amenities of the district'.[3] Less than two weeks later, Britain was at war, and the construction of civilian evacuation camps took precedence over objections from hoteliers like Heath.

Ironically, the Second World War contributed to the growth of holiday camps and domestic tourism, reconfiguring the position of the countryside as a place of safety as well as leisure for the nation's urban population. The public and parliamentary discussion surrounding planned peacetime holiday centres and evacuation sites began in early 1938 as the international situation in Europe deteriorated. Many in Britain believed that the tactics of warfare would be to target urban industrial centres in aerial bombing raids and that civilian casualties would be high. Plans to evacuate women and children from towns and cities began in earnest as war looked imminent.[4] In January 1939, Parliament debated a Camps Bill and began to plan the construction of fifty wartime evacuation centres in, which could be used as children's school holiday camps in peacetime.[5] Although the Bill stipulated the use of the buildings as sites for children's leisure, many in Parliament also argued for their use as inexpensive family centres to cater for the increased number of workers who received annual paid holidays under the provision of the Holidays With Pay Act (1938), passed a few months earlier.[6]

The construction of the camps created anxiety amongst hoteliers and boarding-house proprietors. The mass holiday camps of the coastal regions threatened to move inland. Nevertheless, as hoteliers and local residents protested the construction of government camps in their locales, the risk of war legitimated holiday camps as centres both of worker leisure and for the preservation of civilian life. At the outbreak of war in 1939, the construction of evacuation camps continued alongside facilities to house war workers and service personnel. The reaction of local residents and businesses, however, reveals the levels of social conflict present during the 'people's war'.[7]

War presented an unexpected bonanza for holiday-camp entrepreneurs. It unwittingly facilitated the growth of the industry and simultaneously legitimated the expansion of holiday camps in the postwar period. Because of the interruption to the peaceful expansion of their leisure empires, both Harry Warner and Billy Butlin worked for the Ministry of Supply throughout the war. Their reputation for mass catering made Warner and Butlin particularly suitable to oversee the construction of industrial villages and wartime camps for service personnel. When asked to find suitable sites for military training camps, Butlin agreed, and also negotiated to buy them from the government at the end of the war. At the end of the war in 1945, Butlin took possession of three new sites that he transformed into luxury holiday camps, and Warner expanded his leisure empire to include several former military camps on the south coast of Britain.

Indeed, other domestic leisure industries, such as circuses, fairgrounds, and the cinema, also expanded during the war years.[8] Throughout the Second World War, the British government encouraged leisure activities and traditional travelling entertainments to help boost civilian morale.[9] In addition, as historian John Walton points out, the number of holidays with pay agreements increased, despite the hostilities, and many Britons enjoyed some kind of holiday as a distraction from work.[10] Thus the expansion of leisure begun in the interwar years continued, even if the sites of leisure were somewhat restricted.

At the same time, a new vision for postwar Britain emerged during the war years that centred attention on the state provision of citizen welfare. Sir William Beveridge presented his plan for the reconstruction of postwar Britain in November 1942, which served as a blueprint for the development of a welfare state that would abolish 'want, disease, ignorance, squalor and idleness'.[11] Beveridge envisioned a new type of citizenship where the state took responsibility for the social needs of its citizenry from the 'cradle to the grave'. As the ideas encapsulated in the Beveridge Report became public, plans to expand postwar leisure intersected with the needs of the new social citizenship and a redefined relationship to the state. The idea of a State Holiday Corporation emerged as the Ministry of Supply planned to derequisition wartime facilities for use as peacetime holiday camps. This chapter explores the impact of war on the holiday-camp industry. Just as the camps garnered government support in the interwar years as a potential solution to the problem of mass leisure, the industry also received a boost from wartime policies. Rather than halting leisure, war stimulated the need for mass camps to billet troops and civilians. As a result of war, the government built a political and economic infrastructure that increased the number of camps and ensured their availability for leisure in the immediate postwar period.

The Camps Bill and war

Early in 1938 Members of Parliament recognised the need to prepare for possible air attacks on Britain's cities and ports. The eastern coastal areas appeared especially vulnerable. When Butlin opened his second holiday camp at Clacton in 1938, former Labour MP Lord Strabolgi spoke at the opening ceremony and expressed a great interest in the camp as a potential venue to accommodate troops. In the event of a European war, Strabolgi claimed, '8,000 soldiers could be housed in the [Clacton] camp' immediately. The importance of holiday camps to the strategic interests of the nation lay not only in the 'set purpose of entertaining visitors during the summer season', but also in their ability to house British troops in time of war.[12] Later that year high-ranking officers of the British and French armed services inspected Butlin's Clacton and Skegness camps in anticipation of their use by the military in wartime.[13]

Holiday camps were also used as blueprints for civilian evacuation centres. As early as May 1938, an area Medical Officer of Health, Dr P. D. H. Chapman, made recommendations in his quarterly report to elevate the sanitation standards of all holiday camps for future wartime use. Chapman indicated that the government viewed existing holiday camps as a valuable evacuation resource in the event of air raids. The government therefore would help to fund efforts necessary to bring existing sites 'up to a good standard of sanitation and order'.[14] In January 1939, Parliament debated a Camps Bill that promoted and financially supported the construction of additional large-scale holiday camps for use as evacuation centres in the event of war. The Bill estimated the cost of each individual camp at £20,000 with a further £200,000 needed to pay management costs. The proposals included plans for the state and private organisations to jointly manage and fund the project as a non-profit enterprise. The Bill overrode the local autonomy gained via the Town and Country Planning Acts of 1925 and 1932 and allowed only a two-week period for local residents or councils to raise objections to the construction of any of the camps.[15]

Hoteliers and boarding-house proprietors feared increased competition from the camps. Despite assurances from Minister of Defence, Sir John Anderson, that the facilities would be used primarily as children's camps, doubts remained.[16] The Bill proposed to invest £1,000,000 in a scheme to build fifty inland camps to hold a total of 37,000 civilians for evacuation purposes, should hostilities commence.[17] Ostensibly chosen with the health and safety of urban school-children in mind, the sites were inland and not close to the popular coastal resorts. The plans for the facilities, however, replicated holiday camps and featured individual accommodation huts with electricity and hot water rather than dormitories, a general dining room, and a variety of recreation rooms. Hoteliers feared the competition for guests and also staff. Hotels already competed for qualified and capable workers. Fifty new children's camps would further deplete the labour pool and leave hotels inadequately staffed.[18]

While Anderson, an independent MP, attempted to assuage anxieties within the hotel and boarding house industry, Viscount Astor, a Conservative MP, suggested that the camps be built immediately as holiday centres and used to accommodate workers with paid holidays.[19] Despite his Conservative Party politics, Astor recognised the importance of the holiday-camp industry to the movement for democratic leisure and wished to meet the present and future needs of British workers with newly built sites of pleasure. Faced with what it perceived as state-funded competition, the Bexhill Hoteliers' Association hotly criticised the plan as yet another threat to small hotels and boarding houses when it met to discuss the problem in early March 1939. Captain R. C. Bird told the assembled members at the annual meeting of the Association, 'It is no use closing our eyes to the fact that as holiday camps [the proposed evacuation centres] would be a popular choice' to meet the leisure needs of workers.

In order to counter the effect of the holiday camps on local businesses, Bird proposed that the Association make every effort to secure assurances that these government holiday camps would cater solely to the low end of the holiday market and ensure that the less desirable guests did not attempt to stay at the Association's hotels. To do this, Bird suggested that the charges for full board and sleeping accommodation should 'not exceed one guinea per head per week, thus avoiding competition with apartment and boarding houses and giving thousands of poor families the opportunity to take a holiday'.[20] Despite the apparent magnanimity of the Association toward the poorer members of society, hoteliers expressed the desire that the camps be built away from established resorts and far away from their hotels. In a formal statement to Sir George Courthope, Conservative MP for the Rye Division, the Bexhill Association laid out its proposal to keep the poorest families in Britain away from the coastal resorts and contained within inland holiday camps. Thus, Bexhill hoteliers not only addressed the leisure and safety needs of the British worker in war and peace, they also ensured a higher class of visitor at their own establishments.[21]

As hoteliers met to oppose the Camps Bill and to protect their share of the leisure market, the parliamentary debate focused on the difficulty of planning camps for mixed use. If, as the Bill proposed, the camps were intended as evacuation centres in wartime and holiday camps during peacetime, their design and geographical location was of prime importance.[22] While inland camps would serve the needs of evacuated children, they would not attract peacetime holiday makers who desired seaside holidays. Dormitories designed for children, for example, would not serve the needs of adult holiday makers in peacetime.[23] During the debate, Labour MP Mr Creech Jones suggested that 'the camps should be designed mainly as holiday camps'.[24] In response to those members who shared the anxiety of hoteliers, Jones maintained that 'hotels need not be apprehensive' about the camps because they would 'cater for a class' which, up to the recent time, had not enjoyed holidays away from home. State camps, in his opinion, would cater for the new group of consumers created largely through the movement for holidays with pay.[25]

To a certain extent, the disappointing 1938 season supported this view. After the passage of the Holidays With Pay Act in April 1938, many resorts and leisure entrepreneurs expected to provide for the newly leisured workers.[26] Yet for many workers, holidays were still too expensive, or consumers were simply unused to paid leisure time, as interviews conducted by Mass Observation suggested. The observers described the women they interviewed as lower, middle or upper working class, the social groups most likely to benefit from the paid holiday legislation. Of those interviewed, many described holidays as 'too expensive' and had no plans to go away from home. Others stated that they intended to stay with relatives or friends, often on farms, or would take day trips into the countryside. Very few anticipated a seaside holiday without careful saving throughout the year.[27] The local pub, football matches, and gambling often fulfilled workers' leisure needs.[28] As a result, the influx of holidaying workers to seaside resorts did not materialise. Blackpool actually saw a decline in the number of holiday visitors.[29]

An article in the *World's Fair* (the showman's weekly business newspaper) at the end of the 1938 holiday season assessed the effect of the legislation. In the coastal resorts of North Wales, the number of visitors did not increase as expected. 'While these resorts have had their usual quota of visitors they have not had the "invasion" which it was thought would follow the granting of holidays with pay to thousands of workpeople in the industrial north.'[30] For many in the leisure industry the disappointing season suggested the need to counter consumer resistance and promote their resorts as the places to spend newly acquired leisure time. For some, state-sponsored children's camps had the potential to change holiday habits and help to create demand among a new generation of consumers of pleasure. If the children of working people could be persuaded to go to a state-sponsored camp each year they were more likely to continue to take holidays later in life. Children promised a future market as consumers who would habitually holiday away from home as adults. State involvement in the promotion of children as leisure consumers could thus only benefit the domestic industry in the future.

Members of Parliament viewed the Camps Bill differently. Those connected to the tourist industry attempted to limit what they saw as state aid to mass consumption. Mr Roland Robinson, Conservative MP for Blackpool and president of the British Residential Hotels Association, suggested to the House of Commons that the Camps Bill originated with 'certain people' who wanted camps established for reasons other than evacuation.[31] The 'certain people' included Butlin and Warner, who understood the importance of their camps to national security but also viewed the construction of more camps as a potential opportunity to expand their leisure empires. They openly supported the Camps Bill. Robinson, on the other hand, declared that he would speak 'for the small man engaged in the hotel industry and in apartment and boarding houses' and stand firm in his opposition to any proposal to use the camps for any other purpose than evacuation.[32]

Robinson's declaration had little effect. The construction of a state-funded holiday camp four miles from Hindhead in Surrey commenced shortly after the debate in the Commons. It was scheduled for completion in September 1939 and planners hoped to accommodate up to 1,000 urban children in dormitories.[33] While Robinson opposed any kind of camp that might threaten the livelihood of the hotel industry, local hoteliers and residents in Hindhead did not oppose this camp, specifically designed for children, as it would not compete for the age or class of visitor welcomed at the Surrey beauty spot. In addition, the camp was hidden from view and located several miles away from any hotels. Thus Hindhead, as an inland resort accommodating middle-class cultural idealists seeking the seclusion of unspoiled countryside, remained attractive to their target clientele.[34]

Hoteliers and local residents did, however, object strongly to proposals for a second camp in Hindhead because of its closer proximity to the resort and its planned use as an inexpensive family holiday camp in peacetime.[35] After a barrage of letters and a public meeting, the Haslemere Urban Council acknowledged the anxieties expressed by hoteliers such as Mrs Heath of the Manor Hotel and Mr Evans of Highcroft Private Hotel in Hindhead. In an attempt to shore up official opposition to the camp, the council invited the County Medical Officer to inspect the site. The officer duly noted inadequate drainage and sewerage systems in Hindhead that would not accommodate the needs of a further thousand people. Echoing older concerns over the potential danger of the 'unsanitary' urban poor, the officer accordingly declared the site a potential health hazard for Hindhead and unsuitable as either a holiday camp or an evacuation centre.[36] After some discussion, the council voted to address the problem directly and inform the government that the construction of the camp could not take place.[37]

Warner and Butlin followed the parliamentary debate closely. As local authorities opposed the construction of camps in their locales, both men saw the commercial potential of the evacuation centres in peacetime.[38] When Britain declared war on Germany on 3 September 1939, the holiday season came to an abrupt end and Warner and Butlin voluntarily closed their holiday camps. Requisitioned to billet military personnel shortly thereafter, the camps designed to provide a source of democratic leisure for thousands of Britons now provided accommodation for troops determined to protect the nascent social and political democracy forged in the interwar years.[39]

The location of Warner's four camps on the south coast gave them particular logistical value as centres to billet troops prior to deployment. The camps contained individual 'chalets' to house as many as six soldiers, bathroom blocks for communal bathing, laundry facilities, a large, cafeteria-style dining room and kitchen to cater for hundreds of soldiers, and a ballroom large enough to hold all the wartime 'guests' for important briefings. Furthermore, the location of the four holiday camps on Hayling Island made them an ideal base for overflow troops from the naval base at Portsmouth, fewer than twelve miles away by land and even less by sea. On 15 June 1940, the Royal Navy requisitioned Warner's camp and renamed it HMS Northney. The Civil Service Union camp became HMS Northney II, and the Coronation camp HMS Northney III. The fourth, the Sunshine holiday camp, was requisitioned by the Royal Marines.[40] Hayling was now a restricted zone, and the former resort saw few visitors other than troops throughout the Second World War. Butlin's camp at Skegness, renamed HMS Arthur, accommodated a Royal Navy training centre, and his newest Clacton camp housed prisoners of war.

The experience of the interwar holiday-camp entrepreneurs proved useful in wartime. In late 1939, the Minister for War, Hore Belisha, approached Butlin to oversee the building of an army camp at Filey, in Yorkshire.[41] Butlin had had plans to build a new holiday camp there before the war halted work. Aware of the building costs, Butlin offered to build the camp for two-thirds of the projected price on condition that he should have the opportunity to buy back the camp at the end of the war for a fraction of the building cost.[42] The site was situated on the east coast of Britain, and Butlin's proposal gambled that the enemy would not destroy the camp in an air raid. The Minister agreed to the proposal. Butlin then asked his business associate, Harry Warner, to oversee the construction of the Filey camp while he answered the call for a civil defence force and enlisted as a private in the Home Guard.[43] By 1942, the Filey camp housed 8,000 members of the Royal Air Force (RAF) and served as Britain's largest RAF training camp.

War had a heavy financial impact on Butlin's Ltd. The abrupt end to the holiday season meant that net profits for the year ending September 1939 were only £22,735, compared to £88,393 the previous year.[44] Butlin's permanent funfairs, however, still made a profit. At the outbreak of war, Butlin designed a popular rifle range for his Felixstowe funfair. The stall featured a number of moving life-sized figures of Adolf Hitler, Goebbels, Eva Braun and 'Lord Haw Haw' at which customers could take aim.[45] Despite the popularity of this stall and others, Butlin's profits did not reach pre-war levels.[46] Nevertheless, he looked optimistically for new business opportunities throughout the war. While Warner spent the first year of the war overseeing the construction of the camp at Filey, and the remainder as an active member of the Home Guard, Butlin put his organisational skills to work for the Ministry of Supply.[47]

The Ministry of Supply (MOS) was responsible for housing Royal Ordnance Factory workers. The MOS began building hostels close to the factories that were relocated to remote areas of Britain, deemed safe from enemy fire.[48] At the beginning of the war there were sufficient materials and construction workers to build estates as homes for transferred workers and their families. The Ministry employed external contractors to build seventy estates with 7,800 houses for Ministry of Aircraft Production and a further forty-three estates with 5,400 quarters for Ministry of Supply workers.[49] By early 1940, Butlin was advertising designs for 'industrial villages'. An article in the *World's Fair* promoted his services to the 'many British manufacturers who have new or enlarged factories', and who faced the problem of 'how to house your workers – how to house them so they are happily housed'. W. E. Butlin, the article claimed, 'is the one man in Britain who has solved this problem' through his design of industrial villages. The villages consisted of 'single storey concrete buildings' to house twenty-five workers, with central heating and comfortable furnishings. Every building, the article claimed, 'has its own baths, dining room, kitchen, lounge and recreations'. Butlin's first model industrial village was built close to the border between England and Wales, in Monmouthshire, and housed 1,500 men.[50]

By 1941, however, limited building supplies, the poor quality of available labour, and lack of adequate supervision for it, created problems for both the tenants and the management of the industrial villages. Many contractors used substitute materials before they had been properly tested. Consequently, maintenance problems increased costs, and building of houses for married workers ceased abruptly. Despite the problems of construction, Butlin's village designs prompted the Admiralty to engage him to design accommodation for naval employees and their families.[51] When he was asked to scout out a safe place for a new naval training centre, Butlin found Pwllheli in North Wales. 'It was nothing but a series of fields leading down to the sea with the mountains in the background,' claimed Butlin, but it became the site for a spacious camp for 8,000 naval ratings, and was rapidly transformed into HMS Glendower. The Admiralty again asked Butlin to find a site for a naval training centre, this time in Scotland. Butlin chose a site at Ayr, on the coast, overlooking the Isle of Arran.[52] As with Filey, Butlin negotiated with the Admiralty to buy back the Pwllheli and Ayr camps at the end of the war for a fraction of the building costs.[53] Although Butlin was unsure whether he would have the money to pay for the camps, or whether indeed Britain would win the war, his gamble paid off and, at the end of the war, in addition to reopening Skegness and Clacton, Butlin opened his three new holiday centres at Filey, Pwllheli, and Ayr.

Work and leisure in wartime

Although Butlin and Warner closed their camps to holiday makers, over three-quarters of all other resort accommodation remained available, even after the demands placed upon hotels and guest houses by evacuated children and service personnel.[54] The Association of Health and Pleasure Resorts advertised that resorts planned to take special care to cater for the needs of holiday makers despite the war.[55] As a result, for some resorts such as Blackpool, the 1940 season proved a tremendous success, unparalleled in history.[56] Located on the north-west coast of England and perceived to be out of the range of enemy bombers, the large resort of Blackpool catered for thousands of Britons during the first summer of war.[57]

The government recognised the importance of the continued availability of amusements and traditional summer diversions to maintain civilian morale. Unlike the First World War, when the government sacrificed leisure time in the interests of war production, the Second World War government encouraged recreation even as civilian conscription into war work increased.[58] By 1940, the Ministry of Labour introduced and financed entertainment in factories during lunch hours and other breaks. The Entertainment National Service Association (ENSA) toured with performers and mobile cinema units and libraries of music records for use in workers' music clubs. ENSA also assisted workers to give performances themselves. The Council for the Encouragement of Music and the Arts (CEMA) gave concerts in factories and the BBC gave special 'worker's playtime' and 'Works Wonders' broadcasts for workers from the factories.[59] By the end of 1940, ENSA alone had given over 8,600 performances in over 600 factories.[60] Although the work day lengthened in many factories, the interwar legislation to introduce annual paid holiday for all workers continued to apply. As Minister of Labour, Ernest Bevin, one of the chief supporters of the 1938 Act and a member of the Holidays With Pay Committee, also supported the introduction of a three-day weekend in the spring for war workers. In effect, the Ministry of Labour actually extended the number of annual paid holiday days throughout the war years.[61]

The extension of the number of leisure days meant that the availability of activities and traditional entertainment was essential. Serious problems, however, faced entertainers and travelling show-people. Conscription, petrol rationing, curfews, and the difficulty of performing during blackouts put severe constraints on many travelling performers and entertainments.[62] In a public meeting of the Showman's Guild of Great Britain, Lord Strabolgi encouraged the Guild's members to persevere despite the difficulties they encountered. 'Keep going and keep up the spirit of the people', Strabolgi urged, and 'anticipate a very busy summer season'. Most importantly for the domestic leisure industry, 'there is plenty of money among the working people', he claimed, and less unemployment because of war work. Showmen, Strabolgi suggested, were in a position to profit handsomely from the war. Rationing and shortages of material goods made the consumption of pleasure all the more important and potentially profitable. The consumption of pleasure was important to the work of war as well. 'People must have relaxation', Strabolgi argued, and showmen 'provide clean and wholesome entertainment', especially for children. Indeed, the war underscored the idea of children as consumers of leisure in their own right. Children 'are the citizens of the future', Strabolgi encouraged. 'Help brighten their lives and you will be helping the future of the nation.' Just as the pre-war Camps Bill recognised the need for children's leisure, so the wartime government understood that children required distraction and pleasure. Circuses and travelling fairgrounds appeared to provide both. With a promise of official support and financial aid to overcome difficulties experienced by travelling showmen in wartime, Strabolgi left those at the meeting encouraged and optimistic about the coming season.[63]

Despite the promised support, after the fall of France in June 1940 the Treasury cancelled one of the most lucrative days of the year for many showmen, the August bank holiday.[64] The government felt that the occupation of Britain's closest ally by the enemy and the debacle of Dunkirk was a sobering reminder of the danger the nation faced. A national holiday was considered inappropriate. Despite the disappointment this policy caused, the wartime government recognised the value of leisure and swore not to repeal the 1938 Holidays With Pay legislation.[65] Wakes weeks in the cotton industry continued during the war, and union and voluntary agreements for paid holidays increased between 1939 and 1945.[66] Holidays and hotel accommodation actually expanded during the war years.[67] The Ministry of Transport, together with the railways, planned cheap rail travel for holiday makers during the summer weeks.[68] Local authorities throughout the country also organised 'holiday weeks' to enable war workers and their families to enjoy a break from work.[69] There were some restrictions, such as the ban on public bathing and on use of a fifty-mile stretch of the south coast from Selsey to Brighton.[70] Nevertheless, an agreement between Ernest Bevin, the Minister of Labour, the National Joint Advisory Council, and trades unions, ensured that workers' holidays took place between June and September.[71] In addition to the promise of continued annual paid holidays for those workers who had secured agreements prior to the outbreak of the war, public policy encouraged 'holidays-away-from-home' in order that civilians and military personnel could recuperate from the exigencies of conscripted and voluntary wartime work.[72]

Women workers, hostels, and the problem of pleasure

By March 1941, over a million single women between the ages of 20 and 30 were conscripted for war work. The women took jobs as clerical staff, as members of the Land Army, as military drivers, and in armament factories.[73] The unprecedented National Service Bill, which required single women to undertake war work, passed into the statute book in record time, as those in government recognised the need for increased war production. The Bill did, however, give some people cause for concern regarding the effect of conscription on the morals of young women. In a scathing reply to these 'mid-Victorian' critics, Edith Summerskill, MP wrote, 'There is a certain type of individual who is always ready to suspect the morals of women who indulge in activities outside the home.' A young woman may be level-headed, capable and responsible, Summerskill continued, 'but apparently she loses all her graces immediately' upon leaving the house and 'becomes a sub-human moral defective'.[74] Women, Summerskill claimed, had a right to work outside the home without this kind of nineteenth-century censure from the very politicians who were requesting their services in the workforce.[75]

Concerns about the morality of workers continued, as labour needs required the conscripted women to travel considerable distances to their workplaces. By March 1941, the Ministry of Labour needed accommodation for the 270,000 to 300,000 workers now employed in the newly constructed and camouflaged munitions factories built in remote and isolated areas outside large towns and cities.[76] Local residents provided some of the workers with accommodation in homes, boarding houses, and hotels, but the need exceeded the supply of lodgings available.[77] In addition, transportation to and from the factories posed serious logistical problems for the workers and the Ministry of Labour. In an official report, a Select Committee recommended the provision of hostels sited close to the factories as a solution to the dual problem of housing and transportation. Adequate housing close to the factories would also increase the time available for workers' recreation.[78] Recognising the close connection between leisure and work, the report recommended a policy change to address the needs of workers' recreation and maintain morale. By the middle of 1942 the Ministry of Labour had built sixteen new hostels with accommodation for 11,000 single workers. Over the next two years, the number of hostels rose to sixty-five for a total of 35,500 workers.[79] As the number of hostels and workers grew, the Ministry delegated the management of the hostels to middle-class volunteers but maintained control through the oversight of the National Service Hostels Corporation, set up in May 1941.[80] As the conscripts were mainly young working-class women, used to mass commercial types of entertainment, the remoteness of the factories and the inexperience of the volunteer management created tensions.[81] A few months later the newly appointed Minister of Supply, Lord Beaverbrook, approached Butlin to oversee the hostel accommodation and recreation programme.[82]

Beaverbrook recognised Butlin's interwar efforts to accommodate the leisure needs of working people on a mass scale. In particular, the Minister acknowledged Butlin's ability to cater for the needs of the women who were the focus of the new conscription laws. With these needs in mind, Beaverbrook believed that Butlin was the 'only man in Britain' capable of managing wartime hostels, accommodation, and recreation.[83] The hostels built by the Ministry of Supply were based on a standard design chosen largely for economy and speed of erection. Comprised of single-storey buildings in large blocks, the hostels housed between 500 and 2,000 workers, who shared rooms and slept in bunk beds to maximise the accommodation capacity. Each room contained a wash basin, but workers showered communally.[84] According to Butlin, the hostels were hurriedly built, surrounded by barbed wire, and 'dreary beyond description'. In addition to their uninviting exteriors, Butlin claimed, the walls inside the hostels were painted with a 'depressing dingy brown paint'.[85] Women workers deserted these less-than-welcoming hostels in the thousands. In some areas, such as South Wales, they preferred to travel 30 or 40 miles to work rather than stay at the hostels.[86] They arrived tired for work, and production suffered. Despite this, the hostels remained sparsely populated.[87] Butlin toured the accommodation before accepting the unpaid position as Director of Hostels in December 1941.[88] In his memoirs, Butlin claims that the hostels resembled 'internment camps'. As he explained, one basic problem, apart from the decor, 'was that many of the hostels were run by volunteers who, though anxious to help and meaning well, had little idea of how to organise on a large scale'. The hostels contained no leisure facilities and provided simply a bed and meals for the women in barrack-style simplicity. Far from the familiar faces and diversions of their homes, women workers in the hostels had little to do during their off-duty hours.[89]

A study of women in war factories and hostels by Mass Observation, an independent fact-finding body, revealed some of the problems of boredom. Within the hostels, the observer noted a lack of organised leisure activities, but also a lack of initiative among the women in creating their own amusements. For many of the women, the local cinema represented one of two recreational opportunities. In the report, the observer claimed that an evening at the cinema was the high point of the week. 'There is always a lot of talk about films as the weekend approaches', and, the reporter argued, 'going [to the movies] forms a sort of focal point to an otherwise aimless and drifting weekend'.[90] There were also local dances. However, as the observer noted, although well attended, the dances 'were not very lively affairs'. Women outnumbered men, and the local men who did go tended to hang about in corners and not dance. One of the dance planners told the observer, 'You know, at the end of the evening I feel … [a]s if I'd been pushing heavy weights about for hours'.[91] For this inexperienced volunteer, the work involved in the organisation of leisure time was a heavy burden. The lack of recreation decreased morale and production, but also presented an opportunity for Butlin to use his skills to remedy the situation.

Butlin confronted the challenge with experience and set to the task of remedying the multiple shortcomings of the hostels. Although he had assumed a voluntary position, Butlin asked for a paid staff to help inspect and supervise the work of the hostels.[92] The first suggestion from the group, apart from applying more colourful paint to the walls, was a change of name. The working-class-based name 'Hostel' was changed to a more middle-class-sounding 'Residential Club', with facilities where working women could invite men friends to play pool, watch a movie, play tennis, or dance.[93] Dancing was especially popular in the interwar years and, according to Mass Observers, one of the most popular activities of the war years.[94] For those workers lodged in government hostels, however, the love of dancing was constrained by the absence of music and a lack of male partners. Up to this point, men, even brothers and husbands of the women workers, were strictly kept out of the hostels.[95] Although these divisions replicated others in working-class leisure, Butlin believed a change was necessary. In an effort to facilitate a new hetero-social working culture and to raise awareness that munitions workers contributed greatly to the war effort, Butlin suggested opening the hostels to men. He argued that the working-class munitions workers deserved to be treated in the same way as the middle-class WRNS, WRAF, and ATS,[96] who enjoyed dances and other entertainment alongside servicemen.

The effort to allow servicemen to attend dances at the clubs landed Butlin in unexpected trouble. When African-American servicemen attended the dances, Butlin was accused in Parliament of 'allowing British girls to be seduced' by black American GIs.[97] Butlin blamed the attitude of his critics in Parliament on a generalised racism in 1940s Britain.[98] Yet historian Graham Smith has argued that the British government had specific anxieties about the sexual exploits of British women and African-American soldiers and the effect it might have on the wartime Anglo-American relationship.[99] Nevertheless, the black GIs fascinated many sections of the civilian population, while the open hostility shown them by white Americans caused disgust.[100] Despite the interest shown by some members of the population, African-American GIs 'became racial "others" when it came to sexual relations with British women'.[101] Even the most liberal-minded Briton feared 'race mixing'.[102] To give the appearance of promoting and even encouraging relationships between civilian conscripts and black GIs in government hostels alarmed Parliament. To counter the racialised criticism of the new-style clubs, Butlin's team brought in older, married women to live in the clubs and act as chaperones and confidantes to the younger women workers, who continued to dance with American GIs.[103]

The presence of older women gave the impression of order in the residential clubs. Yet the low recruitment and morale of women in the hostels prompted the Ministry of Information to commission a film to address the 'female problem'.[104] In response, Gainsborough Films made *Millions Like Us* (1943), a film about the nation's need for 'mobile' women to leave home, find accommodation in hostels, and undertake factory work. The protagonist, Celia, is appalled by the idea of factory work but eventually comes to understand that her sacrifice is equal to that of the servicemen battling in the air and on land.[105] It is unclear whether the film's message was read as such by the audience, or whether the film reached its target audience.

The same year, socialite and novelist Amabel Williams-Ellis was sent to investigate the hostels. She expected to find 'something rigid, mechanical, and rather horrible' with 'old spinsters' orchestrating the daily routine.[106] Instead, she found the 'nicest of clubs' that resembled a well-organised, 'one-class cruise'.[107] The chaperones proved friendly and approachable, and although the war forced a certain austerity on the architects, the colours and furnishings were bright and comfortable, and the bedrooms 'beautifully planned'.[108] Most of the hostels Williams-Ellis inspected contained a large assembly hall with a stage, modern stage lighting, and dressing rooms, as well as good film projectors. Many encouraged dances and the provision of 'bus-loads of RAF or soldiers for partners'.[109] Other activities included discussion groups and travel talks, sewing clubs or 'homely, restful activities', much like an earlier culture of working-class girls' clubs.[110] Overall, the author claimed, the hostels were managed by those 'used to having to please or amuse people, but also with a sense of social responsibility'.[111] For this author at least, the hostels appeared to promote an atmosphere that maintained acceptable social standards while providing activities that encouraged interaction between servicemen and women war workers.[112]

Morale in the hostels increased. The residents enjoyed the introduction of dancing, whist drives, amateur theatricals, and variety shows put on by ENSA, CEMA, or the women themselves.[113] The aim of the music and drama provided by the two organisations was, in the words of one member, to lift morale and 'calm the human soul' in the 'supreme turmoil' of war.[114] A report at the end of 1942 praised the effort and care taken to make the hostels 'attractive and home-like', as well as the work undertaken to 'foster a community spirit' among the residents.[115] Butlin's efforts to brighten the walls and atmosphere in the hostels proved partially successful. The report noted, however, that while improvements in furnishings and fittings made the hostels a more pleasant place to live, the atmosphere still depended to a large extent on the personality of those in charge.[116] This was one of the key problems noted by Butlin and his team, but the one that proved the most intractable.

Despite the material changes in the hostels and the leisure facilities available, many young women still preferred the freedom of living at home. Even the financial subsidies introduced by the Ministry to lure women to the hostels failed to fill all the accommodation.[117] As a result of the subsidies, the hostels ran at a weekly loss.[118] Notwithstanding the continued problems, in September 1942 Butlin resigned from his position as Director of Hostels because, he claimed, the hostels were now running smoothly and there was no need for his post.[119] The Ministry accepted his resignation and expressed gratitude for Butlin's hard work in placing the Hostels Organisation on a firm footing.[120] After some negotiation, Butlin agreed to remain as an honorary consultant and Chairman of the Hostels Advisory Panel and a member of the Hostels Council.[121]

Holidays-at-Home and the extension of wartime leisure

Butlin's resignation as Director of Hostels came at the same moment he was offered a potentially lucrative position directing a new government policy – Holidays-at-Home. The new policy replaced the earlier 'holidays away from home' policy as the government faced severe fuel shortages in 1942. The new policy encouraged leisure but limited travel in an effort to prevent unnecessary travel and petrol consumption. The poster campaign that asked, 'Is Your Journey Really Necessary?' failed to persuade Britons to stay at home, as did a decrease in available public transport and petrol.[122] Even the physical restrictions of petrol rationing and the inconvenience of congested and disrupted transport services did not prevent wartime Britons from summer travel. According to the official history of the Ministry of War Transport, the policy of discouraging passenger travel was 'at best, a limited success'.[123] Civilians appeared determined to holiday during the war. Indeed, the Ministry of Labour believed holidays aided production and kept the workforce healthy. In fact, The Ministry of Labour discussed a 'National Holiday Scheme' for insured workers as a way of providing 'wholesome accommodation' for workers and their families in the winter of 1940. Although the scheme did not materialise on a national scale, the Ministry did requisition nine large houses (eight for women and one for men) at seaside resorts or in rural areas to meet the 'special rest needs' of munitions workers.[124] At the beginning of 1944, 300 factories sent over 2,400 women workers to holiday hostels in Colwyn Bay, Weston-super-Mare, and Abergele.[125] Nevertheless, the recognition of the recreational needs of the workforce directed other policy. For the first two years of the war, the government encouraged workers to holiday away from their homes.

Butlin was asked to assist local authorities to organise six weeks of continuous entertainment for civilians and troops in their cities and towns, including circuses, funfairs, theatre performances, concerts, and children's competitions.[126] The underlying motive for providing a variety of leisure activities in the cities and towns was to maintain morale and provide a form of consumption that brought satisfaction without increasing the demand for scarce material goods. Holidays-at-Home created new opportunities for Butlin, who had large amounts of fairground equipment in storage and was able to purchase other travelling fairs inexpensively and make considerable wartime profits.[127] At the same time, the policy change presented a new notion of 'home' as thousands of children and mothers returned from evacuation centres all over the countryside to the towns and cities. The arrival of the evacuees guaranteed an audience, while the dearth of consumer goods and the elevated war wages provided the necessary spending money for leisure activities.[128] Holidays-at-Home policies ensured work and pleasure for millions of Britons and foreign military personnel stationed throughout the British Isles.

Holidays-at-Home encouraged a variety of amusements and activities. Despite the conscription of many musicians, performers, and showmen into the armed forces, programmes included a selection of 'high-brow' entertainment in the form of classical music concerts, operas, and Shakespearean plays, as well as more popular 'low-brow' amusements such as circuses and fun fairs.[129] Liverpool's holidays-at-home programme attracted three-quarters of a million people during the course of eleven weeks and included open-air concerts, children's shows, fun fairs, circuses, plays and opera, band concerts, dances, and organised games in the city parks.[130] In Birmingham, the council proposed forty-eight sites for continuous fairgrounds and entertainment alone during the summer of 1942.[131] Butlin recruited two of his old fairground friends, Billy and Charlie Manning, to help form three travelling fun fairs with forty-four rides between them,[132] and used his fairground equipment during the summer weeks in various towns and cities throughout Britain. He even procured more fairground equipment at discount prices, especially the popular galloping horses and switchback rides left idle by the constraints of war.[133]

Other catering industries felt threatened by Holidays-at-Home. Vocal members of seaside resort associations made a strong case against the new policy on the grounds that 'war workers and others are showing a strong preference for holidays away from their everyday environment'. In a speech to the United Textile Factory Workers' Association Conference, the Mayor of Blackpool, Alderman Percy Round, reiterated his view that 'people [want] holidays at the seaside or at an inland resort'. Workers, the Mayor claimed, 'were entitled to a change of environment, otherwise it was no holiday at all'.[134] Indeed, the ban on travel would severely affect businesses in Blackpool that depended on the thousands of annual urban tourists who travelled considerable distances to the coast for their holiday. For traditional resorts such as Blackpool, Holidays-at-Home threatened an end to wartime profits.

Many Britons continued to travel for pleasure, despite government attempts to limit civilian journeys. Railway companies accommodated the demand and profited from authorised and unauthorised civilian travel. For example, the LMS Railway Company laid on duplicate trains to cope with the tourist traffic between Manchester and Blackpool over the Easter bank holiday in 1943, and described the twelve extra trains to the Ministry of War Transport as part of a 'readjusted service', in order to subvert the official order that limited the number of civilian trains during the holiday season.[135]

Butlin profited greatly from his travelling fun fairs in the summer of 1943. Butlin's Ltd. announced a gross profit of £61,500 for the year to 30 September in 1943, compared to £18,666 the year before. Even the war effort appeared more promising and Butlin was in a more stable financial position to 'buy back' his new holiday camps. Once 'normal activities' recommenced, Butlin believed, his company's profits would exceed pre-war levels because holiday-camp accommodation would double with the new camps.[136]

Butlin continued to seek new business opportunities outside the country. Lord Kenmare, an Irish peer, invited Butlin to assist his plans to transform Killarney in south-west Eire into a popular holiday resort. Lord Kenmare believed that 'Organised villages and camps, built for the purpose, are the order of the day.' The Earl maintained that 'Visitors require and will demand constant entertainment – starting on a special train and continuing to the very end, even to the last moment of their holiday.' Butlin, however, did not see Killarney as suitable for a popular and mass holiday camp. Instead, Butlin persuaded the Earl to build a holiday village that would attract 'the professional classes of England and the United States', and proposed to overcome the problem of the Irish weather by offering every type of indoor amusement in the village, namely 'swimming pool, billiards, squash courts, indoor tennis, dancing, roller-skating, etc'. When asked if he could 'underwrite the arrival of this class of tourist', Butlin assured the Earl that he could and would, as well as guarantee the financial backing for the scheme. Unfortunately, the death of Lord Kenmare in October 1943 brought a temporary halt to these ambitious plans for Killarney, and for Butlin.[137]

Butlin's plans for a postwar camp in North Wales came under attack. The campsite, originally built for wartime use, had been chosen by Butlin for postwar leisure use. In March 1944, Mr James Griffiths, MP for Llanelly, asked the Minister of Health if his department, or indeed the local authorities concerned, had been consulted about the site of Butlin's camp on the Welsh coast. Griffiths pointed out that the original nature of the camp was to be temporary. He understood that another government department had agreed to hand the site to Butlin at the end of the war. Was this move, Griffiths asked, done 'with the consent of ... the Welsh Board of Health, or any of the local authorities?' Apparently neither government department had given consent. However, when the Caernarvonshire County Council met later in the week, it passed a resolution that approved of the proposed holiday camp subject to 'safeguards' deemed reasonable by the Joint Planning Committee.[138]

Opposition to the proposed holiday camp mounted. Two local groups formed to prevent the development of a Butlin's holiday camp on the northern Welsh coast. The first group, the Defence Committee, prepared a petition against the scheme and claimed that opposition mounted daily. Local residents, like themselves, proposed that the campsite should be used as a postwar rehabilitation and recuperative centre controlled by the Society of Friends. The second group, the Action Committee, suggested that the campsite should simply be pulled down at the end of the war. Members of the Action Committee looked for signatories to support this idea among other residents of seaside resorts, towns, and villages in Caernarvonshire.[139] By October of 1944, a third group began a fresh campaign against the holiday-camp proposal. The Lleyn Defence Committee sent a telegram to the Welsh Parliamentary Party to express its members' determination to 'press for the retention of Government ownership and control of the camp, or, failing that, demolition'.[140]

Butlin's postwar plans for Ireland and Wales remained uncertain. Nevertheless, his wartime work expanded when General Montgomery invited his to become honorary advisor to his staff on all aspects of Army Leave Centres in the spring of 1944.[141] Butlin agreed and, after the D-Day landings, scouted Normandy for suitable places to build leave camps for Allied troops.[142] He chose Brussels and requisitioned several restaurants, hotels, and a dance hall, which he renamed the 21–Club after the 21st Army Group. Butlin then approached several Belgian women's organisations to ask for help to find Belgian girls with 'solid family backgrounds who would act as hostesses to troops, perhaps give them a little language tuition, and dance with the boys from time to time'.[143]

Butlin was immediately thwarted by army regulations. British troops were forbidden to fraternise with women who had been 'too friendly' with the Germans. In other words, British servicemen were expected to be able to recognise women who had consorted with the occupying German army in any capacity! Butlin, however, saw the underlying intention of the ban. Under no circumstances should British soldiers have sexual relationships with women who had had sexual contact with their German counterparts. He wrote, 'There was good reason for the ban. Brussels, when I arrived, was absolutely overflowing with prostitutes' who had serviced the German force in order to survive the exigencies of wartime occupation. While fear of sexually transmitted disease drove army policy surrounding 'fraternization' with local women, Butlin simply wanted to create an alternative space where British troops could meet local women socially without having to pay for sexual services.[144]

Local newspapers severely criticised the 21–Clubs. According to Rex North, a war correspondent in Brussels at the time, 'the local press in Brussels, for reasons that completely baffle me, came out with a violent attack on Bill Butlin for exposing local Belgian girls to the possible un-British conduct of the British soldiery'.[145] The front page of one Belgian paper featured a large picture of Butlin with the caption, 'A procurer for the British Army' written in bold print beneath it. To counter the criticism that he was 'pimping' for British servicemen, Butlin called a press conference of British, Belgian, and American representatives and defended the centres and the conduct of the troops. 'I put it to them', Butlin later claimed, 'which was better – that our boys should have decent girls to dance with and talk to, and relax with inside one of the 21–Clubs ... or would you prefer that our troops, after being starved for female company for months, should go and look for it, in the brothels?'[146] Years later, Butlin saw the irony of the accusations. 'What a contrast to earlier in the war', Butlin claimed, 'when I was accused of allowing *British* girls to be led astray by [black] GIs' [my emphasis].[147]

The real issues in Belgium were political and economic. Butlin maintained that collaborators and communists wanted to embarrass the British in any way they could. Designating Butlin 'a procurer' for the British army certainly embarrassed some in the armed forces. Yet the campaign against the 21–Clubs was also fuelled by the commercial interests of the owners of 'sleazy clip-joints who saw the Club taking away their business'. Indeed, one British reporter saw the whole smear campaign as rooted in economics. Approximately 75 per cent of all Allied troops spent their leave in the service clubs. This meant that Belgian nightclub owners lost millions of francs from potential customers. The 21–Clubs offered non-alcoholic drinks and snacks, as well as lager at reasonable prices.[148] A soldier could enjoy a whole evening for roughly a quarter of the price of one drink at a privately run club.[149]

British newspapers also criticised Butlin as he expanded the recreation centres into Antwerp and Liège.[150] The press, aware that Butlin had secured agreements to takeover wartime military camps in Britain after the war, assumed that the entrepreneur had similar claims to the 21–Clubs on the Continent. An article in the *Daily Mail*, written by an early critic of Butlin's holiday camps, Guy Ramsay, explained that Butlin had planned to expand his leisure empire into Europe even before the war. The recreation centres for troops were simply part of the bigger plan.[151] 'In 1939, Billy Butlin – the man who put holiday camps so effectively on the British map that 100,000 people spent their holidays in one or another of his establishments – opened a funfair in Liège', and planned to open an all-inclusive holiday hotel in Ostend for Britons who wanted a cheap holiday abroad. Butlin, Ramsay claimed, was stopped by Hitler, who took over the Butlin hotel as a German post office. In 1944, once the Germans had withdrawn from Belgium, Butlin opened recreation centres in Brussels, Antwerp, and Liège. 'These centres', Ramsay claimed, 'are now facing a raking criticism' as dens of sexual immorality.[152]

The critique of the recreation centres in Belgium reflected contemporary concerns about wartime sexual activity, disease, and citizenship. The incidence of venereal disease in Britain rose dramatically with the arrival of US servicemen, who, according to government discussions, attracted a camp following of 'loose women'.[153] Women who had sexual relationships with foreign soldiers were often seen as prostitutes and considered less-than-ideal citizens.[154] Critics perceived Belgian women in the same way and feared that they would infect British soldiers, using Butlin's 21–Clubs for their 'immoral' assignations.

For Ramsay, however, the real problem was Butlin's naked ambition. Ramsay pointed to a statement Butlin had made in the late summer of 1939. 'If there is no war', Butlin had claimed, 'I shall make money on the holiday camps. If there is a war, the camps can be used for the troops.' This statement, Ramsay argued, revealed Butlin for who he really was – an opportunist. No longer a 'fairground "boy-o" but Big Business', Butlin's advertising 'claimed him a philanthropist' because of the funds raised to buy Spitfires and because of his voluntary position at the Ministry.[155] Ramsay, however, disagreed. He went on to explain that at the outbreak of the war Butlin's camps had been valued at £1 million and requisitioned by the government. Butlin had then been 'co-opted' in 1941 to organise hostels for the Ministry of Supply. 'By the time he had finished the task', Ramsay claimed, 'you could do anything in one of them from have a baby to getting a permanent wave. You could amuse yourself with activities ranging from jitterbug to chess, from fencing to bridge.' If Butlin could transform every hostel or recreation centre into a holiday camp, worried Ramsay, what was to stop him doing just that after the war?[156]

There was some truth to Ramsay's accusation. Part of the problem lay in the report published by the Catering Wages Commission. Set up to create a derequisitioning plan for wartime accommodation, the Commission suggested the conversion of some of the Ministry of Supply hostels into peacetime holiday camps. The report suggested that a combination of Holidays With Pay and the 'travel habit' generated by wartime evacuation and conscription had effectively stimulated a demand for holiday facilities after the war. The conversion of wartime hostels was therefore necessary to avert the potentially 'serious social problem' of inadequate postwar facilities for workers' holidays.[157] The preliminary report to the Minister of Labour, Ernest Bevin, in October 1944 specified some of the adaptations necessary for the transformation of the hostels. In February 1945 the Commission published an official report that reiterated this and recommended that 'wherever practicable those hotels or camps which are regarded as suitable for holiday purposes should be released as quickly as possible' and any necessary work be completed as soon as possible. The report further recommended that the camps deemed suitable for such transformations 'should be offered at a nominal rent to the voluntary organisations at the present managing them to be run on a non-profit making basis'. The remainder of the hostels, the report suggested, should be managed by the National Service Hostel Corporation.[158] Furthermore, the converted hostels would remain in voluntary or public hands and not, as Ramsay had suggested, be exploited by ambitious men like Butlin for financial gain.

In June 1944, Butlin received an official honour for his work as Director of Hostels. He was made a Member of the British Empire (MBE).[159] The honour, reserved for those who gave outstanding service to the British Empire, aroused suspicions that Butlin would manage the proposed state holiday camps.[160] In the last few months of the war, the creation of a 'National Holiday Corporation' seemed likely and Butlin appeared the likely candidate to run the organisation. The pre-war Camps Bill had specified plans to convert all wartime hostels and military camps into postwar leisure centres in order to provide holiday sites for every worker, and support grew in response to the 1942 Beveridge Report, which fuelled the discussion of an all encompassing welfare state.[161] If the postwar vision for Britain included state-funded healthcare, education, housing, childbirth, disability, and unemployment, many wondered, why should the state not involve itself in the provision of state-funded holidays?

Many believed the wartime camps would be converted into state-run holiday centres after the war. Butlin countered the idea that he, or the British government, had plans to transform all the wartime hostels into holiday camps at the end of the war under a 'State Holiday Corporation' idea. In an article in the *Caterer and Hotel Keeper*, he claimed that it was difficult to induce workers to live in the industrial hostels even after heavy subsidies. The limitations of the facilities and their location in industrial areas made the wartime camps unpopular. Those same reasons would prevent their transformation into 'adequate pleasure sites after the war'. British holiday makers wanted quality accommodation and coastal holidays. The hostels had been simply too hurriedly built, and in the wrong places.[162]

Butlin's assessment upset former colleagues in the Ministry of Supply. In a series of angry letters those volunteers charged with the oversight of the hostels indignantly claimed that Butlin had no right to speak with an authority he did not have and make such a public announcement.[163] The Ministry of Supply actually agreed with Butlin's assessment of the unsuitability of the construction and location of the hostels, but tried to placate the volunteers.[164] Despite the attempt to soothe their concerns, the volunteers threatened to abandon their management role unless the Ministry dismissed Butlin as Director of Hostels.[165]

The secretary to the Minister of Supply requested Butlin's resignation in order to prevent a mass walk-out by the volunteers.[166] In a personal note to Butlin accompanying the official letter, the Minister wrote, 'In a certain way I envy you. We shall be for some time engaged in clearing up and in adjusting ourselves to a smaller sphere, whereas the invitation which recently faced me in a bus suggested that you were already reaching out with both hands to touch the new era of peace and enjoyment.'[167] Indeed, in the closing months of the year, Butlin stood poised to re-establish his leisure industry and build an empire of pleasure on a scale that dwarfed his pre-war enterprises.

Planning for postwar leisure

The discussion of the state provision of holidays, or a 'National Holiday Corporation', continued.[168] Throughout the war years various individuals and groups met to discuss ideas for postwar leisure, in anticipation of a full implementation of the 1938 Holidays With Pay Act. The idea that all workers should receive annual paid holidays marked a shift in institutional attitudes to workers' leisure. The experience of the work of war also altered the notion of citizenship and the idea of national leisure took on a new meaning.[169] As the report of the Catering Wages Commission suggested, the provision of sites for workers' leisure was necessary to prevent social unrest.[170] Yet the idea of annual periods of relaxation for all Britons was also inextricably linked to a vision for citizenship in the postwar nation. The calls for state intervention in leisure and tourism did not seem so far fetched, in view of the discussion of an all-encompassing welfare system that would take care of Britons 'from the cradle to the grave'. Institutional support for a variety of 'nationalised leisure services' came from a variety of sources, including the Ministry of Education. The second report of the Youth Advisory Council appointed by the Minister of Education in 1943, for example, suggested that the nation had an urgent need for holiday camps to allow urban children the opportunity to go to the seaside or rural areas with or without their parents for recuperation from the exigencies of life in the towns and cities. A State Holiday Corporation might provide the nation with sufficient amenities to do this.[171]

The Minister of Labour, Ernest Bevin, supported the idea of national holiday centres. In a speech to the House of Commons in 1943, Bevin argued the need to plan for postwar leisure. He claimed, 'Our people have had no holiday, no rest, no recuperation since the war broke out; they have had winters of blackout one after another, and, if I read the people of Britain right, when the whistle blows the first thing they will want will be a holiday.' Bevin promised, 'large sums of money will be spent on organised leisure' to facilitate worker holidays. Yet this postwar 'organised' leisure need not be purely commercial pleasure. In postwar Britain Bevin envisaged workers' leisure as a 'health-giving … social service', with the provision of facilities a national concern.[172]

Bevin's vision for postwar leisure necessitated a relatively well-paid work-force. The Minister knew that, given the choice, women conscripted into the workforce chose well-paid and unionised jobs and avoided the service industries and catering work. While interwar hotels and the leisure industry in general relied heavily on poorly paid part-time and seasonal workers, who were most often women, well-paid alternatives in postwar Britain could cause a potential labour shortage and challenge the idea of national holidays. Thus the Minister proposed to work with the Wages Commission to study several problems, including minimum wages, holidays with pay, and possible unionization for service industry workers, as well as the provision of good-quality and extensive low-cost postwar holiday accommodation for planned pleasure.[173]

By January 1944, with plans for the Normandy invasion in place, the end of the war seemed imminent. The problem of accommodating those who wished to take a holiday immediately after the cessation of hostilities concerned politicians. The Wages Commission met to discuss the problem and assist the government in regard to the idea of building holiday camps, a project which, naturally, did not meet with the approval of the hotel industry.[174] Many hotel-iers saw the idea of a national chain of holiday camps as unfair competition, and Bevin's attempt to raise wages and encourage unionization as a direct attack on the industry. Captain Peter McDonald, MP for the Isle of Wight, claimed that the hotel industry needed tax cuts, not further burdens such as higher wages and potential labour unrest.[175] Others saw the minimum wage as an attempt to 'place a large, important, and honourable industry to some degree upon a footing of order and self-respect' through adequate wages and union representation.[176] For some hoteliers and members of the catering trade, the attempt to regulate wages in the catering industry was viewed as an opportunity to gain government assistance and as a means to distinguish hotels from holiday camps. The Association of Hoteliers and Boarding-house Proprietors urged government action and the creation of a Ministry of Tourism to aid the development of Britain's postwar leisure industry. The association suggested that the government sponsor a large 'Come to Britain' campaign to encourage overseas visitors after the war. As one member of the London City Council put it, the war gave 'Britain the biggest and best advertisement that any country had ever had. Thousands of people would want to come here after the war.'[177] In the view of this council member, the hotel industry needed financial help from the government to provide high-class service and accommodation to attract foreign tourists and foreign currency so as to help stimulate the postwar economy.[178] Wartime hostels transformed into low-cost holiday camps for working Britons would leave hotel accommodation for overseas guests.[179]

Criticism of government wages policy and holiday camps continued. The extension of paid holidays, however, promised to increase the profits from the domestic tourist industry immediately. While mass catering continued to create social tensions, the industry re-imagined workers with cash. The editor of the *Caterer and Hotel Keeper* argued that the increase in the number of holidays-with-pay agreements during the war promised to yield payments of '£200,000,000 a year for holiday expenditure'.[180] Hoteliers, the editor urged, should plan for this leisure boom and be prepared to made 'drastic adjustments' in the provision of amenities, comfort, and space. In other words, hotels should be prepared to provide facilities for overseas and domestic guests that surpassed the luxury, availability, and service of pre-war hotels and holiday camps.[181]

In March 1945, a deputation of the Federation of Permanent Holiday Camps requested the release of some of the requisitioned camps.[182] The war in Europe was not officially over but the Federation predicted the need to accommodate large numbers of summer holiday makers. The Ministry of Supply sympathised with the desire to reopen the camps. The government continued to require the camp accommodation for service personnel, but agreed to review the situation in three months.[183]

Butlin's Filey camp was derequisitioned in June 1945.[184] Only 50 per cent of other holiday-camp accommodation, however, was available for the 1946 season. This was due largely to difficulties in finding sheets and other textiles and because 'some camps suffered badly from occupation by the military'.[185]

Butlin's camps at Clacton, Skegness, and Filey were derequisitioned in 1946 and reopened to the public between March and November that year.[186] Butlin used his wartime position to circumvent rationing and shortages. Rocky Mason, a former manager, remembers the immense concave mirrors that covered the dining hall walls. He later found out that the unique decorations were recycled searchlight reflectors from the wartime occupation. The curtains in the chalets were also ex-military, as were the knives, forks, and crockery used by the postwar campers.[187] In August 1947, Butlin's Ltd. assumed control of the Glendower naval training camp at Pwllheli and converted the property into a holiday camp to accommodate 5,000 to 6,000 guests per week.[188] Just ten years after his first camp opened with accommodation for a thousand guests a week, and less than two years after the end of a six-year war, Butlin's camps stood poised to entertain over half a million visitors each season.

Conclusion

The war expanded the opportunities and forms of entertainment. The government recognised the leisure needs of civilians in what came to be known as the 'people's war'. The recreational possibilities that emerged in the wartime hostels and camps focused the attention of the postwar government on the idea of a collective leisure market for 'the people'. The war intensified efforts to democratise leisure time and transformed the cultural importance of holidays for the postwar world. As Parliament debated the extension of welfare measures in the immediate postwar years, the idea of social citizenship expanded the right to annual paid leisure time.

The war aided social planning and welfare, but it also boosted capitalism. Wartime policies provided an unexpected boon to holiday camps in general, and to Warner's and Butlin's postwar leisure empires in particular. Both men benefited from their association with the Ministry of Supply and utilised wartime structures for commercial gain in peacetime. The mixed economy of the postwar years supported and promoted particular forms of mass leisure. At the beginning of the 1946 season, both Warner and Butlin expanded their commercial concerns to include many sites obtained through wartime negotiations.

The war also shifted ideas about the worker and the consumption of pleasure. The leisure industry re-imagined workers as consumers with cash because of the experience of war and full employment. The war also highlighted the possibilities surrounding leisure and the child consumer, and demonstrated that children were consumers in their own right and not just potential consumers for the future. Perhaps most importantly, the war was also a transformative moment in shaping consumer expectations of leisure and holidays. Indeed, the provision of leisure in wartime altered expectations of the state. The wartime experiences underscored the idea of leisure as a right and paid holidays as an entitlement of citizenship. The provision of postwar leisure was therefore envisioned as an essential part of reconstruction. Where the private sector failed to provide adequate holiday facilities, the state was expected to intervene.

Nevertheless, despite these altered expectations and the idea of the 'people's war', mass catering continued to create social tensions. The next chapter explores the growth of the leisure industry in the years immediately following the Second World War. As a result of the joint wartime enterprise, numerous camps throughout the country were available for postwar leisure activity, although not immediately. While the transition from leisure to war use was apparently seamless, more time and resources were required to transition back to peacetime use, as the following chapter illustrates. Constrained by austerity, entrepreneurs like Warner and Butlin packaged their holiday camps to meet the needs of 'the people' and provide a welcome distraction from the hardships of everyday life in postwar Britain.

Notes

1 Two tourist attractions included the Devil's Punchbowl and Beacon Hill. See D. Rose, *Villages of Surrey: Photographic memories* (Salisbury: Frith, 2004), introduction.

2 Mrs A. S. Heath, quoted in 'Hoteliers ask "Is camp site suitable?"' *Caterer and Hotel Keeper*, 25 August, 1939, p. 9.

3 Ibid.

4 Evacuations began in September 1939. Approximately 1.5 million people left Britain's cities. See M. Cole and R. Padley, *Evacuation survey* (London: George Routledge &Sons, 1940) and J. Welshman, 'Evacuation and social policy during the Second World War: Myth and reality', *Twentieth Century British History*, 9:1 (1998), pp. 28–53.

5 The Camps Bill proposed that non-profit organisations would run the camps in peacetime as school camps and as evacuation centres in wartime. Camps Bill, 20 March 1939, *House of Commons Papers* (London, 1939), p. i.

6 Many local authorities provided annual camps for schoolchildren and discussed expanding the camps to accommodate families. 'Holidays for all', *The Economist*, 4 June 1938, pp. 527–8.

7 For other aspects of social conflict during the Second World War see S. Rose, *Which people's war? National identity and citizenship in wartime Britain, 1939–1945* (Oxford: Oxford University Press, 2005).

8   C. Sladen, 'Holidays at home in the Second World War', *Journal of Contemporary History*, 37:1 (2002), pp. 67–89, and T. Murphy, *A History of the Showman's Guild, 1939–1948. Part II* (London: The Showman's Guild of Great Britain, 1950).

9   The government-sponsored Entertainments National Service Association (ENSA) performed ballet, plays and variety shows for the armed forces in the Second World War. In October 1943, ENSA included circuses in the itinerant shows. See E. Graves, 'Circus for ENSA', *World's Fair*, 17 October 1943, p. 17 and S. Nicholas, *The echo of war: Home front propaganda and the wartime BBC, 1939–45* (Manchester: Manchester University Press, 1996), p. 133.

10 Walton, *British seaside*, ch. 4. By 1949, 25 million Britons received paid annual holidays. '25,000,000 now get holiday – here's how they spend it', *Daily Herald*, 14 April 1949, p. 3.

11 W. Beveridge, *Social insurance and allied services* (London: HMSO, 1942), pp. 41–2. The Beveridge Report was based on a number of interwar social surveys that covered topics of old age, poverty, and declining birth rates. See J. Harris, 'Political thought and the welfare state 1870–1940: An intellectual framework for British social policy', in D. Gladstone, ed. *Before Beveridge: Welfare before the welfare state* (London: IEA Health and Welfare, 1999), pp. 43–63.

12 'Opening of Butlin's luxury holiday camp', *Clacton News*, 18 June 1938, p. 9.

13 Butlin offered to convert the Clacton camp into an air-raid shelter for townspeople in the event of a war. 'Butlin's offer to Clacton hoteliers – campaign for boosting Clacton', *Clacton News and East Essex Advertiser*, 15 January 1938, p. 1.

14 'Holiday camps and A.R.P.', *World's Fair*, 28 May 1938, p. 14.

15 The Town and Country Planning Acts of 1925 and 1932 gave local authorities greater power to plan and control the growth of towns. The Camps Bill negated the earlier acts in the name of national security. Camps Bill, *House of Commons Parliamentary Papers*, 29 March 1939, Vol. 345 (London, 1939), pp. 2073–174.

16 Sir John Anderson, 16 February 1939, *HCPD*, Vol. 343 (London, 1939). See also 'Government camps will not compete with hotels', *Caterer and Hotel Keeper*, 17 February 1939, pp. 2, 14, and 'No reference to holiday centres in Government Camps Bill', *The Caterer and Hotel Keeper*, 24 March 1939, p. 17.

17 Camps Bill, paragraph 3 (1) pp. 33–41.

18 'Hoteliers still anxious about state camps', *Caterer and Hotel Keeper*, 24 February 1939, p. 11.

19 Ibid.

20 This was half the cost of a week at a Warner or Butlin holiday camp. See rates in *Make this year's holiday your best*, p. 10.

21 'More criticism of state camp scheme: Bexhill hoteliers send resolution to M.P.', *Caterer and Hotel Keeper*, 10 March 1939, p. 15.

22 The sites chosen were criticised as too far from town amenities, creating difficulties for construction workers. Mr Kennedy, MP. Questions to the Minister of Labour, *HCPD*, Vol. 344 (London: 1939) 2 March 1939, p. 1434.

23 Mr Elliot, MP. Camps Bill, Second Reading, 29 March 1939, *HCPD*, Vol. 345. (London, 1939), p. 2078.

24 Mr Creech Jones, MP, Camps Bill, Second Reading, 29 March 1939, *HCPD*, Vol.

345 (London, 1939), p. 2120.

25 Ibid., p. 2122. See also 'More doubts about state camps: Mr. Roland Robinson's protest in the House', *Caterer and Hotel Keeper*, 31 March 1939, pp. 15–16.

26 'SOS for Easter workers – Blackpool shortage', *Daily News Chronicle*, 13 April 1938, p. 1.

27 'Holiday questionnaires', Reel 35 46/A Worktown Papers, 1937–1940, Mass Observation Archive, Adam Matthews Publication.

28 A. Davies, 'Leisure in the classic slum, 1900–1939', in A. Davies and S. Fielding, eds *Workers' worlds: Cultures and communities in Manchester and Salford, 1880–1939* (Manchester: Manchester University Press, 1992), pp. 102–32.

29 'Holidays with pay no boon to seaside resorts', *World's Fair*, 27 August 1938, p. 1.

30 Ibid.

31 Mr Robinson, MP. Camps Bill, Second Reading, 29 March 1939, *HCPD*, Vol. 345 (London, 1938), p. 2131.

32 Mr Roland Robinson, quoted in, 'More doubts about state camps', *Caterer and Hotel Keeper*, 31March 1939, pp. 15–16.

33 By 1941, thirty camps were available for use as evacuation schools. H. C. Dent, *Education in transition: A sociological study of the impact of war on English education, 1939–1943* (London: Kegan Paul, Trench, Trubner & Co. Ltd., 1944), pp. 95–6.

34 For a discussion of middle-class cultural ideals of landscape see A. Potts, 'Constable country between the wars', in R. Samuel, ed. *Patriotism: The making and unmaking of British national identity*, Vol. III (London: Routledge, 1989), pp. 160–86.

35 'Hoteliers ask "is camp site suitable?" Objections to be sent to the Ministry of Health', *Caterer and Hotel Keeper*, 25 August, 1939, p. 9.

36 S. Koven, *Slumming: Sexual and social politics in Victorian London* (Princeton: Princeton University Press, 2004), introduction.

37 'Hoteliers ask "Is camp site suitable?" Objections to be sent to the Ministry of Health', *Caterer and Hotel Keeper*, 25 August, 1939, p. 9.

38 'More doubts about state camps: Mr. Roland Robinson's protest in the House', *Caterer and Hotel Keeper*, 31 March 1939, pp. 15–16.

39 Soldiers were also billeted in private homes, boarding houses and hotels. Accommodation needs were exacerbated by bombing and by billeting of foreign soldiers. See D. Reynolds, *Rich relations: The American occupation of Britain, 1942–1945* (London: Harper Collins, 1999), pp. 149–51.

40 Olive Houghton, interview with author, 14 September, 2001.

41 Butlin with Dacre, *Butlin story*, p. 130.

42 Building costs for service establishments were approximately £250 per person. Butlin built the Filey camp at a cost of £175 per occupant. Butlin with Dacre, *Butlin story*, p. 130.

43 Butlin with Dacre, *Butlin story*, pp. 130–1.

44 'Butlin's report', *World's Fair*, 21 December 1940, p. 23.

45 'Butlin's park at Felixstowe', *World's Fair*, 6 April 1940, p. 7. 'Lord Haw-Haw' was the nickname given to William Joyce, a member of the British Union of Fascists, who began broadcasting on Radio Hamburg on 11 September 1939. Nicholas, *Echo of war*, p. 45.

46 'War's effect on Skegness – Butlin's staff on government work', *World's Fair*, 20 August 1940, p. 7.

47 The Home Guard was commissioned to defend Britain in the event of an invasion. A. Marwick, *The home front: The British and the Second World War* (London: Thames and Hudson, 1976), p. 39.

48 The Ministry of Supply was created in April 1939 with powers to buy or manufacture, store, and transport, any article required for the public service. J. D. Scott and R. Hughes, *The administration of war production* (London: HMSO, 1955), pp. 68–78.

49 P. Inman, *Labour in the munitions industries* (London: HMSO, 1957), pp. 242–4.

50 'W. E. Butlin builds new type of industrial village', *World's Fair*, 20 April 1940, p. 7.

51 A directive from the Prime Minister in November 1941 cancelled any further accommodation for married workers. The Admiralty secured permission to build two estates, each with 200 dwellings for married workers. Inman, *Labour in munitions industries*, pp. 244–5.

52 Ibid., p. 244.

53 Butlin with Dacre, *Butlin story*, p. 134.

54 'Ample room for visitors at holiday resorts', *World's Fair*, 24 February 1940, p. 7.

55 'Blackpool Tower Circus carries on: war or no war, the show must go on', *World's Fair*, 21 October 1939, p. 23.

56 T. G. Hearney, 'Blackpool in war-time – amusements in full swing', *World's Fair*, 17 August 1940, p. 7.

57 The 'phony war' lasted from September 1939 to April 1940. Aerial bombing of British towns and cities began in September 1940. Smith, *Britain and 1940*, pp. 70–90.

58 H. M. D. Parker, *Manpower: A study of war-time policy and administration* (London: HMSO, 1957), pp. 445–7.

59 *Ministry of Labour and National Service Report, 1939–1946* (London: HMSO, 1947), pp. 119–20. See also F. M. Leventhal, 'The best for the most: CEMA and state sponsorship of the arts in wartime', *Twentieth Century British History*, 1:3 (1990), pp. 289–317.

60 Parker, *Manpower*, p. 409.

61 Ibid., p. 446. The paid Whitsuntide holiday began in 1941. Bullock, *Life and times of Ernest Bevin*, pp. 78–81.

62 The ranks of showmen were depleted by conscription, voluntary service, and internment as enemy aliens. 'Police at Mills circus – Italian clowns detained', *World's Fair*, 22 June 1940, p. 17.

63 'Travelling Showmen's difficulties in wartime: renewed assurance of support from MPs', *World's Fair*, 27 January 1940, pp. 8–9.

64 'No August Bank Holiday', *World's Fair*, 6 July 1940, p. 1.

65 Workers covered by the Holidays With Pay Act had until March 1941 to take their holidays. 'Holiday with pay announcement', *World's Fair*, 21 June 1940, p. 12.

66 'Cotton holidays to be resumed', *World's Fair* 20 July 1940, p. 4 and Walton, *British seaside*, p. 62.

67 'New hotel opened at Buxton', *Caterer and Hotel Keeper*, 4 October 1940, p. 3.

68 'Cheap trains for holiday-makers: Sir Walter Womersley on 1940 prospects', *World's Fair*, 27 January 1940, p. 7.

69 'Canteens to provide meals for holiday makers', *Caterer and Hotel Keeper*, 10 July 1940, p. 18.

70 'Beach ban at south coast resorts', *World's Fair*, 13 July 1940, p. 7.

71 'Holidays as usual', *World's Fair*, 9 March 1940, p. 29.

72 *Ministry of Labour Report, 1939–1946* (London: HMSO, 1947), p. 120. 'Holidays in wartime', *World's Fair*, 23 March 1940, p. 29.

73 The National Service Number 2 Act was passed in December 1941 and conscripted all single women aged 20–21. A year later the Order was extended to include all women up to age 40. P. Summerfield, *Women workers in the Second World War: Production and patriarchy in conflict* (London: Routledge, 1989), pp. 35–36 and T. Benson, *Sweethearts and wives: Their part in the war* (London: Faber and Faber, 1942).

74 E. Summerskill, 'Conscription and women', *The Fortnightly*, March 1942, pp. 209–14.

75 See S. O. Rose, 'Sex, citizenship and the nation in World War II Britain', *American Historical Review*, 103:4 (1998), pp. 1147–76.

76 'Management of National Service Worker's Hostels', Statement from the Ministry of Labour, 26 March 1941, TNA: PRO, T161/1192 Box 3.

77 Evacuees were willing to pay more for accommodation than were factory workers. Parker, *Manpower*, pp. 397–9.

78 *Seventeenth report from the Select Committee on National Expenditure, 1940–1941* (London: HMSO, 1941), pp. 2–3.

79 Inman, *Labour in munitions industries*, p. 246.

80 Letter to E. Hale, Treasury Department, from Mr Todd, Ministry of Labour, TNA: PRO, T161/1192 Box 3.

81 For a larger discussion of conscripted women and government accommodation see S. Dawson, 'Busy and bored: The politics of work and leisure for women workers in WWII British government hostels', *Twentieth Century British History*, 21:1 (2010), 29–49.

82 Letter to E. Hale from Mr Todd, 11 September 1941, TNA: PRO, T161/1192, box 3. The Hostel Board retained control of finances. The National Service Hostels were incorporated in 1941. Articles of Association, National Service Hostels, 23 May 1941, 3, TNA: PRO, T161/1192, box 3.

83 Butlin with Dacre, *Butlin story*, p. 132.

84 C. M. Kohan, *Works and buildings* (London: HMSO, 1952), pp. 372–4.

85 Butlin with Dacre, *Butlin story*, p. 136.

86 Dawson, 'Busy and bored'.

87 Minutes Number S.48141 TNA: PRO, T161/1192, box 3.

88 Ministry of Supply Memo No. 350, 6 December 1941, TNA: PRO, SUPP 20/2.

89 Butlin with Dacre, *Butlin story*, p. 136.

90 *War factory: A report by Mass-Observation* (London: Victor Gollancz, 1943), p. 81. Mass-Observation (MO) was established by Tom Harrisson, Charles Madge and Humphrey Jennings in 1937 to collect information about everyday life. Teams of observers and voluntary informants documented social change, political trends and public and private opinion. During the Second World War, MO prepared some reports for the Ministry of Information.

91 Ibid., p. 82.

92 Butlin's assistant director was Captain J. Pickering, an accountant with Butlin's enterprises. W. Hayden to W. E. Butlin, 19 December 1941, TNA: PRO, SUPP 20/2.

93 Colour schemes, furnishings and leisure facilities in the hostels changed in 1942 because of concern for the comfort and contentment of the workers. Bunk beds were replaced by single beds and laundry and hairdressing facilities were added, as were sick bays. Kohan, *Works and buildings*, p. 373.

94 *War begins at home*, T. Harrisson and C. Madge, eds (London: Chatto & Windus, 1940), pp. 222–5.

95 Some hostels allowed invited guests to come for tea or supper for an additional fee. *War factory*, pp. 105–12.

96 Women's Royal Naval Service, Women's Royal Air Force, and Auxiliary Territorial Service.

97 Butlin with Dacre, *Butlin story*, 137, G. Smith, *When Jim Crow met John Bull: Black American soldiers in World War II Britain* (London: I. B. Tauris, 1987), pp. 37–96, and Reynolds, *Rich relations*, pp. 164–82. By D-Day, in August 1944, there were 130,000 black GIs in Britain, at a time when the total black community in Britain was 8,000. P. Clarke, *Hope and glory: Britain 1900–1990* (London: Allen Lane, 1996), p. 205.

98 J. L. Keith of the Colonial Office claimed that racial prejudice was widespread in Britain in 1940 as incidents of discrimination against people of colour increased. H. Adi, *West Indians in Britain, 1900–1960: Nationalism, pan-Africanism and communism* (London: Lawrence & Wishart, 1998), ch. 4.

99 Smith, *Jim Crow*, pp. 37–9.

100 Ibid., pp. 120–7.

101 S. Rose, 'The "sex question" in Anglo-American relations in the Second World War', *International History Review*, 20 (December 1998), pp. 884–903.

102 Smith, *Jim Crow*, p. 94.

103 The Ministry of Labour set up separate hostels for West Indian and South Asian workers. A. Spry Rush, 'Imperial identity in colonial minds: Harold Moody and the League of Coloured Peoples, 1931–50', *Twentieth Century British History*, 13:4 (2002), pp. 356–83.

104 S. Harper, 'The years of total war: Propaganda and entertainment', in C. Gledhill and G. Swanson, eds *Nationalising femininity: Culture, sexuality and British cinema in the Second World War* (Manchester: Manchester University Press, 1996), p. 202.

105 *Millions Like Us*, 1943, 98 mins. dir. F. Lauder and S. Gilliat, Gainsborough Films.

106 A. Williams-Ellis, *Women in war factories* (London: Victor Gollancz, 1943), p. 72.

107 Ibid., p. 73.

108 Ibid., p. 76.

109 Ibid., p. 77.

110 D. Fowler, *The first teenagers: The lifestyle of young wage earners in interwar Britain* (London: Woburn Press, 1995).

111 Williams-Ellis, *Women in war factories*, p. 78.

112 Ibid.

113 Ibid., p. 77. See *War factory*, p. 77 for worker responses to ENSA concerts.

114 E. Kisch, 'Music in wartime', *Our Time*, July 1943, p. 6.
115 *Health and Welfare of women in war factories, third Report from the Select Committee on National Expenditure, 1942–1943* (London: HMSO, 1942), p. 18.
116 Ibid.
117 Parker, *Manpower*, p. 402.
118 Memo S.48141/2 12 June 1944, TNA: PRO, T161/1192 Box 3. The weekly loss amounted to 7s per resident.
119 Letter from W. E. Butlin to Sir Andrew Duncan, 30 September 1942, TNA: PRO, SUPP 20/2.
120 Letter from A. R. Duncan to W. E. Butlin, 6 October 1942, TNA: PRO, SUPP 20/2.
121 Ministry of Supply Memorandum no. 532 from W. S. Douglas, October 1942, TNA: PRO, SUPP 20/2.
122 Railway Executive Committee slogan quoted in Sladen, 'Holidays at home', p. 68. See I. McLaine, *Ministry of morale: Home front morale and the Ministry of Information in World War II* (London: George Allen & Unwin, 1979), p. 254.
123 C. I. Savage, *Inland transport* (London: HMSO, 1957), pp. 518–19.
124 *Ministry of Labour Report, 1939–1946* (London: HMSO, 1947), p. 120.
125 Parker, *Manpower*, p. 410.
126 'Holidays at home scheme – drawing power of showland attractions', *World's Fair*, 7 March 1942, p. 1.
127 Murphy, *Showman's Guild*, pp. 34–5.
128 Young working women earned higher wartime wages but were expected to increase their contributions to the family income. Todd, *Young women, work and family*, p. 83.
129 CEMA provided much of the classical and 'high brow' entertainment. Leventhal, 'The best for the most', pp. 289–317.
130 'Liverpool holidays at home success', *World's Fair*, 28 October 1944, p. 1.
131 'Holidays at home – big plans at Birmingham', *World's Fair*, 6 June 1942, p. 1.
132 Butlin and Dacre, *Butlin story*, pp. 138–9.
133 Butlin bought gallopers and switchbacks for a fraction of their pre-war value. Butlin with Dacre, *Butlin story*, p. 140.
134 'Holidays away from home – workers entitled to a change', *World's Fair*, 8 May 1943, p. 1.
135 'Holiday trains', *World's Fair*, 8 May 1943, p. 1. The Parliamentary Secretary to the Ministry of War Transport claimed to know about the unscheduled trains. The rules governing civilian transport meant that the LMS technically did not break the law because, in order to meet the demand for holiday traffic between Manchester and Blackpool, other local trains did not run, thus the total number of trains used did not exceed the usual number.
136 'Butlin's make £61,500 Profit', *World's Fair*, 4 March 1944, p. 1.
137 'Holiday village in Killarney: W. E. Butlin's Ideas', *World's Fair*, 9 October 1943, p. 1.
138 'Butlin's camp on Welsh coast – questions in the Commons', *World's Fair*, 4 March 1944, p. 1.

139 'Petition against holiday camp', *World's Fair*, 6 May 1944, p. 1.

140 'Fresh campaign against holiday camp', *World's Fair*, 28 October 1944, p. 1.

141 'Mr. Butlin's new job', *World's Fair*, 28 October 1944, p. 1.

142 North, *Butlin story*, p. 83.

143 Ibid., p. 85.

144 Butlin and Dacre, *Butlin story*, pp. 144–51.

145 North, *Butlin story*, p. 85.

146 Butlin and Dacre, *Butlin story*, p. 145.

147 Ibid., p. 147.

148 The only alcoholic beverage offered in the *21–Clubs* was lager. Sir J. Grigg, MP, *HCPD*, 24 October 1944 (London, 1944), p. 40.

149 Butlin and Dacre, *Butlin story*, p. 148.

150 Butlin opened eight 21–Clubs in Belgium, Holland and Germany. Butlin with Dacre, *Butlin story*, p. 148.

151 See G. Ramsay, 'Man in the news – battling Butlin', *Daily Mail*, 6 February 1945, p. 6. Although the article was critical of Butlin, some at the Ministry of Supply thought Butlin's publicity machine may have co-written the article. See Memo to the Ministry of Supply from Miss Powers dated June 1945, TNA: PRO SUPP, 20/2.

152 Ramsay, 'Man in the news', p. 6.

153 Smith, *Jim Crow*, 194–5 and J. Virden, *Good-bye Piccadilly: British war brides in America* (Chicago: University of Illinois Press, 1996), pp. 25, 33.

154 Rose, *Which people's war?* pp. 71–106.

155 Ramsay referred to the publicity surrounding Butlin's Spitfire Fund. Butlin advertised the amount he and his employees raised for the fund. 'Butlin's staff Spitfire Fund: first £2,500 paid to Lord Beaverbrook', *World's Fair*, 12 April 1941, p. 1, and 'Butlin's Spitfire Fund now £4,175', *World's Fair*, 8 November 1941, p. 1. Lord Beaverbrook was Minister of Supply from 1941 and offered Butlin his wartime job.

156 Ramsay, 'Man in the news', p. 6.

157 *Catering Wages Commission, First Annual Report, 1943–1944*, 26 September 1944 (London: HMSO, 1944), p. 8.

158 'Commission's recommendations for assisting hotels', *Caterer and Hotel Keeper*, 23 February 1945, p. 10.

159 'Personalities: W. E. Butlin receives MBE on King's Birthday Honours list', *Caterer and Hotel Keeper*, 16 June 1944, p. 16.

160 '"Billy" Butlin awarded M.B.E.', *World's Fair*, 17 June 1944, p. 1.

161 Lloyd, *Empire, welfare state*, pp. 256–69 and R. Lowe, 'The Second World War, consensus, and the foundation of the Welfare State', *Twentieth Century British History*, 1:2 (1990), pp. 152–92.

162 Butlin quoted in 'No evidence for state holiday corporation idea', *Caterer and Hotel Keeper*, 23 March 1945, p. 1.

163 Letter from E. W. Wimble, Secretary and General Manager of the Workers Travel Association Ltd. to Miss Power, Ministry of Supply, 29 March 1945, TNA: PRO, SUPP 20/2.

164 Letter from Miss Power to E. W. Wimble, 7 May 1945, TNA: PRO, SUPP 20/2.

165 Letter from E. W. Wimble to Miss Power, 14 May 1945, TNA: PRO, SUPP 20/2.

166 Letter from D. C. V. Perrott to W. E. Butlin, 15 June 1945, TNA: PRO, SUPP 20/2.

167 Letter from A. F. Dobbie-Bateman to W. E. Butlin, 15 June 1945, TNA: PRO, SUPP 20/2.

168 'National Holiday Corporation: recommendations made in group report', *Caterer and Hotel Keeper*, 10 August 1945, p. 12.

169 The government feared social unrest after the Second World War because of the experience of such unrest after the First World War. Lloyd, *Empire, welfare state*, pp. 98–103. For a discussion of citizenship and the Second World War, see Rose, *Which people's war?* and D. Morgan and M. Evans, *The battle for Britain: Citizenship and ideology in the Second World War* (London: Routledge, 1994).

170 See 'Workers' holidays', *Catering Wages Commission, First Annual Report, 1943–44* (London: HMSO, 1944), p. 8.

171 'Catering for youth in community centres', *Caterer and Hotel Keeper*, 20 July 1945, p. 23.

172 Mr Bevin, MP, quoted in 'Mr. Bevin on postwar holidays', *Caterer and Hotel Keeper*, 12 February 1943, p. 12.

173 Ibid. Bevin argued that workers in the catering industries should receive adequate wages and the right to unionise.

174 'Postwar holidays problem for hotels – Wages Commission considering subject', *Caterer and Hotel Keeper*, 28 January 1944, p. 9.

175 Captain P. McDonald, MP, quoted in 'Mr. Bevin on postwar holidays', *Caterer and Hotel Keeper*, 12 February 1943, p. 16.

176 'More comprehensive bill needed', *Caterer and Hotel Keeper*, 12 February 1943, p. 16.

177 Mr A. Emil Davies quoted in 'Postwar Britain needs first class hotels: Plan to make this country a Mecca for tourists', *Caterer and Hotel Keeper*, 11 December 1942, p. 12.

178 'Postwar Britain needs first class hotels', pp. 11–12.

179 'Postwar plans of Travel Association: Government considers national publicity abroad', *Caterer and Hotel Keeper*, 20 November 1942, pp. 9–10.

180 Editorial opinion, 'Holidays with pay', *Caterer and Hotel Keeper*, 19 May 1944, p. 4.

181 See 'Postwar boom for country hotels and inns', *Caterer and Hotel Keeper*, 15 December 1944, p. 10.

182 The deputation was headed by Mr W. J. Brown, MP, General Secretary of the Civil Service Union.

183 'Holiday camps want release', *Caterer and Hotel Keeper*, 16 March 1945, p. 10.

184 'Butlin's camp at Filey', *World's Fair*, 2 June 1945, p. 1.

185 '50 percent holiday camps this year', *Caterer and Hotel Keeper*, 19 April 1946, p. 12.

186 'Butlin's holiday camps', *Caterer and Hotel Keeper*, 15 February 1946, p. 13.

187 R. Mason in *Secret lives*.

188 'A Welsh holiday camp', *World's Fair*, 31 August 1946, p. 1.

5

The 'people's peace': postwar pleasure and austerity

In July 1945, after campaigning on a platform of socialism and consumer constraint, Labour took office in a landslide victory.[1] The new government, led by Clement Atlee, continued rationing and committed Britain to an extended period of austerity that especially had an impact on the service industries.[2] Although politically the physical and psychic postwar reconstruction of the nation emphasised the importance of workers' leisure, austerity curtailed the expansion of the domestic tourism industry in an unprecedented way.[3] Policies intended to 'level the playing field' for all Britons affected individuals and industries unevenly. Building materials, able-bodied workers, and a steady cash flow to fund wages and repairs were in short supply. Thus, even as the postwar Labour government sought to expand worker leisure, rationing and a commitment to austerity constrained the leisure industry, complicating efforts to plan pleasure for millions of newly leisured workers and their families.

At the same time, however, the postwar politics of want and austerity also enhanced the appeal of mass leisure facilities like Warner's and Butlin's holiday camps.[4] Labour, despite – and indeed because of – austerity and the perceived ethos of equality, gave special help to holiday camps, but not to other forms of domestic tourism. Because holiday camps were 'for the masses', the government underwrote efforts to expand existing camps and build new ones. Postwar policies enabled entrepreneurs like Warner and Butlin to transform the infrastructure of wartime production – industrial villages and hostels – into an integral part of the welfare state. Just as the Holidays With Pay legislation had given political legitimacy to the interwar holiday-camp industry, so did the ideology of the postwar Labour government. By lending support to the holiday-camp industry, the government implicitly endorsed Butlin and Warner's efforts to make their holiday camps emblematic of British national culture.

This chapter reveals the ways in which the holiday-camp industry shaped and was shaped by the politics of the postwar government. As the nation renewed its commitment to the right of the worker and the workers' family to leisure time, the Labour government led efforts to ensure equal access to the welfare state, including national healthcare, unemployment pensions, and, as this chapter demonstrates, leisure. At the same time, the BBC and other entities worked to create the foundation of a national cultural heritage that cut across lines of class and region. In the midst of these two trends – towards socialism and a national culture – the holiday camps re-emerged as sites of truly democratic leisure. In addition, entrepreneurs such as Warner and Butlin catered for the increasingly affluent working class and transformed unassuming places like Hayling Island into fashionable resorts, making leisure an important element of the postwar economic recovery.

Rationed pleasure and establishing normalcy

When the Allied forces successfully landed in Normandy on 6 June 1944, the outcome of the war in Europe was no longer in doubt. Many in Britain believed the war would soon end.[5] As politicians planned the 'people's peace', holidays featured prominently in national debates. By October 1944, hoteliers, holiday-camp entrepreneurs and boarding-house proprietors were requesting the release of their property from government use. They argued that the prospect of a summer holiday would increase morale and encourage a sense of normalcy. Sir Reginald Clarry, Conservative MP for Newport, agreed. In Parliament he called for the immediate derequisitioning of holiday camps and similar accommodation so that civilians and demobilised service personnel could enjoy holidays 'long deferred' by six years of war.[6]

The daily press joined in and stressed the need for holidays in 1945 for the health and welfare of the nation. Newspapers estimated that eighteen million workers received paid holidays, compared to four million before the war, and claimed that holiday camps could provide mass accommodation and inexpensive holidays for millions of workers if derequisitioned immediately. Under pressure from the industry and the popular press, the government promised to release the camps as soon as possible.[7]

By March 1945 the government still had not released the camps. In response to the inaction, the NFPHC went to the press and claimed that although the government knew that the 'requisitioned camps … could accommodate 250,000 campers per week', the delayed requisitioning meant that the 'huge army of holidaymakers' who could only afford a cheap holiday were prevented from enjoying one.[8] Federation members claimed that huge numbers of applications came daily from the welfare officers of large war factories, requesting accommodation for the up-coming Easter holiday.[9] The situation, predicted the NFPHC, would only worsen as summer approached and could potentially stimulate worker unrest.[10]

Although the war was not officially over, camp owners did not see the immediate derequisitioning of their property as an unreasonable demand.[11] Indeed, the majority of the requisitioned camps appeared to be underused and contained few occupants. One of Warner's camps on the Isle of Wight, for example, housed only two fire-fighters. Camp owners described the release of their facilities as a 'national necessity' and argued that they could provide holidays for at least 5,000,000 workers during the 1945 season.[12] Despite this pressure, the majority of the former holiday camps remained in government hands throughout 1945.[13]

At the end of January 1946, the government finally derequisitioned fifty holiday camps and planned to release a further seventy later in the year.[14] The owners were pleased, but the industry still faced several major obstacles, including shortages of labour and materials for repair, as well as of basic foodstuffs, bedding, and furniture.[15] Without a co-ordinated effort to provide reparations to owners and speed the work of restoration, many camps would still not be ready to open in time for the summer season. The government, owners insisted, should treat immediate assistance to holiday camps as a matter of national importance.[16]

The newly elected Labour government, though, had other pressing concerns. Following the 1945 election landslide, Britons faced stricter rationing than during the war. Queues for basic commodities like dried eggs, meat, fabric, and fuel, continued as key industries such as farming, textiles, and coal remained under tight government control. As the government contemplated bread rationing in 1946, discontent increased.[17] Although the Conservative opposition used this to its political benefit, it did not oppose Labour's radical nationalisation programme. Nevertheless, as key industries such as coal and gas were nationalised, the government assumed responsibility for losses as well as profits, greatly adding to the financial burdens of the state.[18]

In March 1946, Sir Stafford Cripps, President of the Board of Trade, announced plans to help hotels and holiday camps prepare for the coming season.[19] Holiday accommodation was important, Cripps agreed, and establishments damaged by enemy action would be equipped first, followed by requisitioned facilities. Cripps promised to release supplies of unrationed metal, plastic, and other non-wooden furniture, as well as sheets, blankets, and mattresses. Many other supplies, such as carpets, crockery, and glassware, although scarce, were unrationed and therefore available for purchase. Other goods, such as linoleum and curtain materials, remained virtually unobtainable.[20]

Despite government efforts to provide for tourists and holiday makers, rationing severely hampered the leisure industry.[21] Just as the policies intended to 'level the playing field' for all Britons affected women more directly and on a daily basis in their roles as housewives, they also impacted unevenly on private industry.[22] Unlike other industries, rationing and shortages obstructed every aspect of service in hotels and boarding houses. The gendered dimensions of services provided by hotels and boarding houses – meal preparation and grocery shopping, as well as the provision of linens, laundry, and cleaning services – were those usually associated with household management and housewives. The hotel and catering trade grappled daily, even hourly, with the regulations governing the acquisition and consumption of essentials such as sheets, tea, and laundry detergent. As a result, many individuals resorted to obtaining consumer goods on the black market.[23]

When the Association of Health and Pleasure Resorts met in London in mid-January 1946, the constraints of austerity featured largely in the discussions. The scarcity of linen was particularly problematic. 'Single sheets on double beds ... [did] ... not add to the comfort and good temper of visitors', one hotelier claimed, and guests also 'disliked having to bring their own towels'.[24] Tourism could bring in £100,000,000 a year to Britain, hoteliers claimed, but not without an adequate supply of basic linen.[25] A few months later the situation worsened as linens and other necessary supplies became extremely hard to come by, legally or illegally.[26]

The government appeared not to acknowledge the value of domestic tourism to the economy. Adequately equipped, the industry had the potential bring much-needed sterling into the coffers of the Exchequer. Nevertheless, the financially constrained government offered inadequate reparations to the formerly commandeered facilities.[27] The paucity of supplies and the meagre reparations affected boarding houses and small hotels particularly badly.[28] Unlike the holiday camps, whose proprietors received considerable compensation for the wartime use of their facilities, boarding houses used to billet troops and other service workers received a maximum of £10 each for repairs.

In May 1946, the British Federation of Hotel and Apartment Associations (BFHAA) met to discuss its common problems. Highly critical of the compensation offered to the industry, Mr R. O. Whiteman expressed his frustration. Hotel and boarding-house keepers, he asserted, gave 'seven years of valuable national service' during the war. Now they were forced to endure 'injustice' from the government as they attempted to reconstruct their businesses without adequate reparations or supplies, while holiday camps received 'every assistance to put their house in order'. The government gave preferential treatment to holiday camps, Whiteman asserted, giving them a commercial edge. This, an exasperated Whiteman exclaimed, had gone on 'far too long'. It was time, he told members, to take 'a firm stand, and in future expect to be treated with justice and in a manner commensurate with the valuable service … rendered to the country'. BFHAA members agreed and formed an ad hoc deputation to express their frustration to Parliament and demand priority dockets for the purchase of linen, furnishings, and equipment.[29]

Whiteman's claim was accurate: the postwar Labour government did privilege holiday camps. There were several reasons for this. For a government determined to create a vision of social equality in which all citizens had the right to enjoy leisure, holiday camps provided large numbers of people of all ages with cheap accommodation. Military camps were easily converted to civilian usage because holiday camps were more flexible than hotels and guest houses. Camp accommodation, while comfortable, was basic and did not require large amounts of luxury items. Chalets contained beds and a dresser for clothes. Communal bathrooms, and dining rooms furnished with benches and long tables simplified meal times. Additionally, unfinished sections of the camps could simply be cordoned off without affecting the majority of guests. Thus the financial constraints of the postwar Labour government served to promote holiday camps as suitable sites of mass pleasure.

What was perhaps more important than the ease of transition from military to civilian use was the larger social ethos of the camps. Class distinctions seemed to disappear amid the uniformity of accommodations and services offered. This resonated strongly with the agenda of the postwar Labour government, which was eager to rebuild Britain as an egalitarian society.[30] The 1945 landslide victory assured the government of a mandate from the British electorate for its social agenda. Crucial to the programme for social change was the construction of a national memory of the common experience of war. Reconstruction meant more than simply replacing the infrastructure of the nation; it was also forging a new, mythologised national identity in order to withstand the tumultuous changes in the postwar world order. Holiday camps, with their communal canteens, bathrooms, and jovial entertainment, were a constant re-enactment of the already mythical war years, when everyone 'pulled together'.[31] Their transformation from wartime billets to postwar pleasure accommodation literally made holiday camps into sites at which the national wartime struggle for freedom and democracy was transformed into the promise of the postwar welfare state: the equal provision of food, accommodation, childcare, amusements, and (perhaps more importantly for some enduring cramped and crowded postwar accommodation) a degree of privacy. The collective identity forged in the war years – real or imagined – was to be replicated in the culture of the postwar holiday camps. Thus, the experience of war helped to redefine holiday camps as a particularly British institution and holiday-camp culture as emblematic of British national identity. The 1930s critique of holiday camps as sites of uniform mass leisure that subsumed individualism was rendered toothless by postwar policies and a governing ethos that encouraged an idea of 'the people' and a homogenous society.[32]

Indeed, Butlin played on feelings of wartime cohesion to draw people to his camps. Immediately after the war he invited Britain's new breed of entertainers to the camps. 'They were the stars of radio, the artists who had kept up our morale in the dark days of the war,' Butlin claimed.[33] Household names with familiar voices, the radio stars united camp culture with the larger community and the national memory. As historian Sîan Nicholas notes, '[T]he unifying appeal of wartime comedy' received 'much publicity both during and after the war', and Butlin used this to his advantage.[34] He advertised the celebrity concerts each Sunday with the slogan, 'Artistes you have heard but seldom seen'.[35] Irene Chambers remembers the audience rocking with laughter at the antics of Arthur Askey and Frankie Howerd, as well as the hypnotist who hypnotised campers to do comic turns, during her first visit to Clacton in 1951.[36]

Other regular performers included Tommy Handley and the cast of the popular wartime radio comedy show *It's That Man Again*. Catch phrases from the show, such as 'I don't mind if I do', uttered by the alcoholic Colonel Chinstrap (played by Jack Train), became part of the 'nation's language', claimed Butlin in his memoirs. 'Not to mention "Can I do you now, sir?" and "It's being so cheerful that keeps me going" … Or the polite pair who were always saying: "After you, Cecil," "No, after you, Claude."'[37] Other artistes included Richard Murdoch and Kenneth Horne with the cast of *Much Binding in the Marsh*, another popular radio show set in a mythical and hilariously mismanaged RAF station. Butlin invited Anona Winn, a wartime radio star and later panelist on *Twenty Questions*, and comedian Arthur Askey, as well as the ventriloquist Peter Brough and Leslie Welch, the 'memory man'. Butlin maintained that the Sunday-evening shows brought much-needed publicity in the local and national papers and 'invaluable word-of-mouth advertising'.[38] Every Monday, Butlin claimed, 'thousands of guests sent off postcards saying, "Guess who we saw last night?"' to their friends and relatives, thus promoting the camps and the celebrity performers.[39] This use of wartime comedy both aided in the postwar construction of wartime unity and maintained the holiday-camp experience as a continuation of a shared wartime experience. Indeed, the very infrastructure of the camps reminded guests of the war years, as many service personnel returned to the site of their wartime training camp, albeit with fewer restrictions and more colour.

Butlin also attempted to change the image of the camps through the introduction of 'high-brow' entertainment, such as opera. His first effort included the San Carlo Opera Company of Naples. For two weeks, the company performed Puccini's *La Bohème* at Filey for 5,000 campers and invited guests. In addition to the Italian opera, Butlin also hired the Bristol 'Old Vic' theatre company and the International Ballet to perform, and the London Symphony Orchestra to play at the opening of the Pwllheli camp.[40] Guests enjoyed ballet performances of *Aurora's Wedding*, *Swan Lake*, *Coppelia* or *Carnaval*, featuring world-class dancers such as Mona Inglesby, Algeranoff and Jack Spurgeon, or Paul Petroff and the Corps de ballet, accompanied by the International Ballet Orchestra.[41] The inclusion of high-brow entertainment surprised many people, Butlin later recalled, 'particularly those who still looked down on holiday camps' as a particular form of low-brow culture. Although campers reported that they preferred more traditional forms of camp entertainment, such as variety shows, Butlin's experimental ventures in opera, ballet, and the symphony were successful. The war years, Butlin explained, proved that 'the appreciation of classical music, ballet and opera is not limited to any one section of the community'.[42] Indeed, CEMA presented an array of classical music and high-brow performances to appreciative audiences during the war through programmes such as 'Music While You Work' and lunchtime concerts, as well as Shakespearean plays, ballets, and opera in the Holidays-at-Home schemes.[43] After the war, CEMA transformed into the National Council for the Arts and continued to offer 'uplifting' cultural performances to the British public.[44]

Butlin's efforts to bring high-brow entertainment to his guests mirrored similar attempts by the establishment to create a national culture that would raise the 'taste' of the nation. Efforts began in the interwar years as the BBC assumed the role of directing and educating musical tastes. Indeed, the corner-

MONDAY
19th May 1947

9.30 a.m.	*Junior Campers*—P.T. and Games.
9.45 a.m.	Keep Fit in Junior Campers' Room. (This is not a Junior Campers' Item).
10.30 a.m.	**Tombola,** in the Card Room.
10.30 a.m.	Individual Competitions in the Games Room. Lasses : Miniature Bowls. Lads : Table Tennis.
10.30 a.m.	*Junior Campers*—Audition for Junior Campers' Concert. South Theatre.
11.45 a.m.	Old Tyme Dancing Instruction in the Montgomery Ballroom.
11.45 a.m.	Lads' Soccer Practice on the Sports Field.
12.00 noon	*Junior Campers*—Health and Beauty Exercises ; Boxing Instruction. Junior Campers' Room.
2.30 p.m.	Games Time on Sports Field.
2.45 p.m.	*Junior Campers*—Netball Practice, Girls : Team Games. Boys : Sports Field.
3.15 p.m.	**Campers Quiz the Redcoats.**
3.15 p.m.	*Junior Campers*—Sing-Song, Special Junior Campers' Songs. Junior Campers' Room.
3.30 p.m.	*Junior Campers*—'Uncle Jim' entertains, in the Kiddies' Playroom.
4.00 p.m.	**Tea Dance,** in the Montgomery Ballroom to Maurice Sheffield and his 'Butlin Boys'.
4.00 p.m.	*Junior Campers*—Painting Competition. Junior Campers' Room.
4.45 p.m.	*Junior Campers*—Elementary Instruction, Lawn Tennis. Tennis Courts.
5.00 p.m.	Beach Walk. An organized tour of the coast.
7.30 p.m.	**Butlin's present at 7.30 p.m., in the Continental Theatre**

INTERNATIONAL BALLET
Direct from ADELPHI THEATRE, LONDON
PROGRAMME
'Aurora's Wedding,' 'Swan Lake' (Act II), 'Coppélia' (Act III), featuring **MONA INGLESBY, ALGERANOFF** and **JACK SPURGEON,** and Guest Artistes **NANA GOLLNER** and **PAUL PETROFF,** and **THE CORPS DE BALLET.**
International Ballet Orchestra,
Conductor: JAMES WALKER

10.00 p.m.	**Dance** to Maurice Sheffield and his 'Butlin Boys'.
11.15 p.m.	**Goodnight Campers.**

CAMPERS' BADGES. Your camp badge is your passport. Only members of the Butlin Club are allowed to use the bars. Unless you wear your badge, there is nothing to show you are a member.

Special Grand Celebrity Week, Butlin's Pwllheli, May 1947   **20**

stone policy of the BBC in the 1920s and 1930s was as the 'guardian of cultural values', and its mission to expand 'by worthy means' the number of Britons capable of enjoying the BBC's choice of programming.[45] The postwar government continued the interwar mission and engaged in a wholesale effort to raise the taste of the nation for two reasons. First was the belief that Britain had

21   Butlin (centre) enjoying poolside entertainment with campers, Clacton, c. 1947

fought to preserve what was 'best' in European civilisation, and this included predominantly British cultural forms. The second reason entailed the reconstruction of the nation and the 'good citizen' based on an appreciation of cultural roots or cultural art forms. Nationalised culture in postwar Britain acted, then, as a form of social control and also a form of socially directed taste. According to Nick Hayes, the new and powerful cultural establishment made clear its appreciation of 'good' culture by offering financial subsidies.[46] As Butlin rightly perceived, 'good culture' in postwar Britain included classical music, opera, ballet, and Shakespearean theatre.[47] By introducing this type of entertainment into his camps, Butlin positioned them within the spectrum of good culture and transformed Britain's wartime and postwar policies into a more popular form. Just as the wartime efforts of CEMA and ENSA had attempted to re-establish the close relationship between performers and audience that had been lost in the interwar years through broadcasting, so Butlin continued to build that intimacy in his camps in the postwar years. Live variety performances, including high-brow elements as well as the more low-brow audience participation, remained keystones of holiday-camp entertainment and an important aspect of a national postwar culture.

In addition to socially uplifting cultural forms, Butlin invited high-profile politicians and even some members of the royal family to his camps immediately after the war. These invitations demonstrated a different kind of interactive relationship, this time between the governing elites and holiday-camp guests. According to Butlin's memoirs, the Countess of Mountbatten and her daughter Pamela were frequent visitors to the holiday camps, and politician guests included Anthony Eden (Conservative), Herbert Morrison (Labour), and Hugh Dalton (Labour).[48] Bringing politicians to the camps as 'celebrities' reinforced the idea of the 'people's peace' brought about by the 'people's politicians'. Indeed, the Filey camp contained a bar that was an exact replica of one in the House of Commons, making politics central to an important part of the social life of the camp.[49] Thus Butlin used the postwar settlement to his advantage. He made celebrities of the political architects of reconstruction. Their presence at the camps signalled an apparent abandonment of class distinctions as well as political support for holiday camps as a legitimate form of mass leisure in postwar Britain.[50]

The postwar press, families, and the child consumer

The ethos of holiday camps also received attention from the press. When Butlin's Filey camp opened in June 1946, a five-page article written for *Picture Post* by Hilde Marchant captured the journalist's first impressions.[51] 'Most things in Butlin's holiday camp, Filey, go in straight lines', the article began, 'from the sauce-bottles to the chalets, from the dining-tables to the flower-beds.' In the event of a disruption to the order there is a chain reaction, Marchant claimed. The 'dining-room supervisor calls the head waiter, who calls the station waiter, who summons a waitress and the line is reformed'. A large number of people required 'a routine and orderly procedure, very similar to that of an army camp', Marchant noted. The problem, the journalist explained, lay with the guests. 'Some are fat, some are lean, some sit straight in their chairs, others wriggle.' Even in the most organised of camps, the author explained, people behave differently and have an opportunity for self-expression. That, in a sense, was Butlin's answer to 'critics who deride his mass-produced, conveyor-belt holidays'. The Butlin framework allowed all guests to create whatever holiday they desired.[52]

To understand the way this worked in practice, the journalist followed a newly arrived and 'typical family' of eight, including two enlisted sons who were on leave from Germany. The family began their holiday experience at reception, where 'they collected a number for their chalet, a number for their dining-room position, a number for their luggage', and the name of the 'house' they belonged to for the duration of their stay. The house name was, Marchant claimed, the most important aspect of the week because house members 'eat together, play together and compete together against other units in such competitions as the knobbliest knees, the camp "lovely" and the mass keep-fit exercises'. Led by a Butlin employee, each house formed a committee of campers to act as a feedback loop to meet the needs and desires of all campers and to lead the response to the leader's 'Hi-di-hi' call over the camp radio with a resounding 'Hi-di-ho'.[53]

Once the family had collected keys, numbers, and tickets, they were guided to their huts by camp 'Redcoats', who wore a uniform of white flannel pants or skirts and scarlet blazers, with 'B' on the pockets. The Redcoats, Marchant explained, were members of the staff responsible for games and for generating gaiety at all times of the day or night. Enduring a 'maze of lunatic questions, the wear and tear of physical jerks twice a day, the howls of children with scraped knees, the wit of the bowler hat from Bolton, the ogling of the masher from Bradford, or a foxtrot with a fifteen-stone mother-of-six from Newcastle', the Redcoats were 'worthy acolytes of the Spirit of Fun'. With constant smiles, they ensured the pleasure of thousands at the camp 'even when there is gravel in their shoes and they have heard the one about the elephant for the tenth time that day', witnessed the journalist.[54]

22   Knobbly knee competition at a Butlin camp, c. 1959

Marchant noted the day began at 7.45 a.m. when the radio gave a 'hearty rise and shine call' to the camp. The radio voice, for Marchant, was 'cheerful, but relentless' in the daily recitations of 'Good-morning campers. It is a lovely day and the sun is shining (or, the weather has let us down)'. The formless voice continued daily with 'show a leg you lads and lasses, rub the sleep out of your eyes and prepare for another grand day of fun, another Butlin's jolliday'. From that moment on, claimed the journalist, the radio was omnipresent and briefed campers on the day's activities. The radio 'leaks through every door and window', Marchant claimed. 'It calls, croons, marches and agitates all day, until the final dance' and the midnight rule brings silence to the camp.[55]

While the loud-speakers cajoled guests, the camp management recognised a group of consumers prone to chaos and spontaneity and largely neglected by hoteliers – children. The child-centred games and competitions, the nurseries staffed by professional childcare assistants, the talent shows, and the baby-sitting services offered families the luxury of a holiday that accommodated the needs of all. Indeed, holiday-camp advertising in the 1940s and 1950s stressed the family-centred nature of the camps. 'You owe it to yourself and your family to make the most of your holiday', a 1948 advertisement claimed. In fact, the advert suggested, send for a copy of *Butlin's Holiday Book*, 'packed with happy holiday-plan reading for every member of the family'.[56]

Other adverts focused on 'mother'. 'Butlin's, the perfect holiday for mother and, of course, the rest of the family too!' claimed a holiday flyer in the 1940s. 'As well as sharing her children's pleasure at Butlin's, mother may leave them from time to time in safe hands and have a chance to feel a bride again.' At Butlin's, married couples with children could recapture 'the magic of their earlier years together amid all the delights and attractions' without worrying about their children. If those promises did not suffice, a personal note from Billy Butlin on the back of the flyer encouraged families to come to one of his camps. 'Every year more and more families leave their holidays in my hands', assured Butlin, 'knowing that every member, from tiny baby to grandmother, will have a good time.'[57] A holiday-camp holiday included 'fun and entertainment in plenty for every member of the family', claimed another advertisement. 'Children always have someone to play with, and father and mother can for awhile lay aside the burdens of parenthood to enjoy a "second honeymoon" together on their Butlin holiday.'[58] After the enforced family separations, due to evacuation and conscription during the war years, demands for child-centred holiday accommodation increased in postwar Britain and holiday camps like Butlin's welcomed all with the promise of entertainment and family regeneration.

The lack of family holiday facilities surfaced as a specific postwar issue. In a 1951 speech to the British Travel and Holidays Association, Sir Alexander Maxwell, a long-time supporter of holiday camps, expressed his belief that the way to attract families to British resorts was to provide for children.[59] Young people had long been consumers of mass pleasure in Britain and the lack of leisure space and activities for children was not a new issue. Sir Maxwell's insistence on the provision of public sites of children's pleasure did, however, signal a shift in thinking that made children legitimate consumers of leisure rather than a 'problem' for the catering industry. Maxwell rightly identified the lure of holiday camps not only for parents but also for their children. Compared to hotels that featured stuffy and child-free dining-rooms and discouraged noise of any kind, Butlin's holiday camps provided children with their own space and activities, clubs, and competitions. Indeed, Butlin advertised directly to children using fictional 'Billy' and 'Bunty' child characters in holiday brochures. Billy and Bunty encouraged and directed children to enjoy their special facilities and to join in all the activities and fun available at the campsites. The fictional pair exclaimed in 1946, 'Isn't it fun to be at a holiday camp? ... The other day we were lucky and won a prize in the Kiddies' Fancy Dress Tea Party, we hope that you are lucky too.' For those without creative talent, Billy and Bunty offered step-by-step instructions for building sandcastles as well as an introduction to the Redcoats and Nurses who, they claimed, 'are very nice and know lots of nice games to play'.[60]

Each campsite featured playgrounds and playrooms for children, and Skegness even included a fun-fair. The weekly programme scheduled meetings, activities, and events for three specific age groups, 'Infants' (under 2 years), 'Young Campers' aged 2 to 8 years, and 'Junior Campers' aged 8 to 12.[61] Junior Campers and Young Campers were given special club badges, enjoyed games on the sports field, keep fit exercises, entertainment from 'Uncle Jim', health and beauty exercises, instruction in sports such as baseball and tennis, and planned 'rambles' in the countryside. Junior campers also learned to dance, swim, and box, as well as to enjoy competitions, scavenger and treasure hunts, painting contests, and talent shows like the 'Girl with the Silver Voice' or the 'Brains Trust'. The weekly programme included the Fancy Dress, the 'Kiddies Holiday Lovelies' and 'Most Charming Junior Camper' competitions, as well as inter-house tournaments and educational trips to local stately homes.[62] The Redcoats, ever ready to entertain and cajole the young campers, encouraged group singing of songs like 'Penny on the Drum' and 'The Butlin Buddies Song' that helped maintain order and prevent boredom among young campers.[63]

The advertisement reads:

Butlin's the Perfect Holiday for Mother

AND, OF COURSE, THE REST OF THE FAMILY, TOO!

FREE BOOKLET

As well as sharing her children's pleasure at Butlin's, mother may from time to time leave them happy in safe hands and have the chance to feel a bride again, recapturing with her husband the magic of their earlier years together amid all the delights and attractions of their Butlin holiday.

BUTLIN'S—WHERE YOU MAKE NEW FRIENDS

23 *Butlin's the perfect holiday for Mother*, advert, c. 1940s   **23**

One former Redcoat remembers two seasons dressed as 'The Outlaw, Chief Running Bear or … Captain Blood', and being chased around the campsite and eventually thrown into the pool by energised groups of Beavers.[64]

24   *Butlin's Holiday Pie*, 1946

In addition to the regularly scheduled children's programme features, young campers could pay extra for horse-riding lessons, have their portrait sketched by the resident camp artist, or accompany parents to any of the many shows, concerts, and circus acts regularly performed throughout the day. Toddlers received special treatment. Between 9.30 a.m. and 10.30 a.m. each day Butlin staff organised and supervised toddler playtimes. In the afternoon, the very young campers returned for more supervised play at 2.30 p.m. followed by the Toddler Tea Party at 4 p.m.[65]

For Anthony Hutt, Butlin's was a world of fantasy. Hutt was 6 when he and his family first went to Butlin's holiday camp at Clacton in 1952. He remembers that the 'entertainment was like going to a proper theatre with great shows with all the stars and singers of the time'. On one occasion, Hutt was nearly run over by 'Tommy Trinder's Rolls Royce' while holidaying at the Clacton camp. Trinder was one of the greatest comics of the 1950s and, despite the near accident, Hutt was thrilled to see the star. He also enjoyed the 'luxury' of swimming in the heated indoor and outdoor pools and joined in the games organised for his age group by the Redcoats. Loyal Butlin's campers, Hutt and his parents returned year after year to either Clacton or Skegness. They enjoyed the entertainment, the friendly atmosphere, and the child-friendly activities.[66]

The presence of the holiday-camp operator's own children enhanced the child-centred image. Harry Warner's three sons spent many summer days at the camps as young children, playing with guests. Although they lived on Hayling and so did not sleep at the camps, the young Warners ate the same food and enjoyed the same activities as the paying guests. When the three sons took charge in 1965 after the death of their father, they understood the value of retaining a child-friendly atmosphere.[67] Butlin's daughter Shirley and adopted son Bobbie also spent their childhoods at the camps, involved in the activities and events alongside paying campers and sleeping in the same accommodation. In the early postwar years the camps catered for all classes of guests, owners, heirs, and VIPs in the same standardised accommodation.[68]

Both Butlin and Warner understood the need to retain the interest of the child consumer beyond his or her brief family holiday. Butlin set up Beaver Clubs for young campers that sent each member a book for their birthday and a personalised card and 'Beaver Annual' for Christmas. Warner developed similar organisations called Wagtail Clubs for his young campers. Like Butlin, Warner sought to engage the minds of his young guests throughout the year with regular mailings, and activities at the camps. Many of the Beavers and Wagtail Club members became loyal adult campers in later life.

The holiday-camp industry's focus on the leisure of children brought into sharp focus the deficiencies of more traditional resorts. The memory of war and the statistics on the postwar baby boom centred the needs of children and families in postwar Britain. The increased birth rate also challenged the idea that adults were the only legitimate consumers of leisure. Holiday camps were visibly able to meet the needs of this burgeoning market on a mass scale, in a way that largely evaded the hotel industry and resort towns constrained by austerity and the visible remnants of war.

Holiday camps also fuelled a new genre of children's books centring on camp life. *Holiday Camp Mystery* (1959) is a story about four children, Tessie, Sid, Ken, and Judy who spend a week at Butlin's Clacton holiday camp.[69] As the title of the book suggests, the core of the tale is mystery and intrigue. The safety of the camp allows the children the freedom to transform into detectives without parental interference. The activities at the camp provided the backdrop for the mystery and the adventures of the young campers as the novel introduced readers to the amenities of the Clacton camp – the Beavers Clubs for children under 12, where secret signs and special secret activities kept the youngsters amused, as well as the One-Five-Club that organised skating, jiving, and square-dancing lessons for older children. The camp also boasted a children's theatre that produced a play per week for interested youngsters, as well as talent shows for all age groups and competitions like the 'Junior Miss and Tarzan', where girls wore dresses and boys wore swimsuits. Even if readers had never been to a holiday camp, the novel introduced them to the daily activities and even explained what happened during bad weather – the Redcoats laid on extra entertainments and amusements. Indeed, the author explained, the camp slogan proved accurate, 'Even when it's wet it's fine at Butlins'.[70]

Other children's novels set against a backdrop of holiday camps featured child detectives and even the experiences of employees.[71] Many of these books were then distributed to the Beavers and the Wagtail Club members, who read the stories and imagined themselves as the adventurous subjects. In addition, the postwar holiday camps, their guests, and staff were also the subject of films, songs, and adult novels.[72] When Gainsborough Films made the film *Holiday Camp* (1947) on location at Butlin's newly opened Filey camp, the guest activities formed the backdrop and campers became film extras. Thus holiday camps became simultaneously objects and subjects of British postwar popular culture.

The holiday camps of the 1940s and 1950s were far from luxurious by today's standards. But in the postwar years, the accommodation, food, and entertainment exceeded that experienced in everyday life. Additionally, for a modest amount of money, families with children enjoyed a week of distraction in relatively comfortable, if not exactly luxurious, surroundings. During the years of rationing and austerity, the colourful camps appealed to those looking for a week away from food queues and the drudgery of daily life. According to long-time Butlin camper Anthony Hutt, 'The chalets contained a cheap wardrobe and chest of drawers a double bed plus a bunk bed' and were in rows 'with toilet and bath blocks along the rows around 10 baths per 50 chalets'. Despite the spartan sleep and hygiene arrangements, Hutt remembers that the food was plentiful and included a fully cooked English breakfast and three courses for lunch and dinner. He also remembers the year that the roof of the chalet leaked and his mother caught pneumonia.[73] Likewise, Olive Houghton, a long-time employee of the Sunshine camp on Hayling, remembers the early accommodation as pretty basic. The 'chalets' did not have carpets or luxury furnishings, but, as Houghton notes, neither did working-class family homes in the immediate postwar period.[74] Many houses still had outside toilets and so the communal bathroom facilities in the early camps presented little hardship for the guests.

The popularity of the camps as a holiday destination for Britain's families encouraged some hoteliers to reorganise their facilities. To compete success-fully with holiday camps, argued the Mayor of Weston-super-Mare, hotels must provide nurseries and separate play rooms for children. Many potential guests, the Mayor claimed, feared the exclusion of children even as they wrote to enquire about accommodation for their families. The hotel industry could ill afford *not* to cater to the future generation, he maintained. 'The children of today are the grown-ups of tomorrow, and they always remember where they spent a happy holiday.' If hotels catered well to children today they could ensure their business in the future, the Mayor opined.[75]

Indeed, the future looked bright for the leisure industry. Postwar workers demanded more paid leisure time and government policies encouraged family holidays away from home. In May 1946 discussions began to extend paid holidays from seven to twelve working days.[76] Additionally, the National Savings Committee encouraged workplace 'savings clubs' to help workers finance their summer holidays.[77] Full employment seemed certain and workers, unable to buy consumer goods, sought to spend their earnings on leisure. As the first full season after the war approached, the industry waited expectantly for a new generation of postwar leisure consumers to increase profits and rebuild the pleasure business in Britain.

The holiday slump

Britons did not take holidays as expected in 1947.[78] Hotels remained half full and the holiday makers who did come failed to spend money and frugally brought as much as possible with them. This state of affairs existed even as fifteen million people received holidays with pay. Mr W. Teeling, Conservative MP for Brighton, one of the resorts affected, tried to make sense of this new and alarming trend. It could be a 'lack of money', he suggested, 'or a fear of the future'. In a speech to the House of Commons, Teeling emphasised another problem – many hotels still needed considerable repairs. The lack of comfortable accommodation discouraged holiday makers, as did rationing. Those who did venture away from home came supplied, for fear of a dearth of food in the resorts.[79]

Petrol shortages and government policies restricting consumption also affected domestic tourism. A ration of ninety miles per month per household seriously limited travel and the choice of holiday resorts.[80] A survey conducted by the *Caterer and Hotel Keeper* discovered that resorts 'well served by public transport or within easy reach of London and other large cities appear likely to "scoop the pool" as far as holiday visitors are concerned'. The more remote and isolated resorts, the survey suggested, suffered as a result of their 'inaccessibility to motorists restricted to the standard ration'.[81]

In spite of the disappointment of the 1947 season, the leisure industry received an unexpected boost when the government issued a foreign travel ban in October 1947. In an effort to conserve much-needed currency, the British government forbade travel abroad for pleasure or holidays. The editor of the *Caterer and Hotel Keeper* wrote expectantly, 'If the ban remains in force until next summer it will divert … a good deal of money' to British resorts 'as people who had intended to take their holiday overseas will be compelled to stay in this country'.[82] British hotels, still in need of rehabilitation, demanded more state assistance to deal with an anticipated increase in demand for domestic accommodation.

Eight months later the government lifted the foreign travel ban. Restrictions remained, as British tourists could exchange a maximum of only £35 while on a holiday abroad. The spending limit, intended to limit the flow of sterling out of the country, had an adverse effect on the British tourist industry. Foreign hotels, anxious for sterling, offered cheap rates, and British tourists looked for ways to enjoy a cheap holiday abroad. The penchant for camping greatly increased. Additionally, the restrictions reduced peer pressure. The limit applied to all Britons equally, thus decreasing social demands to outspend friends or acquaintances. The sterling limit encouraged more Britons to travel abroad sure of spending no more than £35 each.[83] High hotel tariffs and the cost of travel in Britain, conversely, made domestic holidays almost as expensive as foreign ones, and less attractive to consumers.

Holiday camps, on the other hand, benefited from the restricted travel spending. Assured of a mass of travellers, bus companies and train services accommodated camp schedules. The camps varied in size from 200 to 3,000 and catered for over 7 per cent of the nation's total holiday business.[84] The camps opened from May to early October. Each week of the season, camp guests numbered approximately 70,000, and they totalled over 1,200,000 per year. A survey revealed that in 1948, the camps refused over 200,000 bookings, due to a lack of room.[85]

Holiday camps successfully accommodated families. Special arrangements for taking care of children, ample laundry facilities, flexible, all-weather amusement and recreation arrangements, as well as the convenience of an all-inclusive cost made a camp holiday attractive to guests with children. Camps advertised the fact that they offered 'family' holidays. Rogerson Hall, close to Great Yarmouth, advertised the facilities as 'a holiday camp designed for families'.[86] Many camps reduced the price for children under the age of 14. The NFPHC promoted the family-centred approach and claimed that camps 'provide the only answer to the family problem', because they met the needs of children. 'They know how to look after them, keep them amused, and see that they really do enjoy the holiday to the utmost.'[87]

Camps, like hotels, were forced to deal with the constraints of austerity. Faced with a common problem, camp managers explained that rationing should not interfere with a good time. Visitors need only bring ration books, towels, and soap, and they could leave the rest to the management.[88] Campers could rent the paraphernalia of middle-class leisure such as 'sports and games equipment – Bathing suits etc', from the on-site store.[89] In addition, a 'pre-holiday' brochure gave a handy list of clothes to include in 'the family holiday wardrobe'.[90] The camp management understood the problems everyone faced. Listing the essentials for each family member's wardrobe, taking into account the constraints of rationed goods and emphasising camps as a perfect holiday for mothers, the brochure suggested, 'If any coupons remain Mother should have one nice dress for evening relaxation.'[91] Otherwise, mother's reward for a year of sacrifice was a week of relaxation and choreless entertainment. Indeed, Veronica Scott, the fashion editor of *Woman* magazine, reinforced this idea. Scott recognised that packing for children posed a special problem for mothers. 'As it is just as important that it should be [mother's] holiday as well as the children's, be wise and leave behind those pretty little frocks and suits which need pressing each time they are put on,' she recommended. 'Bring the casual clothes children are happiest in and enjoy the week without the worry of ironing.'[92] Thus the postwar holiday camps reinforced the idea that their facilities accommodated the needs of mothers, and promoted the annual family holiday as a just reward for married women in particular.[93]

Camps tried to keep the cost of a family holiday within the reach of the average worker's weekly wage. While a Tourist Board survey in 1949 calculated that the average cost of a holiday in Britain was £11 5s 2d per person, Warner's camps on the Isle of Wight and the Devon coast charged only £5 10s per person per week, with discounts for children.[94] Warner charged even less at his camps on Hayling – £5 per person per week at Southleigh, and £4 10s per person per week at Northney.[95] The Sunshine holiday camp on Hayling Island ranged between £15 15s and £18 18s for a family of four.[96] Nevertheless, in 1948 a survey revealed that while fifteen million people took a holiday away from home, a further thirteen million Britons did not.[97] They represented a huge, untapped consumer market.[98]

Yet the survey also revealed some criticism of holiday camps. Campers complained about the repetitious weekly entertainment programmes, the mass feeding that lacked a personal touch and any flexibility for dealing with individual preferences, as well as the absence of the kind of 'luxury' obtainable at first-class hotels.[99] Other critics claimed that the camps were indicative of an increasingly indolent postwar citizenry. Signalling his disapproval of the camps and the Labour government's welfare programme, Mr G. L. Reakes, a Wallasey hotelier, claimed, 'Holiday camps fit in with the spirit of the lazy age of today when people, having everything done for them, wanted their holidays planned for them.'[100] Pointing to the political difference of the 'Labour' supported camps versus the 'Conservative' supported hotels and boarding house guests, Alderman G. K. G. Pindar maintained that resorts appealed to 'people who want the freedom to do and spend what they like', unlike the regimented entertainment and standardised accommodation of holiday camps.[101]

The Labour Party did indeed support holiday camps. Some party members advocated state-sponsored camps to increase the provision of inexpensive family holidays. Conservative Party members opposed what they saw as a grossly unfair scheme that was contrary to private enterprise.[102] Roland Robinson, Conservative MP for Blackpool, insisted that 'The duty of the Government was not to compete with its citizens but to create conditions which would help them to earn their bread and butter.' Instead of competing directly with private enterprises, the state should remove the obstacles that the catering industry faced. The leisure industry, Robinson claimed, could meet the demand for cheaper holidays if the government placed price restraints on the raw materials it needed to renovate and run its businesses.[103]

Yet the real problem lay with the postwar policies of austerity and the financial restraints of a managed economy. The postwar British government attempted to rebuild and reconstruct the nation in the same way that the state expected its citizens to – with rationed resources. Austerity constrained the state and the people alike. In order to remake the nation and rebuild the leisure industry, Britain needed foreign investment and foreign tourists. More specifically, postwar Britain needed American dollars.[104]

Chasing the 'Yankee dollar'

In 1949 the state-sponsored British Travel Association (BTA) attempted to lure American tourists to Britain. Set up in 1929 as part of the movement to facilitate tourism, by the 1940s the BTA was determined to establish Britain as the primary destination for American visitors to Europe.[105] While state policies constrained the leisure industry in Britain, the Labour government encouraged tourism as a way to jump-start the economy and encouraged the BTA to entice international guests. This was part of a conscious and deliberate movement to package Britain for American tourists and also to reorient Britain 'economically and administratively in the direction *of* the tourist'.[106]

The director general of the BTA, Mr J. G. Bridges, toured North America. Unlike other tourists, Bridges left home not to see the country but to prepare Americans to see Britain. When he returned, he made several observations. While thousands of middle-class Americans with holiday time 'represented a vast, almost untapped market for travel' in Britain, he claimed, 'the average American traveller is not a millionaire. He is not looking for luxury hotels, but rather for clean, comfortable accommodation at a reasonable cost.' The devaluation of sterling in September 1949, Bridges continued, made Britain 'the world's best travel bargain'. It offered foreigners cheap travel to Britain and inexpensive goods and services.[107] For those who feared that austerity might deter tourism, Bridges gave this optimistic reassurance. Americans, he maintained, 'did not travel across the ocean to eat' and so food rationing was not a deterrent. However, to remain competitive, Bridges insisted, the British tourist industry must cultivate a service ethic and have 'more modern hotels with adequate bathroom facilities at moderate prices'.[108]

Butlin made his own plans to entice American tourists. He negotiated with leading US travel agents, and shipping and airline companies to create an all-inclusive price for fares and accommodation for 10,000 holiday makers. The Americans would pay approximately £10 a week, compared with £8 for British guests. The price difference, according to Butlin, denoted extra bus tours and theatre tickets for the international visitors, but not a difference in the standard of service.[109] Butlin's former business partner conceived a smaller-scale plan to lure American guests and aid the nation's need for dollars. Warner planned the construction of another 500–bed holiday camp on the Isle of Wight and dozens more 100–bed camps close to 'places of historical interest in different parts of the country'.[110]

Although both men wanted to attract overseas visitors to Britain, Butlin also understood that some North Americans preferred an exotic destination closer to home. The Caribbean, 800 miles from New York, was a fast-growing holiday destination for many Americans. In 1948 Butlin leased two hotels in Bermuda and Nassau as a way of making money and bringing US dollars into Britain. The following year, four chartered planes from New York brought American tourists to Butlin's Caribbean hotels.[111]

Despite the relative success of the hotels in the Caribbean, shareholders in London were sceptical. The previous year's profits had not met expectations, and many feared further financial losses in Bermuda. At the 1949 annual meeting, Butlin insisted the hotels were money makers. He protested, 'We wanted to spread our risks and we wanted, and we still want, to get into the US. We want dollars and we are going where they are.' Mr Ian Anderson, the Chairman of Butlin's Ltd, supported Butlin and emphasised the hotels' popularity and the fact that income at both sites exceeded £1,000,000. The shareholders still had reservations and so Butlin offered to forgo his director's salary of £5,000 per year until the company was once again 'paying a dividend of 100%'.[112]

Butlin wanted to continue to expand into the US market by offering low-cost holidays to middle- and lower-income Americans. He chose the small, sparsely populated island of Grand Bahama, lying just fifty miles off the coast of Florida, for his new venture and promoted it as a way for Americans to get to know more about the British way of life.[113] He called his project the Bahama Village and planned to staff it with British entertainers. That way, Butlin explained, Americans 'will get a unique opportunity of finding out what makes us [the British] "tick"'.[114] Indeed, Butlin believed that his Bahama venture might prove to be one of the vital links in 'the chain of Anglo-American understanding'.[115]

The Bahama Village proved popular with the island population as a source of employment.[116] Nevertheless, the venture received a financial blow when sterling was devalued in 1949, increasing the cost of the project by 25 per cent.[117] Butlin also faced political opposition. The Nassau Parliament initially passed the plans for the British venture and agreed to pay half the cost of building a small airport, in return for landing fees and customs duties. Once the runways were built, the government reneged on the deal. Butlin already had bookings for the grand opening in January 1950. He claimed that the change in attitude was the result of jealous hoteliers and businessmen who saw him as competition.[118] Yet the island remained relatively undeveloped until the mid 1950s, suggesting a more complex explanation for the lack of support. More likely, the political opposition in the Bahamas came from the perception of Butlin as British – despite the fact that he was Canadian. The government regarded Butlin as a relic of a recent colonial past (the Bahamas had gained independence from Britain in 1945). Perhaps the construction of the Bahama Village as a little piece of 'Olde England' reinforced fears of a renewed imperial presence.[119]

Despite opposition, the village opened in 1950, 'totally geared to Americans and Canadians, with luxury chalets set in "olde worlde" English atmosphere', and staffed by imported British entertainers and local workers.[120] Like the organisers of the Festival of Britain, Butlin understood the value of 'selling the nation' in an era of increasing affluence and expanded foreign travel.[121] Butlin named the lines of chalets after English counties, and facilities included a pub called Ye Olde Pig and Whistle. In the main street, Butlin placed some medieval-looking pillory and stocks. As the choice of name suggests, Butlin designed his holiday village to look like an imagined 'old England'.

In the holiday village, Social Directors, not Redcoats, directed entertainment, and their activities took place in the evenings. During the day the guests sunbathed and swam on the magnificent beaches, or fished for dolphin, barracuda, and tarpon in boats provided free of charge.[122] According to Tom and Margaret White, former employees at Butlin's Clacton camp as well as at the holiday village, the Bahaman venture differed from the camps in Britain in other ways as well.[123] While the camps in Britain catered for predominately working-class guests, the entertainment in the Grand Bahama holiday village was tailored to suit a clientele who were mainly middle-class Americans from New York, West Palm Beach, and Miami. The Whites, along with other Butlin employees, spent three weeks in New York to learn square dancing so that it could be included in the entertainment programme. While square dancing hardly fitted the 'olde worlde' English theme, Butlin believed that it would appeal to American guests.[124]

As in Britain, the holiday village employees wore jackets, but as the Whites recalled, 'the British Redcoat was a bit warm for the climate', and so the hosts and hostesses wore red shirts instead.[125] The entertainers spent their daytime hours teaching swimming lessons and tennis. In the evenings, aside from cabaret and dancing, they organised crazy-golf competitions, bingo, and card games. Many of the domestic workers included local residents, and a few Canadians worked at the reception desk. Visitors were exclusively white and came from the United States or Canada. Unlike the camps in Britain, the staff of the Bahaman venture ate separately, unless invited by individual guests. The democratic ethos of the British camps gave way to a class-conscious atmosphere where the staff remained strictly separate from the guests. Indeed, the segregation of the staff at the holiday village retained a racial divide that resembled 1940s and 1950s American society. Workers were mainly black, but Redcoat entertainers were white Britons or white Canadians. According to Vernon Jenkins, Butlin insisted that black employees wear white gloves to prevent 'black fingerprints' on the plates, revealing a deep-seated racism.[126] Thus, in Butlin's holiday village, class and racial distinctions were heightened, not deliberately blurred as in the British camps, where guests and staff mingled. Butlin sought to package 'old Europe' for Americans in the Bahamas rather than to celebrate a 'democratic' form of 'Britishness', as in the pre-war holiday camps.

Although Butlin's holiday village attracted 17,000 guests – a third of the total visitors to the Bahamas – in only six months, without government support, the project needed more capital to continue.[127] The project cost £2.5 million but needed another £1 million in the first year.[128] Butlin believed that the venture's financial troubles were exacerbated by the outbreak of the Korean War, which made American investors hesitant to invest in tourism. However, Rocky Mason points out that the reluctance had more to do with the fact that the holiday village was built in the path of hurricanes.[129]

Yet, in reality, Butlin failed to translate a successful British cultural form into one that would attract Americans. Holiday camps and the culture fostered within them appealed to British consumers in a way that could not be replicated for a non-British audience. The communal entertainment and singing, the socially levelled atmosphere and informal relationships between staff and guests simply did not appeal to Americans in the way that it did to Britons. Constant and organised activities that incorporated comedy and humour eased social tensions in Britain, but did not have the same effect on an American audience.

In addition, menus offered only British-style meals, like porridge and bacon and eggs, that didn't appeal to American palates and the holiday village provided games like billiards, when Americans played pool.[130] Butlin's desire to create a uniquely British culture in his holiday camps had succeeded to the degree that it could not and did not appeal to non-British guests. In 1952, Butlin sold the holiday village at a personal loss of a quarter of a million pounds.[131] The fiasco in the Bahamas almost cost Butlin control of his company in Britain.[132]

Despite Butlin's failure to translate his vision so as to appeal to international guests, the popularity of his camps grew in Britain. Bookings increased even in the face of competition from the Festival of Britain. In 1950, Butlin's Ltd took 8,389 more bookings than in 1949, and the 1951 season looked even better, with over 15,100 more guests than the year before.[133] More guests did not, however, signal more profits. Rising food and other raw material costs, as well as new development taxes and building licences prevented the company from opening new camps.[134] To avoid higher taxes, Butlin decided to extend the accommodation and facilities in existing camps rather than to develop new sites. Filey eventually accommodated 10,000 guests per week, making it the largest holiday camp in Britain and the world.

In 1953, Butlin opened the first of three hotels in Brighton. The Ocean Hotel featured 'sundecks, gay canopies, roof gardens and sports decks, central heating and constant hot water, endless bathrooms, and all the usual amenities of a Butlin's holiday camp plus the added comforts and advantages of a modern hotel'. Butlin's company made history when the Bishop of Chichester conducted the dedication service for the hotel. Although each holiday camp contained Roman Catholic and Anglican chapels, in view of the disastrous Bahamas venture that almost resulted in the removal of Butlin as the Chairman of his own company in London, Butlin may well have felt that he needed the intervention of the Bishop to ensure the success of his new business enterprise. As one observer wrote, one couldn't help feeling that 'the Bishop's grace was shed not only upon the new building and all who would work and all who would holiday within it, but also upon Mr. Butlin himself'. After the events of the previous two years, Butlin certainly needed to feel that grace.[135]

The domestic industry: obstacles and opportunities

While Butlin opened hotels in Britain and planned to extend his British facilities to meet the demand for inexpensive holidays, the hotel industry worried that millions of Britons did not holiday at all.[136] Official figures claimed that 22

25   Butlin's Ocean Hotel, Brighton, c. 1953

million Britons worked, and the majority received holidays with pay. Nevertheless, the statistics compiled by the British Tourist Board indicated that over 10 million Britons did not holiday in 1951. 'If this figure is accurate', noted the editor of the *Caterer and Hotel Keeper*, 'there exists a vast untapped source of potential business for resort hotels'. If this population could be mobilised, hoteliers could 'extend the present holiday season' and increase profits. Indeed, the key to increased profits and a longer holiday season appeared to centre on forcing a change in the holiday habits of the British worker.[137]

Consumers, however, continued to resist the lure of the catering industry, preferring to improvise holidays and pleasure. The extension of paid holidays encouraged the annual rush to the coastal areas. Many of the new holiday makers, especially those with families, turned to holiday camps, rented caravans, disused tram cars, or other types of improvised shelter. Holiday makers who lived within sixty miles of the ocean preferred to sleep at home and make day trips by bus, car or motor-bike. As London housed one-fifth of the total population, the southern and south-eastern resorts received the majority of these visitors. The habits of the day trippers were frugal. Visitors carried their own food and spent little in the seaside towns, and so added little to the local economy. Day trippers maximised their enjoyment by choosing towns with 'esplanades and lawns and illuminations'. In addition to spending little money, they left the beaches strewn with litter. Not only did local businesses make little profit, residents were forced to use local tax monies to foot the bill for cleaning up after the day trippers. Indeed, claimed one caterer, day trippers

ALL-IN HOLIDAYS
ALL YEAR ROUND
at
Butlin's
HOLIDAY HOTELS

OPEN FOR ALL FOUR SEASONS—FOR EVER

BRIGHTON: Butlin's Ocean Hotel, Saltdean, is an ultra-modern hotel with acres of glass-screened sun-roofs and a marvellous ballroom and games rooms. Plenty of indoor entertainment for winter holidays.

BLACKPOOL: Butlin's Metropole Hotel is in the heart of Blackpool's entertainment area. See the famous illuminations and enjoy the all-year-round holiday attractions.

MARGATE: Here Butlin's offer you the amenities of 4 first-class hotels for the price of one. They are among the few places on the south coast offering a full programme for autumn and winter holiday-makers; whichever hotel you eat and sleep in you are quite free to enjoy the attractions of the other three also.

ALL-IN TARIFF includes many of the famous Butlin holiday entertainments and novelties

And, of course,
the popular 'BUTLIN REDCOATS'!

Remember—the Butlin Hotels are open winter and summer

Butlin's Hotels at Brighton, Blackpool and Margate, advertisement, c. 1955   **26**

'are apt to leave more nuisance than cash behind them'.[138]

But the types of attractions offered in the seaside towns encouraged day trippers and excursionists. Boardwalks, big wheels, and fun-fair games, as well as the beaches, appealed to young people and families seeking a day's amusement. Some local authorities, such as Worthing Council, tried to make their resort less attractive to day trippers by refusing permission for the placement of 'juvenile rides and games' near the sea front.[139] Wartime debris posed another impediment to restricting the numbers of day trippers. Britain's coastline, off-limits to civilians throughout the war years, still retained some remnants of war materials years later. For example, Eastbourne, one of the most fashionable pre-war beaches was 'disfigured by large holes, sandbags and ... miles of barbed wire ... and the jagged edges of submerged anti-invasion devices'.[140] On the one hand, this debris posed a danger to careless beachcombers. On the other hand, austerity and a learned frugality led many Britons to use the discarded war materials as holiday shelters. As a result, spontaneous recreation areas emerged in and around many resorts, without adequate sanitary or refuse disposal. Additionally, camping sites and caravan parks, as well as cheap amusements, scattered Britain's coastline, providing alternative spontaneous and inexpensive holiday sites.[141]

In an effort to make the coastal areas more attractive to tourists, one local authority used the 1947 Town and Country Planning Act to clean the beaches, prevent the erection of holiday 'shanty towns', and collect more residential taxes. As a relatively undeveloped resort, Hayling Island presented the local authorities with a potential income from residential taxes.[142] Empowered by the 1947 Act, Havant Council granted planning permission for permanent dwellings, as opposed to temporary holiday structures, designed to provide seasonal accommodation for the increased number of visitors in the summer months. The council collected taxes from permanent dwellings, and even life-long residents were prohibited from maintaining caravans or non-permanent structures on their property because doing so would encourage sub-standard (and non-taxable) development in the area.[143] Requests to expand existing campsites were denied. An application to extend St Mary's caravan site, which already housed dozens of caravans, with a further seventy caravans met with refusal because the council rezoned the area for permanent and taxable residential development only.[144] Plans to erect toilet facilities at Eastoke to cater for the needs of seasonal campers met with the same refusal on the grounds that the 'toilet block', would 'encourage sub-standard living accommodation at excessive density'.[145] In other words, these facilities would encourage the development of temporary and seasonal buildings from which the council would exact no revenue.

Although Havant Council encouraged the growth of residential property and restricted the development of new businesses, it did sanction improvements

Aerial view of Warner's Southleigh Camp on Hayling Island, c. 1950   **27**

and some contained expansion of Hayling Island's four holiday camps, which by 1953 attracted almost 43,000 visitors to Hayling during the nineteen-week season (approximately 2,300 per week).[146] The council approved an application to make additions to Warner's Northney camp,[147] as well as plans to build a swimming pool and filtration plant at the Sunshine camp.[148] The council also gave approval for additional chalet accommodation at the Coronation camp,[149] and permitted the construction of a television room, amenity and reception building at Warner's Southleigh camp.[150] Thus, in addition to the continued popularity of day trips, forms of low-cost holidays offered at holiday camps, camp grounds, and caravan parks suggested that Britons did habitually enjoy leisure away from home. The form that those leisure habits took simply did not include more exorbitant expenditure in the resort towns.

Conclusion

Labour's policies, aimed at securing the welfare and relaxation of a war-weary workforce, gave a boost to the postwar holiday-camp industry, but not to the more traditional hotels. The mass catering of the camps complemented the social ethos of the Labour government in a way that hotels did not. Planned pleasure took on a new meaning as the common experience of war gave legitimacy to holiday-camp uniformity. Catering for thousands of workers, the camps gained more government support and access to scarce resources. Additionally, the problems created by continued rationing and nationwide shortages of food, clothes, and luxury items were overcome more easily in the holiday-camp atmosphere, where every guest received the same service. Indeed, holiday camps successfully capitalised on both wartime and continued austerity in their entertainment and accommodation in a way that hotels could not. When the Conservative government took power in 1951, hoteliers hoped to gain from changed policies. The Conservatives, however, continued Labour's domestic agenda, including austerity, for another three years.

In February 1954, the Conservative government's Ministry of Food announced the final step in dismantling the wartime food rationing system. The leisure industry in Britain celebrated the end of austerity and, optimistically surveying the 1954 holiday season prospects, promised holiday makers pre-war menus.[151] Nevertheless, hoteliers still harboured a grudge against the postwar government which, it claimed, regarded the hotel industry as the 'Cinderella' of domestic tourism and gave preferential treatment to holiday camps.[152]

Unlike most hotels and boarding houses, camps catered for the needs of the postwar families. The provision of childcare facilities and activities proved popular and signalled the importance of a new consumer market – children. As the memory of wartime disruptions centred the family as the locus of concern for the postwar welfare state, children became legitimate consumers of leisure in their own right. While the British leisure industry saw children as legitimate consumer groups, the growing demands of British workers from the mid 1950s onwards forced those in the industry to recognise the importance of providing inexpensive accommodation for all. The competition from holiday camps forced hoteliers and resorts to reconstruct their facilities so as to provide for children. Thus the contours of postwar pleasure were shaped by the political ideology of postwar Britain and concern for children as the citizens of the future.

Despite the popularity of holiday camps in Britain, the same vision of pleasure did not appeal to international guests, as Butlin's failed endeavours in the Caribbean suggested. Butlin's efforts to entice North Americans with the same leisure model as in Britain did not succeed. The communal activities and entertainment that gave pleasure to thousands of Britons each year failed to interest North Americans. The 'democratic ethos' of holiday-camp culture that developed so successfully at home did not have the same appeal to the American consumer, who expected a separation of service staff from guests. The failure of the holiday village in the Bahamas illustrates the uniquely British nature of the mass camp culture – its entertainment and activities.

By the mid 1950s, the leisure industry had turned back to British workers. The domestic tourism industry looked for ways to capture this huge potential market. The next chapter explores the efforts of the leisure industry to expand to meet the increased demands for inexpensive pleasure and package holidays 'for the people' in post-austerity Britain.

Notes

1 S. Fielding, P. Thompson and N. Tiratsoo, *'England arise!' The Labour Party and popular politics in 1940s Britain* (Manchester: Manchester University Press, 1995).
2 I. Zweiniger-Bargielowska, *Austerity in Britain: Rationing, controls, and consumption 1939–1955* (Oxford: Oxford University Press, 2000), pp. 209–25 and S. Howson, *British monetary policy, 1945–1951* (Oxford: Clarendon, 1994).
3 Not all historians agree that there was a cross-political consensus in post-Second World War Britain. See H. Mercer, 'Industrial organisation and ownership, and a new definition of the postwar "consensus"', in P. Catterall and H. Jones, eds *The myth of consensus* (Basingstoke: Macmillan, 1996), pp. 139–56 and Ellison, 'Consensus here, consensus there', in ibid, pp. 17–39.
4 Vernon, 'Ethics of hunger', pp. 693–725.
5 Nicholas, *Echo of war*, p. 213.
6 Sir Reginald Clarry, question to the Prime Minister, *HCPD*, 24 October 1944, p. 25.
7 'Plea for release of holiday camps – big demand for accommodation', *World's Fair*, 3 March 1945, p. 1.
8 Ibid.
9 Welfare officers were responsible for finding holiday accommodation for workers.
10 During 1944, over 716,000 workers were involved in strikes. D. Childs, *Britain since 1945: A political history* (London: Routledge, 2001), p. 22.
11 Threats from German V1 and V2 rockets in the final months of the war made the government wary of derequisitioning the coastal camps, often the first line of defence. Clarke, *Hope and glory*, pp. 201–6.
12 'Plea for release of holiday camps – big demand for accommodation', *World's Fair*, 3 March 1945, p. 1 and 'Holiday accommodation (Derequisitioning)', Prime Minister, *HCPD*, 24 October 1944, p. 25.
13 The Cunningham holiday camp on the Isle of Man was sold for £500,000 while still occupied by troops. 'Big holiday camp deal', *World's Fair*, 5 May 1945, p. 1.
14 The LMS Prestatyn camp opened in 1946. 'Prestatyn holiday camp to re-open', *World's Fair*, 12 January 1946, p. 1.
15 'Holiday resorts', questions from Wing-Commander Robinson to the Minister of Food, Dr Summerskill, 13 March 1946, *HCPD*, Vol. 420 (London, 1946), pp. 1099–100.
16 'Holiday camps want Government action – labour and materials needed', *World's Fair*, 16 March 1946, p. 1.

17 Bread was not rationed until July 1946.

18 Lloyd, *Empire, welfare state*, pp. 284–94.

19 Sir Stafford Cripps served as Labour's President of the Board of Trade (1945–47); Minister of Economic Affairs and Chancellor of the Exchequer (1947–50).

20 'Supplies for hotels and holiday camps: Government aid promised', *World's Fair*, 23 March 1946, p. 1.

21 'Catering and tourist industries', questions and answers, 28 September 1944, *HCPD*, pp. 399–400 and Zweiniger-Bargielowska 'Consumption and consensus: Rationing, austerity and controls after the war', in *The myth of consensus*, pp. 79–96.

22 Zweiniger-Bargielowska, *Austerity in Britain*, pp. 99–150.

23 Black-marketeering was extensive during and after the war. D. Hughes, 'The spivs', in M. Sissons and P. French, eds *The age of austerity* (Westport, CT: Greenwood Press, 1976), pp. 81–100, and Lord Woolton, *The memoirs of the Rt. Honourable the Earl of Woolton* (London: Cassell, 1959), pp. 230–1.

24 Mrs Alderman C. Leyland, quoted in, 'Holiday resorts to have more power', *Caterer and Hotel Keeper*, 25 January 1946, p. 36.

25 'Hotel equipment', Sir S. Cripps, reply to Lieut-Colonel Mackeson, 10 December 1945, *HCPD*, Vol. 417, p. 10.

26 Textile rationing began in 1941 and textiles remained at between 20 per cent and 40 per cent of pre-war availability until the early 1950s. Zweiniger-Bargielowska, *Austerity in Britain*, p. 46.

27 Postwar economic constraints came from the rapid termination of the Lend-Lease in August 1945 and the worldwide food and fuel shortages. Henry Pelling, *Labour governments, 1945–51* (London: Macmillan, 1984), ch. 4.

28 Sir H. Webbe, questions to Mr Tomlinson, 11 December 1945, *HCPD*, Vol. 417 (London, 1946), pp. 345–7.

29 'Holiday camps given preference, say hotels', *Caterer and Hotel Keeper*, 24 May 1946, p. 10.

30 B. Conekin, *'The autobiography of a nation': The 1951 Festival of Britain*, (Manchester: Manchester University Press, 2003), and Francis, 'Not reformed capitalism', pp. 40–57.

31 Smith, *Britain and 1940*, pp. 91–110.

32 D. Dworkin, *Cultural Marxism in postwar Britain: History, the New Left, and the origin of cultural studies* (Durham, NC: Duke University Press, 1997), ch. 1.

33 Butlin with Dacre, *Butlin story*, p. 163.

34 Nicholas, *Echo of war*, pp. 130–2.

35 *Programme of attractions: Butlin's Filey*, week commencing 14 September 1946.

36 Irene Chambers, Bygone Butlins, www.bygonebutlins.com/stories/irene_chambers.html (accessed 8 August 2009).

37 Butlin with Dacre, *Butlin story*, p. 163.

38 Ibid., p. 164.

39 Ibid.

40 Ibid., pp. 165–6.

41 *Programme of attractions: Special grand celebrity week, Butlin's Pwllheli*, week commencing 17 May 1947.

42 Butlin with Dacre, *Butlin story*, 165–6. The high-brow ventures were successful but guests preferred traditional camp entertainment and 'Variety'. For a discussion of wartime preferences see Nicholas, *Echo of war*, pp. 274–5.

43 R. Mackey, 'Safe and sound: New music in wartime', in N. Hayes and J. Hill, eds *Millions like us? British culture in the Second World War* (Liverpool: Liverpool University Press, 1999), pp. 179–208, and N. Hayes, 'More than music while-you-eat? Factory and hostel concerts, "good culture" and the workers', in ibid., pp. 209–35.

44 B. Ifor Evans and M. Glasgow, *The arts in England* (London: Falcon Press, 1947).

45 Scannell and Cardiff, *British broadcasting*, p. 201.

46 N. Hayes, 'An English war: Wartime culture and millions like us', in Hayes and Hill, eds *Millions like us?* pp. 1–32.

47 Evans and Glasgow, *The arts in England*, ch. 3.

48 Anthony Eden was Foreign Secretary in 1945 and 1952, and Prime Minister in 1955. Herbert Morrison was Foreign Secretary from 1945 to 1951; Hugh Dalton was Chancellor of the Exchequer from 1945 to 1951.

49 Butlin with Dacre, *Butlin story*, p. 164.

50 Butlin's holiday-camp kitchens were used to advertise new gas kitchen equipment offered by the newly formed British Gas Council. See British Gas Council advert, *Caterer and Hotel Keeper*, 20 September 1946, p. 6.

51 Hilde Marchant was a successful high-profile freelance journalist who also wrote for the *Daily Express* in the interwar years. Bingham, *Gender, modernity, and the popular press*, p. 40.

52 H. Marchant, 'Life in a holiday camp', 13 July 1946, in T. Hopkinson, ed. *Picture Post* (London, 1970), pp. 192–6.

53 Ibid., p. 193.

54 Ibid., p. 195.

55 Ibid., p. 196.

56 *It's fun in the sun at Butlins*, holiday advert, *Picture Post*, 14 February 1948, p. 30.

57 'Butlin's the perfect holiday for Mother', Butlin's advertisement flyer, c. 1940s.

58 'Butlin's for a REAL family holiday', Butlin's advertisement flyer, c. 1940s.

59 'Public demand cheaper holidays: Sir Alexander Maxwell on future problems', *Caterer and Hotel Keeper*, 16 June 1951, p. 27. Sir Alexander encouraged families to go to holiday camps because of the special provision for children. Sir Alexander H. Maxwell, 'Where shall I spend my holidays?' *Holiday Camp Book* (London: Clerke and Cockeran, 1949), p. 5.

60 'Children only', *Butlin's holiday pie*, 1946, pp. 20–1.

61 *Holiday time at Butlins* (London: Sun Printers, 1950), p. 50.

62 *Programme of attractions, Butlin's Filey*, week commencing 7 September 1946, and *Programme of attractions: Special grand celebrity week, Butlin's Pwllheli*, week commencing 17 May 1947.

63 The words and music for both songs were printed in *The Butlin holiday book, 1949–50* (Ipswich: W. S. Cowell, 1949), pp. 78–83.

64 'Skegred', Bygone Butlins Memories, www.bygonebutlins.com/forum/viewtopic.

php?t=255 (accessed 4 August 2009).

65 See for example *Programme of attractions, Butlin's Filey*, week commencing 14 September 1946.

66 A. Hutt, e-mail correspondence with author, 25 April 2005.

67 H. Warner, WFSA, AV632/16/S1. See also a photograph of the Warner boys at Northney holiday camp in *Warner news*, 1964, p. 2.

68 Butlin with Dacre, *Butlin story*, p. 152.

69 M. A. Cole, *Holiday camp mystery* (London: Robert Hale Ltd, 1959).

70 Ibid, p. 58.

71 See A. M. Miall, *The holiday camp mystery* (Leicester: Brockhampton Press, 1950), M. Cole, *Another holiday camp mystery* (London: Robert Hale Ltd, 1967) and P. Deal, *Nurse at Butlin's* (London: Arthur Barker Limited, 1961).

72 *Holiday Camp*, 97 mins. Gainsborough Films, 1947, K. Porlock, *Holiday camp: the book of the film* (London: World Film Publications, 1947), Michael Carr 'At a holiday camp' (London: Peter Maurice Music, 1945). M. Cole, *Romance at Butlins* (London: Robert Hale, 1958) and J. Creasey, *The toff at Butlin's* (London: Hodder and Stoughton, 1954).

73 A. Hutt, e-mail correspondence with author, 25 April 2005.

74 O. Houghton, interview with author, 14 September 2001. See A. Olechnowicz, *Working-class housing in England between the wars: The Becontree estate* (Oxford: Clarendon Press, 1997) and J. Burnett, *A social history of housing, 1815–1985* (London: Methuen, 1986), Part III.

75 'Hotels and holiday camp menace', *Caterer and Hotel Keeper*, 23 May 1947, p. 12.

76 'Paid holidays bill urged', *Daily Mail*, 23 May 1946, p. 1.

77 'Staff savings group', advert for the National Savings Committee, *The Caterer and Hotel Keeper*, 4 October 1946, p. 30.

78 T. Blackwell and J. Seabrook, *A world still to win: The reconstruction of the postwar working class* (London: Faber and Faber, 1985), pp. 63–110.

79 'MP's questions on holiday slump: hotels only half full', *Caterer and Hotel Keeper*, 25 July 1947, p. 19.

80 Zweiniger-Bargielowska, *Austerity in Britain*, pp. 192–102. Petrol remained rationed until May 1950.

81 'Petrol the key to holiday prospects: facts revealed by survey', *Caterer and Hotel Keeper*, 7 May 1948, p. 15.

82 'Effect of foreign travel ban: increased business for British hotels', *Caterer and Hotel Keeper*, 5 September 1947, p. 17.

83 'Resorts find the boom is over: lean business in many places', *Caterer and Hotel Keeper*, 9 July 1948, p. 15.

84 The large camps included Butlin's Filey (5,000), Skegness (3,000), Clacton (3,000), Pwllheli (2,500) and Ayr (2,500).

85 'Holiday camp menace to resorts: survey and suggestions by Tourist Board', *Caterer and Hotel Keeper*, 14 January 1949, pp. 15–18.

86 Rogerson Hall advert, *Holiday camp book* (London, 1949), p. 126. Rogerson Hall was managed by the Worker's Travel Association.

87 W. E. Butlin, MBE 'Holiday camps of today and tomorrow', in ibid, p. 93.

88 Campers gave their ration coupons to the camp management on arrival. The catering department calculated meals based on the official rations allowed per person.

89 *Sunshine Holidays, 1948*, Hayling Island Holidays Ltd. brochure, 1948, PCL Pamphlets Collection, 5.

90 Ibid.

91 Ibid.

92 V. Scott, 'What to pack for a week at a holiday camp', *Holiday camp book*, p. 96.

93 The number of working married women increased dramatically after 1945. D. Smith Wilson, 'A new look at the affluent worker: the good working mother in post-war Britain', *Twentieth Century British History*, 17:2 (2006), pp. 206–29.

94 Warner's holiday-camp advert for Puckpool and Seaton, *Holiday camp book*, p. 58.

95 Ibid., p. 100. The average cost of a boarding house holiday was £3 15s per person per week.

96 *Sunshine holidays 1948*, Hayling Island Holidays Ltd. brochure, 1948, PCL, Pamphlets Collection, p. 4. W. F. F. Kemsley and D. Ginsburg, *Holidays and holiday expenditure* (London, 1950) and 'How 20 million use their holidays: facts revealed in new survey', *Caterer and Hotel Keeper*, 13 January 1951, pp. 23–6.

97 'Why seaside visitors are fewer?' *Caterer and Hotel Keeper*, 18 June 1948, p. 18. The survey was undertaken by the Home Holidays Division of the British Tourist and Holidays Board in September 1948. Kemsley and Ginsburg, *Holidays and holiday expenditure*, and 'Why holiday season is limited: result of official survey', *Caterer and Hotel Keeper*, 3 September 1948, pp. 17–18.

98 '9,000,000 more will take holidays: survey of future prospects', *Caterer and Hotel Keeper*, 22 April 1949, pp. 15–16.

99 'Holiday camp menace to resorts: Survey and suggestions by Tourist Board', *Caterer and Hotel Keeper*, 14 January 1949, pp. 15–18.

100 'Why seaside visitors are fewer?' *Caterer and Hotel Keeper*, 18 June 1948, p. 18.

101 'Holiday makers prefer hotels to camps', *Caterer and Hotel Keeper*, 4 February 1950, p. 53.

102 J. R. Robinson, MP, quoted in 'Critic of state holiday centres: Unfair competition with hotels', *World's Fair*, 3 November 1949, p. 1.

103 J. R. Robinson MP, quoted in 'State-built holiday camps: Threat to hotel industry', *Caterer and Hotel Keeper*, 5 November 1949, p. 11. Raw materials for construction remained in short supply as homes took precedence over holiday accommodation in the 1940s.

104 See K. O. Morgan, *Labour in power, 1945–1951* (Oxford: Oxford University Press, 1984), pp. 339–58 for a discussion of Britain's dependence on the dollar.

105 J. Buzzard, 'Culture for export: Tourism and autoethnography in postwar Britain', in S. Barbaowski and E. Furlough eds *Being elsewhere: Tourism, consumer culture and identity in modern Europe and North America* (Ann Arbor, MI: University of Michigan Press, 2004) pp. 299–319.

106 Ibid, p. 301.

107 In 1945 sterling was fixed at $4 to the pound; it was devalued in September 1949 to $2.80. Lloyd, *Empire, welfare state*, pp. 274–5.

108 'All-in holidays for Americans: Travel Association scheme', *Caterer and Hotel*

Keeper, 26 November 1949, pp. 7–8.

109 'Americans to fill Butlin camps: Plans for 10,000 to tour Britain next year', *Caterer and Hotel Keeper*, 2 September 1949, p. 25.

110 'Holiday camp for U.S. visitors: Warner's plans going ahead', *World's Fair*, 16 September 1950, p. 1.

111 Butlin with Dacre, *Butlin story*, p. 187.

112 'Why Butlin's bought two hotels in the West Indies', *Caterer and Hotel Keeper*, 15 July 1949, p. 36.

113 The population of Grand Bahama in 1949 was approximately 500.

114 L. Blair, 'The Butlin holiday villages', in L. Blair, ed. *Butlin holiday book, 1949–50* (London, 1949), p. 46.

115 Ibid.

116 Butlin with Dacre, *Butlin story*, p. 188.

117 Howson, *British monetary policy*, pp. 238–58, Butlin with Dacre, *Butlin story*, p. 189.

118 Ibid., p. 190.

119 The islands were under British rule from 1717 to 1945.

120 Butlin with Dacre, *Butlin story*, pp. 188–9.

121 M. Grant, '"Working for the yankee dollar": Tourism and the Festival of Britain as stimuli for recovery', *British Journal of Studies*, 45 (July 2006) pp. 581–601.

122 Butlin with Dacre, *Butlin story*, p. 190.

123 M. White, e-mail correspondence with author, 24 August 2006.

124 M. White, e-mail correspondence with author, 21 September 2006.

125 M. White, e-mail correspondence with author, 24 August 2006.

126 V. Jenkins in *Secret lives.*

127 Butlin with Dacre, *Butlin story*, p. 191.

128 'Butlin's camp in Bahamas: more capital or …' *World's Fair*, 23 September 1950, p. 11.

129 R. Mason in *Secret lives.*

130 R. Mason in *Secret lives.*

131 Butlin with Dacre, *Butlin story*, p. 194.

132 'Changes on board of Butlin's', *Caterer and Hotel Keeper*, 16 September 1949, p. 25.

133 'Butlin's bookings up this year: popularity of holiday camps', *Caterer and Hotel Keeper*, 21 July 1951, p. 23.

134 'Butlin camps have more visitors but less profit', *Caterer and Hotel Keeper*, 19 July 1952, p. 34.

135 'Butlin's Ocean Hotel opened: Bishop conducts dedication service', *World's Fair*, 9 May 1953, p. 1.

136 In 1950, total revenues from overseas visitors were £81 million, £16 million more that the year before. 'Tourism once more Britain's chief dollar-earner', *Caterer and Hotel Keeper*, 23 June 1951, p. 25.

137 Editorial opinion, 'The ten million who stay at home', *Caterer and Hotel Keeper*, 15 March 1952, p. 19.

138 Editorial opinion, 'The holiday scene: New policy needed', *Caterer and Hotel*

Keeper, 9 August 1952, p. 17.

139   'Resort wants to be select – objection to juvenile rides and games', *World's Fair*, 3 November 1950, p. 1.

140   Hassan, *Seaside, health and the environment*, p. 134.

141   'How camping and caravanning affect hotels', *Caterer and Hotel Keeper*, 23 October 1954, p. 39.

142   In 1951 the population of Hayling Island was 7,147; in 1971, 13,170.

143   Havant and Waterloo Area Development Sub-Committee of Havant County Council (hereafter Sub-Committee) 31 March 1958, HRO 15M74/DDC 140.

144   Application 1570/2, Sub-Committee, 31 March 1958, HRO 15M74/DDC 140.

145   Application 888/1, Sub-Committee, 31 March 1958, HRO 15M74/DDC 140.

146   Warner's Holiday Camps Ltd to the Hayling Island Development Committee, 26 May 1954. Coronation Holiday Village, Hayling Island Holiday Camps Limited to the Hayling Island Development Committee, 25 May 1954. Sunshine Holiday Camp, Hayling Holidays Ltd, May 1954, HRO 15M74/DDC 247.

147   Application 3305/2, Sub-Committee, 28 April 1958, HRO 15M74/DDC 140.

148   Application 4756/I, Sub-Committee, 24 February 1958, HRO 15M74/DDC 140.

149   Application 4842/4, Sub-Committee, 28 February 1958, HRO 15M74/DDC 140.

150   Application 4990/1 and 4990/2, Sub-Committee, 27 January 1958, HRO 15M74/DDC 140.

151   'Caterer surveys the holiday season prospects', *Caterer and Hotel Keeper*, 15 May 1954, pp. 31–49.

152   'Hotels the Cinderella of Whitehall: bold comments in the B.T.H.A.', *Caterer and Hotel Keeper*, 24 July, 1954, pp. 19–20.

Planned pleasure, labour shortages and consumer resistance in the 1950s and 1960s

Despite what seemed to be a promising untapped market in the postwar years, Britain's domestic tourist industries had a hard time exploiting the potential because of outdated, class-based facilities, persistent labour problems, and consumer resistance. While full employment and the extension of paid leisure time increased the demand for holiday accommodation in the mid 1950s, it also created difficulties for the domestic tourism industry, which failed to provide inexpensive lodging or attract employees willing to work unsocial hours for low wages. The problems associated with labour shortages meant that the domestic industry was slow to make the changes necessary to create an enticing and affordable holiday package for the untapped market of working-class consumers. The industry blamed consumers for their unwillingness to alter holiday habits and enjoy what was offered in the traditional resorts. Yet consumer resistance was in part the fault of an industry that misjudged the needs and desires of its target market – working-class consumers. While businesses tried to alleviate the labour shortage and revitalise domestic tourism, consumers created their own low-cost holidays in tents and caravans, or travelled abroad.

Holiday camps, on the other hand, offered affordable planned pleasure in facilities that showcased popular bands and entertainers and featured promising new talent. The opportunity to pursue an entertainment career prompted some guests to seek employment as camp performers. The camps also attracted students with lengthy summer holidays as willing seasonal workers. Lured by the inclusive bed and board at the camps as well as by the perceived opportunity for sexual adventure, students accepted low wages and the long hours entertaining guests and themselves.

Although the planned and unplanned pleasure available in the mass holiday camps attracted a loyal following of holiday makers and seasonal staff, by the late 1970s even Butlin's camps were failing to lure potential campers away from cheap foreign package holidays. This chapter explores the way that holiday entrepreneurs and the British tourist industry attempted to plan pleasure and deal with labour shortages in order to overcome consumer resistance in the 1950s and 1960s.

Planned pleasure

By mid 1955, the demand for holiday destinations in Britain had increased, with full employment and the provision of paid holidays for workers. Yet critics constantly complained about the dearth of affordable holiday resorts for the expanded market. Sir William Holford, architect and past president of the Town Planning Institute, claimed that the facilities in Britain's resorts were a carry-over from the nineteenth century. What Britain needed in the second half of the twentieth century, Holford argued, was planned 'holiday districts' that would cater for all classes and all tastes. These districts would be designed around existing resorts and include 'the historic town and village, the crowded seaside resort, the stretch of country, the conference centre, the holiday camp, camping sites and a range of country houses and gardens'. In fact, the resort of the future would meet the needs of all categories of holiday makers.[1]

Holford envisioned a new generation of planned pleasure districts for all Britons that mirrored postwar town planning. The physical reconstruction of Britain required immediate action to rehouse the millions of homeless Britons.[2] At the same time, town planners strove to rebuild the nation with meaningful markers of a new society based on the policies of 'social balance'.[3] This was not, however, social equality. Rather, the policies of social balance sought to 'bridge class cleavages within British society by encouraging members of the different classes to live close together'.[4] Holford's plan for holiday districts extended these policies to include leisure. Resorts would create centres where different classes of tourists could enjoy various types of leisure side by side but not actually together, reflecting postwar politics. In the 'new' Britain, separate, class-specific resorts of the past would give way to the democratic pleasure centres of the twentieth century.

Holford also believed that a shortage of available holiday venues was cramping the development of domestic tourism. The industry, on the other hand, blamed overcrowding on consumer rigidity, particularly the stubborn commitment to holidays in July and August. The domestic industry lobbied endlessly for a change in public policy and the public perception of alternative holiday periods. The campaign to stagger holidays begun in the interwar years grew as supporters argued that the success of wakes weeks proved that staggering holidays for different industries could relieve resort congestion without decreasing workers' pleasure. With the nationalisation of key industries in the 1940s and early 1950s, the tourist industry hoped that the state would also intervene and direct the timing of workers' pleasure. Sympathetic MPs debated the 'peak holiday' problem in the House of Commons, while tourist associations lobbied local authorities and the Board of Education for a change in the timing of school examinations and holidays to help facilitate staggered holidays.[5] When the Board of Education remained firm and refused to alter the schedule of external examinations, the state-funded British Travel and Holiday Association (BTHA) convened a conference to discuss alternative solutions.[6]

The consumer response to the criticism meted out by the industry was to continue to go to crowded resorts during July and August.[7] Workers did not want to holiday outside the peak holiday months, claimed Mr H. Baker, a member of the Birmingham Trades Council, because they feared that the facilities would be inferior and the number of holiday makers less than at the peak of the season. Mr Swinnerton, another consumer representative, put it this way. 'No girl', he declared, 'is going to walk along the [sea] front wearing a little hat saying "Kiss me" if there is no-one there to kiss her'. Working-class people, he argued, 'delight in having plenty of noise and plenty of company'. In fact, Swinnerton claimed, working people would not go to the seaside resorts unless they could be sure that 'there was the company of their own types and friends there'.[8] In other words, while overcrowding was a problem for the catering industry, it was not necessarily one for holiday makers.

Yet resort congestion in Britain did persuade some companies to organise foreign travel alternatives. By 1954 the coal industry was encouraging miners and their families to take holidays abroad and offering a weekly payment plan. Colliery offices distributed leaflets that described tours, explained passport formalities and foreign currencies, and turned the pithead into a small travel agency. The scheme appalled British resorts, which expected to meet the holiday needs of nationalised industries. They felt betrayed by unions that encouraged members to spend money abroad as well as by a Conservative government that failed to stop the out-going flow of consumer cash.[9] One exasperated resort spokesperson claimed that the scheme constituted a very real threat to countless seaside towns. Many resorts relied on working families who returned to the same place for their holidays year after year. Should the idea spread to other major industries, it would be a catastrophe for these resorts. British workers, claimed the spokesman, needed to understand the impact of their decision to holiday abroad on their fellow countrymen.[10]

Despite the perceived threat to the domestic industry even the BTHA encouraged foreign travel as a way to avoid congested British resorts. In a speech to the industry, the director general, Mr J. G. Bridges, stressed that foreign travel could solve the problem of overcrowded British resorts in July and August. At the same time, Bridges also criticised British resorts for not meeting the needs and desires of holiday makers. If consumers resisted staying at domestic resorts, Bridges claimed, it was because the industry failed to provide attractive and reasonably priced accommodation.[11]

Indeed, the lack of inexpensive holiday destinations was a significant problem. Wages increased in real terms in the 1950s, but the affluence of workers was regional and patchy. The cost of a week's holiday was still out of reach for many Britons.[12] No longer considered a luxury in postwar Britain, holidays for all were deemed an essential aspect of workers' welfare.[13] Hotels lacked experience in catering for the masses and were fast losing the market and any governmental support. By contrast, the holiday-camp industry's willing-ness and ability to provide inexpensive holidays to large numbers of workers garnered state support. Although hoteliers perceived the issue to be one of unfair competition, the problems were compounded by postwar politics and economies of scale. Small private hotels were unable to provide inexpensively for hundreds of workers. Holiday camps, on the other hand, offered affordable and all-inclusive holidays for thousands of consumers.

Holiday camps were also able to break down resistance by connecting with consumers outside the holiday season in a way that hotels did not. Campers could purchase camp souvenirs, including books like *Tommy Handley in Holidayland*, a slapstick comedy starring the popular comedian himself or *The Spotlight on your Holiday Memories*, the official camp souvenir, or even Beauty at Butlin's with ample pictures of the Arthur Ferrier 'pin-up girls'.[14] These were all available at the camp shop. Then, in 1949, the first annual *Butlin Holiday Book* was marketed to former and potential guests. The holiday book included articles about Butlin and the organisation, plenty of photographs of camp activities, as well as a short history of each camp. Former and prospective campers were introduced to, and made familiar with, details of camp layouts and activities as a way to promote a connection to the leisure empire.[15] The book included short stories to appeal to all age groups, as well as quizzes,

The Butlin Holiday Book, 1949–50

competitions and fancy-dress ideas to help guests prepare in advance for camp activities. The musical scores of several 'Butlin Buddies' songs meant that the entire family could learn the lyrics and join in the community singing that was such an integral part of the holiday-camp experience. Knitting patterns, recipes, and beauty tips were designed to appeal to mothers and young women, while the sporting news was directed at male readers. The holiday book emphasised the family-centred nature of the camps and offered tips about when and how to book a holiday at Skegness, Filey, Clacton, Pwllheli, Ayr, or Mosney.

The holiday books detailed the layouts of the camps and their surrounding locales thus promoting the unique experience available at each individual camp.[16] Photographs and articles highlighted distinguished guests, such as the Duke of Edinburgh talking to a group of children, Herbert Morrison, MP, arm-in-arm with smiling campers, Anthony Eden, MP, signing autographs, Laurel and Hardy delighting campers with their antics, comedian Tommy Trinder relaxing with a group of holiday makers, or heavyweight boxing champion Lee Savold entertaining children.[17] The pictures advertised the camps as exciting places to holiday, but they also promoted them as a social space where even royalty and members of the government felt at home. It was a truly British experience, shared by all levels of society. For veteran campers, the annual books extended the experience far beyond the holiday week. For those who had never set foot in a camp, the books offered a glimpse of camp culture.

Butlin's holiday books were a way to advertise the growing number of Butlin Social Clubs around Britain. The clubs were a postwar phenomenon with roots in the interwar years, when campers had requested a 'winter' club. In addition to the annual camp reunions, the clubs were re-established in 1946 at the request of campers. Fifteen thousand guests enrolled immediately. The clubs were located closer to home and extended camp activities and culture outside the holiday week. By 1948 there were over 50,000 members in a hundred clubs all over Britain.[18] Social clubs, like the holiday books, functioned in several ways: they continued the camp experience closer to home, they served to continue friendships begun at the camps, they promoted brand consciousness, and they advertised camp culture to potential guests in a way that hotels and boarding houses could not.

Holiday camps also recognised the growing of consumer power of Britain's youth. Youthful campers were encouraged to enrol in Wagtail, Beaver, or One-Five Clubs while on holiday at Warner's or Butlin's camps. Membership continued throughout the year through birthday gifts and Christmas annuals that, like the holiday books, contained stories, activities, games, and puzzles to encourage young readers to remember their camp experiences and the staff who had worked to make their holidays so memorable.[19] Holiday painting books as well as *Bunty and Billy at Butlin's* illustrated story books were available for purchase at the camp shop as souvenirs replete with pictures of all the children's activities.[20]

By marketing specifically to young consumers, holiday-camp annuals contributed to the emerging pop culture. An article by teen idol Cliff Richard told readers 'how to' become a pop star. Richard, a former entertainer at Butlin's Clacton camp, claimed that all anyone needed to become a pop star was a 'Big Break'.[21] Richard didn't actually get his big break at Butlins. Butlin had thought Richard was 'a good-looking boy' but didn't like the way he sang and eventually fired him because the managers complained that he 'killed all the business'. The holiday-camp guests listened to the music and didn't buy drinks. A couple of years later, 21–year-old Richard, the 'boy' who Butlin thought 'would never make it', was awarded the Variety Club of Great Britain's top entertainment award.[22]

Other entertainers, like Des O'Connor, did get their 'big break' at Butlin's. A former guest, O'Connor caught Butlin's attention when he won most of the sporting events as well as the talent contest. Butlin was so impressed that he offered O'Connor a job as an entertainer. This, claimed O'Connor, was his first break in show business. 'Mind you', he told readers of the *Beaver Annual*, 'lots of other entertainers have started their careers at Butlin's.' These celebrities included 'Charlie Drake, Russ Hammilton, Clinton Ford, Jimmy Tarbuck and yes, Ringo Starr played drums for a group at Butlin's for three seasons before joining the Beatles'.[23] Thus, according to O'Connor, the musical and comedy culture developed at holiday camps produced celebrity and shaped a popular national culture, and campers were part of the whole process.

The annuals also offered a sense of national pride and community conscience through stories of war heroes like Leonard Cheshire, who opened rehabilitation homes for wounded veterans after the war.[24] Readers were encouraged to contact the nearest Cheshire Home and organise fundraising activities. 'But above all', the article concluded, 'think of other people ... particularly anyone who is ill or sick. Just a letter or a word from you might make all the difference' and brighten their lives.[25] Requests like this offered young campers the opportunity to become caring and integrated members of society and positioned holiday camps as promoting social decency.

While it is unclear whether the holiday book and annual readers responded to the dominant messages, the holiday-camp industry in Britain flourished.

Campers at Butlin's camp, Clacton, c. 1948   **29**

Fifty thousand campers went to Butlin's camps each week and over a thousand guests to his four hotels.[26] More expensive than the camps, the Butlin hotels included many of the holiday-camp activities and entertainments, and so the holiday books and annuals continued to appeal to hotel guests as well as to campers. Warner also extended his leisure empire, and opened several new camps and the luxury Sinah Warren Hotel on Hayling Island.[27] Warner claimed that the catering and accommodation standards at Sinah Warren surpassed those of his holiday camps, to attract a higher class of guest.[28] Warner's new hotel represented a successful incursion into the more traditional hotel market. As Butlin and Warner ventured into the hotel industry, others, most notably Fred Pontin, continued to develop more mass holiday camps along Britain's coast.[29]

Labour shortages

As the holiday-camp industry prospered and expanded, hoteliers feared the competition for seasonal workers as well as for guests. How would small hotels and boarding-houses attract chambermaids and waitresses when they were lured to Butlin's by the 'excitement of camp life?'[30] Employees and their families could use the same facilities as the campers on days off – the fairground rides, swimming pools, theatres, and dancehalls. In addition, camp employees were encouraged to mingle with guests after work hours or, if part of the entertainment staff, during working hours. These 'perks' kept wages low but gave many employees the opportunity to socialise and enjoy quality entertainment at no cost. These added attractions, hoteliers feared, would lure young women looking for fun and relationships away from hotel work.

In truth, the single, young, unskilled women historically employed in hotels were no longer willing to work long hours for low wages. The postwar expansion of other industries with higher-paying jobs meant that hotels were deprived of their former labour pool.[31] Although the Catering Wages Act (1943) regulated wages and raised the prestige of hotel work, labour shortages became more acute in the 1950s.[32] An editorial in the *Caterer and Hotel Keeper* claimed that the industry was at an enormous disadvantage when competing with other businesses for available labour because 'no other industry … asks from its workers the same toll of long, inconvenient hours, with its most exacting demands at the very times when the rest of the world is enjoying its leisure'.[33] Unlike workers at a holiday camp, where employees were encouraged to join in the activities with guests, hotel workers maintained a distance from guests and were discouraged from using facilities even in off-duty hours. The clear separation of work and pleasure, in addition to low wages, contributed to the shortage of hotel workers.

One former hotelier creatively suggested a solution to the problem – a self-service hotel where guests looked after themselves. The 'Seltels', as Mr J. E. Cracknell named his proposal, would require only a small workforce. 'Under my plan', claimed Cracknell, hoteliers would offer rooms, 'the use of the kitchen, dining room and other amenities to guests but provide absolutely no service'. Seltels, estimated Cracknell, could reduce hotel wages by 75 per cent and dispense with the need for 'difficult-to-obtain, expensive-to-hire staff'.[34]

Another solution to the staff shortage was to import workers from the British colonies.[35] The 1948 British Nationality Act granted the right of citizenship to all members of the British Empire.[36] This meant, in theory at least, that Empire workers could find employment in Britain. In practice, however, postwar housing shortages created problems for immigrant workers who faced racial bars and competed, often unsuccessfully, with British-born citizens for apartments and rooms.[37] Hotels needed live-in staff to deal with the unexpected demands of guests at any hour of the day or night. Hoteliers were able to offer accommodation as an integral part of the job and as a subsidy for low wages.

At the height of the tourist season in August 1955, an article in the *Caterer and Hotel Keeper* revealed a plan to recruit workers from Barbados, because, claimed the author, Barbadians were 'particularly suitable' for hotel work in Britain. Further, workers from Barbados are 'hard working and reliable, and are taught English in government controlled schools'. Two hundred house-maids, chambermaids, kitchen porters, pantry-men and handymen between the ages of 21 and 40 years were on their way. All the workers had received a medical examination and the government of Barbados had advanced their fare to Britain and thus assumed any risk. If the project proved successful, the government of Barbados planned to train waiters and cooks as needed for export to Britain.[38] The first thirty-one hotel workers from Barbados arrived in Britain on 2 October 1955. The *Caterer and Hotel Keeper* celebrated their arrival with a photograph and claimed that the project was a 'valuable step towards easing the crippling shortage of staff' in British hotels. The workers, expected to stay a year, took the lowest-paid, unskilled jobs in the industry and lived in the hotels.[39]

Despite the welcome given to this group of willing workers, some potential guests experienced racial discrimination. In 1958 the manager of the Goring Hotel in London asked three African women with reservations to find alter-native accommodation.[40] A few months later, Mr Bola Ogun, a Nigerian law student, threatened to take civil action against three Huddersfield hotels that had refused to accommodate him and his 'lady friend' because of the colour of his skin.[41] Empowered by the 1958 anti-discrimination legislation making it 'illegal to refuse admission to hotels, restaurants, dance-halls and similar establishments on the grounds of colour, race or religion', Ogun claimed that when he and Miss Maureen Head, a white Briton, had requested separate rooms at several hotels they had been refused because he was black. Both were then forced to spend the night together in a waiting room at Huddersfield railway station.[42]

The accused hotels argued that accommodation was refused not because of the colour of Ogun's skin, but because the couple had arrived late at night without luggage, a circumstance that suggested a relationship other than friend-ship. In other words, Ogun and Head were refused accommodation, even in separate rooms, because the hotels believed Head was a prostitute. Why else would a white woman seek a hotel room with a Nigerian? The Huddersfield and District Licensed Victuallers' Association supported the hotels, claiming that Ogun's requests for accommodation were 'of such a nature, and made in such circumstances' that they would have been refused by any respectable establishment.[43]

A television documentary revealed that racial prejudice in hotels was widespread, despite fervent denials by the governing bodies of the industry. An African telephoned twenty-five London hotels and was told by fourteen that there was no room. Ten minutes later, an Englishman called same fourteen and was offered accommodation by ten.[44] When the BTHA declared itself unable to police discrimination in hotels, the National Council for Civil Liberties issued a statement deploring the 'complete lack of leadership on this evil of colour bar and race discrimination' within the hotel industry.[45] Despite the 1958 legislation, the industry's governing bodies continued to support an informal colour bar.

Indeed, the colour bar issue also had an impact on the Barbados hotel worker scheme. The experiment faltered after the first thousand workers arrived in Britain because, hoteliers claimed, the workers were 'unreliable' and left hotel work when offered better wages elsewhere. Hoteliers then cancelled requests for West Indian labour.[46] In 1950s Britain West Indian immigrants often faced homelessness because of racial prejudice.[47] Despite this claim, therefore, even if offered higher wages, workers from Barbados were less likely than other hotel workers to leave employment that included accommodation,. The attitude of the hoteliers and the cessation of the Barbados project was thus more likely a reflection of growing racial intolerance during the late 1950s. Although the number of West Indian immigrants to Britain was relatively few, the perception, fed by the press, was of considerably more. Journalists represented the migrants as a threat, 'often regurgitating urban myths about drugging and abducting young [white] women'.[48] A 'West Indian immigrant problem' entered public discourse as politicians blamed housing shortages on competition from immigrant workers. By 1958, the Notting Hill Riots, stoked up by press reports and decolonisation, illustrated the pent-up racial tensions within Britain.[49] The equation of whiteness with Britishness was not new, but by the mid 1950s it had assumed a new salience, and the hotel industry adopted racialised practices that excluded non-white workers and, sometimes, non-white guests.

Unlike hotels, holiday camps were able to avoid negative press about racial discrimination because they attracted a largely white, lower-middle and working-class clientele, and because bookings were taken by phone or in writing, not face to face as in hotels. Nevertheless, employees were closely vetted, especially female applicants, who were required to enclose a photograph with their application. This, claimed one manager, was to 'ensure a selection of attractive types of girls who will be pleasing to the eyes of the holiday-makers as well as helpful in their needs'.[50] Although all employees were encouraged to fraternise with campers, women were recruited for jobs that involved close contact with guests at the reception desk, as waitresses at meal times, barmaids, cashiers, and chambermaids. Men, on the other hand, were employed as porters, chefs, and cooks, all behind the scenes and often not directly in contact with the guests during working hours. Thus the gendered division of labour in holiday camps meant that women applicants underwent greater scrutiny and experienced greater discrimination in employment.

Yet the labour shortage did affect the growing number of holiday camps in Britain. The camps required large numbers of seasonal workers to meet the needs of campers from Easter until mid October. Like the Seltel idea, some camp owners experimented with self-catering options at their camps, which reduced the cost of the holiday and the need for so many staff. Others noted that the length of the season coincided with the university summer break. Many students – the great majority of whom were middle and upper class and white – looked for seasonal work. All camp employees were given the option of accommodation and full board and, unlike in hotel work, were encouraged to mix freely with the guests and enjoy all the camp amenities and entertainment when off duty. Work at holiday camps appealed to many students as a way to make money, live independently, and have fun at the same time.[51]

The 'perks' of the job often encouraged students and other potential employees to apply for work at the camps but they also kept wages low. One former camp employee, William Stewart, remembers the manager describing the duties of his job as a Redcoat. Stewart then complained about the weekly wages. The manager turned to Stewart and replied, 'You didn't come for the money did you? You came for the girls.' Stewart, a little taken aback, realised that the manager was partly right. One of the reasons Stewart had chosen to work in the camp was the sexual opportunities reportedly awaiting employees and guests alike.[52]

According to Rocky Mason, a former Butlin's camp manager, the opportunities were legendary, so much so that the male Redcoats employed a points system to determine the 'shagger' of the week. Every Friday evening, as guests received prizes for week's competitions, the Redcoat who had scored the largest number of points for having sex with female guests (five points), the winner of the beauty contest (ten points), or the general manager's wife (fifteen points), received a ram's-head trophy.[53] The proof of sexual conquests, former Redcoat Peter Everet explained, came from the number of women's knickers taken back to the Redcoats.[54] Female employees also enjoyed some of the same perks. According to Butlin's nephew Vernon Jenkins, many of the waitresses were prostitutes and used their position to ply their trade and supplement the meagre wages.[55] This gave a new meaning to fraternising with the guests.

Yet the guests enjoyed the informality, especially the novelty, of subverting the British class system. While many of the seasonal staff were university students from the educated middle and upper classes, most of the guests came from a lower-middle and working-class background. Provision of services by the students thus turned the traditional class system upside down. Lower-class guests experienced the novelty of having their meals served and their chalets cleaned by people who belonged to the same class as their employers.

However, the class mix among employees created conflicts and a high turnover of staff. University students were most often employed as Redcoat entertainers, whose jobs were perceived by other members of staff as less demanding. 'A. J.' Marriott worked at Butlin's for seventeen seasons and claims that the total number of staff at Skegness the first year was approximately 2,000. During the first ten weeks of the season the turnover rate was 100 per cent. This changed when the waiters went on strike. 'The Redcoats had to do all their normal details and then serve meals at two sittings. It nearly killed us,' Marriott recalls. The waiters returned to work after two days with a new appreciation of the Redcoats. 'Up till then', Marriott claims, 'they'd resented the Redcoats as just a bunch of posers who walked around doing nothing but cadging fags [cigarettes] and drinks off the guests. When they saw that we could do our jobs and THEIRS as well … we had a lot more respect from them.'[56]

As mass holiday camps required more employees than did hotels to function smoothly, staff conflicts and high staff turnover exacerbated labour shortages. Nevertheless, guests appeared not to notice and even eagerly coveted jobs as camp comedian or as part of the entertainment staff. Former guest Des O'Connor saw work at Butlin's as a way to practise his comedy routine in front of a mixed audience and as a means to get into professional show business. O'Connor, a successful comedian and television host, began work at Filey in 1953.[57] During the day he organised games and competitions; in the evening he danced with guests. On Friday evening the Redcoats performed a revue that often drew national talent scouts. It was as a comedian one Friday evening that O'Connor landed a job at the Palace Theatre in Newcastle-upon-Tyne. Within ten years, he was a major television star with his own show.[58]

'A. J.' Marriott couldn't 'resist the lure of that red coat' either. Marriott was a guest at Butlin's Filey twice, when aged 12 and 16. He returned to Filey as an adult a few years later and was interviewed for a job at Skegness the following year. Marriott worked for two seasons as a Redcoat at Skegness and was then offered a job at Butlin's Metropole Hotel in Blackpool where he worked all year round.[59] Marriott maintains that the 'Redcoats worked pretty well like collie dogs. They herded the guests into the dining room, herded them out onto the sports field; into the dining room, to the swimming pool, into the theatres, into the ballroom and the bars.' Yet the atmosphere generated friendships and, Marriott claims, everyone got to know one another, as the same families came to each event. At the end of the week, campers went home 'with a list of names and addresses, and plans to meet up again the following year'.[60]

Marriott remembers the guests and his experience at Butlin's as an unrivalled opportunity to build a career as a comedian. 'Between the races in the Cine Race films, when people were placing bets', Marriott recalls, he 'would get on the mike and do gags'. The eager comedian stole time 'during bingo sales, Donkey Derby and any other events where a mike was available'. Without these stolen moments, Marriott claims, his time as an entertainer would 'have been limited to an eight-minute solo comedy slot in the Redcoat Show' every other week, because it was the camp host who controlled access to the microphone. The camp host during Marriott's first Filey season was a struggling comic who 'resented anyone else getting on the mike', especially Marriott. The following year that host didn't return, and when his replacement walked off the job, Marriott eagerly took the coveted position and the microphone.[61]

Overcoming the British weather and consumer resistance

Holiday camps were able to attract new talent like Marriot and O'Connor inexpensively, as part of the camp entertainment staff, while traditional resorts relied on well-known and highly paid performers to attract holiday makers to their area. Unlike the multiple nightly concerts, shows, and routines at the mass holiday camps, traditional resorts often had a limited number of venues for expensive, quality performances that might not appeal to all guests. In 1956, a Southwick resident complained bitterly that his holiday in Bournemouth had been ruined by a lack of something to do after 10 p.m., by the licensing laws that prevented the consumption of alcohol after 11 p.m., and by the rigid hotel dining times that dictated his entire holiday schedule. In addition, he claimed, Bournemouth was full of 'pseudo American-style' entertainment that had little appeal to holiday makers like him. If things did not change, he maintained, more Britons would holiday abroad.[62] A response from a spokesman for the Association of Resort Publicity Officers pointed out the increasing number of foreign visitors to Britain and suggested that if the Southwick resident took the time to explore his own country, he would find the 'forgotten treasures' that attracted foreign visitors. Surely, concluded the spokesman, the appreciation

Butlin's Continental Holiday brochure, 1957

of Britain's beauty should come before the 'importance of obtaining another drink after 11pm'.[63]

Although more foreign guests visited Britain in the 1950s, an increasing number of British holiday makers chose foreign destinations and the certainty of warm weather. Unable to control the deleterious effects of a sunless season, the tourist industry claimed that the BBC exacerbated the issue. The daily BBC weather bulletins, according to hoteliers, had a detrimental effect on their industry. Every evening, hoteliers complained, the BBC used 'propaganda' against the industry when the weather forecast was broadcast. The weather bulletins exercised enormous influence on tourists and dictated their movements. If the BBC predicted bad weather, holiday makers simply stayed at home.[64] As if that was not bad enough, claimed hoteliers, the BBC's 'Holiday Hour' described foreign destinations and encouraged Britons to holiday abroad.[65] Despite claims by the BBC that 'Holiday Hour' discussed holiday destinations both at home and abroad, hoteliers insisted that the programme was detrimental to the domestic industry.[66]

Others recognised the desire of Britons to travel abroad in search of more predictable weather as a business opportunity. In 1952, Butlin announced his plans to establish a holiday camp in Switzerland for British tourists. This project, conceived shortly after the debacle in the Bahamas, required no investment of sterling. The campsites of twenty and thirty chalets at 'favourite Swiss beauty spots', were planned to open in time for the 1952 winter sports season. Butlin reasoned that selling winter holidays would extend the British holiday season and his company's profits. If the venture was successful, Butlin planned to expand the project throughout Europe.[67] It was, and the following year Butlin's Continental Holidays offered British tourists all-inclusive tours by bus and accommodation in a variety of European resorts, towns and cities – in Belgium, France, Spain, Italy, and Switzerland. The company also organised independent holidays in Rome, Palma (Majorca), Nice, Interlaken, Lucerne, and Venice for a price that included the cost of travel by train or air.[68] Another holiday-camp entrepreneur, Fred Pontin, followed Butlin's lead and created Pontinental Holidays in 1962. He opened the Pineta Beach Hotel in Sardinia as the company's the first all-inclusive foreign package holiday.[69]

Despite the success of these foreign ventures, the holiday-camp industry looked for more domestic opportunities for growth. In 1958 Butlin met the Duke of Bedford to discuss building an inland camp on the grounds of Woburn Abbey. Despite support from the Duke the trustees, of his estate were so horrified by the idea that Butlin withdrew.[70] Plans to build a coastal camp at Bognor

Regis also met with stiff opposition from council members and local hoteliers, who claimed that Butlin's would detract from the quiet family character of the town and result in losses for local hoteliers and boarding houses. Opponents claimed they did not object to 'the type of person who resorts to Butlin's', rather, they wanted to retain the patronage of the 'type of person' who presently enjoyed the quiet town.[71] Thus, despite the official postwar politics of 'social balance', critics in Bognor feared a Butlin's holiday camp would mark the locale as a working-class resort and deter their middle-class consumers.[72]

In spite of the vocal criticism, 1960 proved a very profitable year for the holiday-camp industry. That year a total of over two million guests stayed at Butlin's and Pontin's holiday camps, and a further half a million holidayed at Warner's and other smaller camps throughout Britain.[73] Increased demand and profits continued, so that Warner's shareholders received a dividend of 15 per cent in 1961.[74] The same year Butlin's profits increased, as did bookings at all his camps.[75] An aggressive advertising campaign in two weekly journals, the *Illustrated* and *Blighty Parade* paid off. The adverts were in colour and showcased photographs of campers during activities and amusements, with the claim that 'Butlin's is better than ever', and 'a holiday at Butlin's brings colour into your life'.[76] Butlin needed more accommodation. Plans to build a holiday camp in Minehead, on the edge of Exmoor National Park, to accommodate 5,000 alarmed some local residents. However, when polled, the majority of rate payers believed the holiday camp would increase the tourist trade for the

BUTLIN'S
Typical Children's Playroom

31   A typical children's playroom at a Butlin camp, c. 1962

town and benefit local businesses.[77] A few weeks later Pontin announced an annual dividend of 35 per cent to shareholders, emphasising the potential profits from the lucrative and popular domestic industry.[78]

The success of British holiday camps, according to Arthur Eperon of the

Butlin's advert for a camp holiday to meet other single adults, c. 1950s   **32**

Sun, was their ability to 'defeat the British climate' and ensure exciting and interesting activities, whatever the weather. A holiday at a British camp was the best value for money because few resorts could provide the same quality and quantity of entertainment, claimed Eperon. 'There are at least three theatres working nightly – revue, variety, and repertory', and guests simply 'walk in without paying ... walk out to a bar or to [their] own bed', without the worry of parking, driving, or catching a train. The theatres 'draw top stars but ... also give a break to newcomers'. Although the mass activities might not appeal to everyone, holiday camps were great for families with small children. Nurseries, playrooms, infant feeding and childcare all for 'around £12–£14 a week' made holidays affordable for the average working man and his family, whatever the weather.[79]

Indeed, the first year that Wendy Kilshaw and her family went to Butlin's, in 1964, it rained all week long. It didn't matter. 'Everyone loved [the camp] because there was so much to do,' remembers Wendy. She and her brother enjoyed the activities, the jokes, and the competitions. They especially liked the talent shows. 'Of course, we never thought the right people won,' Wendy recalls. Although the meals were at set hours, the meal-time entertainment and competitions made them seem like just another exciting activity. The inexpensive camp holiday cost far less than a holiday abroad, although more than a boarding house. Looking back on the experience, Wendy claims to have 'only good memories', so much so that when she had children of her own the family often went to Butlin's Minehead camp.[80]

For Butlin, Warner, and Pontin, returning campers like Wendy Kilshaw and her family were key to the success of the holiday-camp industry. Yet throughout the 1960s British holiday camps subtly changed. To meet a growing demand for increased 'luxury', Warner and Butlin introduced a graded system of accommodation and service into their camps in the early 1960s. Guests could choose the class of accommodation that best fitted their needs and their wallets. Abandoning the ethos of the interwar years that promised each camper uniform service and accommodation, British holiday camps offered full-board, half-board, self-catering, and 'gold star' chalets. All entertainment and activities, however, remained open to guests on an equal basis. Indeed, the quality and quantity of entertainment remained emblematic of the mass camp appeal.

Yet by the 1960s, some of the appeal of a holiday camp was the virtual guarantee of a sexual experience. Rocky Mason claims that 'sex' became an open selling point in Butlin's advertising. Butlin marketed aggressively to the new teenage market, with the result that many teenagers came to holiday in groups without their parents. Mason remembers carefully ensuring that there were equal numbers of single young women and men and that all their chalets were in one part of the camp, known, appropriately enough, as 'dodge city'. The advertisements made it clear that sexual adventures were available at the camps, and many guests came for that reason.[81] By the mid 1960s, then, the anxieties voiced by pre-war critics appeared fully justified as the 'sexual revolution' altered attitudes and behaviours.

The perception of a guaranteed sexual experience at a camp holiday may well have contributed to their continued success. In an interview at the beginning of 1965, both Butlin and Pontin expected increased profits in the coming season and both men planned to expand their leisure empires.[82] Butlin intended to open two new camps – one at Barry Island in South Wales, the other in Weymouth, and to double the accommodation in his camps because the demand was so great. 'People would go without paying the butcher, the baker and the candlestick maker rather than tell their kids that they were not going on holiday,' Butlin claimed. He decided to concentrate his efforts so as to meet the needs of the twenty-seven million people who stayed in Britain for their holidays, as opposed to the four million who chose holidays abroad. Pontin, on the other hand, focused his company's expansion on the foreign holiday market. 'Holidays have become a habit' for Britons, claimed Pontin, and so we can expand 'indefinitely' because packaged pleasure is here to stay.[83]

Conclusion

Indeed, Pontin was right. Holidays had become a habit for most Britons by the mid 1960s. Many consumers enjoyed all-inclusive holidays, increasingly abroad. Nevertheless, holiday camps in Britain remained profitable until the 1970s because they met the specific needs of a section of the domestic market and because the industry adapted its product when those desires changed. The introduction of half-board and self-catering options gave guests greater control over their meal times and budgets, while talent shows offered campers the opportunity for 'stardom' and even camp employment.

Yet by 1970, British holiday habits were changing dramatically. That year almost six million Britons holidayed abroad. Within ten years the number had doubled.[84] As the domestic tourism industry faced increased competition from foreign travel and the challenges of neo-liberalism in the 1980s, holiday camps were forced to reorganise and redevelop their sites as leisure centres and to appeal to a more corporate consumer. The Thatcherite reforms of major industries such as coal and steel all but destroyed the loyal consumer base of the mass holiday camps, while big leisure conglomerates like the Rank Organisation and Haven Leisure altered the Butlin and Warner camps so as to more accurately meet the desires of the 1980s consumer of pleasure. The holiday revolution promised and delivered by men like Warner and Butlin appeared to be at an end.

Notes

1 'Break with tradition for resorts? Planning expert looks to future', *Caterer and Hotel Keeper*, 14 May 1955, pp. 27–8.
2 Burnett, *Social history of housing*, ch. 10.
3 Catterall, 'The state of the literature', p. 221.
4 P. Dunleavy, *The politics of mass housing in Britain, 1945–1975: A study of corporate power and professional influence in the welfare state* (Oxford: Clarendon Press, 1981), p. 11, and A. Homer, 'Planned communities: the social objectives of the British New Towns, 1946–65', in L. Black, ed. *Consensus or coercion?: The state, the people and social cohesion in post-war Britain* (Cheltenham: New Clarion, 2001), pp. 125–35.
5 'Hotels the Cinderella of Whitehall', *Caterer and Hotel Keeper*, 24 July 1954, pp. 19, 45.
6 'Off-peak holidays fight reinforced: BTHA supported by holidaymakers', *Caterer and Hotel Keeper*, 6 November 1954, pp. 21–2.
7 'Millions pack the seaside resorts: Peak period rush greater than ever', *Caterer and Hotel Keeper*, 30 July 1955, pp. 19–20.
8 Ibid., p. 20.
9 'Holidays abroad', *World's Fair*, 9 October 1954, p. 27.
10 Ibid.
11 'Resorts spurred to attract the stay-at-home millions', *Caterer and Hotel Keeper*, 2 July 1955, p. 21.
12 K. Jeffreys, 'Social class, affluence and electoral politics, 1951–64', in S. James and V. Preston, eds *British politics since 1945: The dynamics of social change* (Houndmills, Basingstoke: Palgrave, 2001), pp. 51–76.
13 '21 nations plan holidays for millions', *Caterer and Hotel Keeper*, 16 June 1956, p. 23.
14 *Butlin's holiday pie*, 1946, p. 3.
15 Blair, ed. *Butlin holiday book, 1949–50*.
16 *Holiday time at Butlins, 1950–51*.
17 'Some famous visitors', in ibid., pp. 48–9.
18 C. F. Johnson, 'The story of the Butlin social clubs', in Blair, ed., *Butlin holiday book*, pp. 59–70.
19 *1962 Beaver annual*, N. Spain, ed. (London, 1962). Annuals first appeared in 1898, published by daily newspapers. P. Hunt, *Children's literature: An illustrated history* (Oxford: Oxford University Press, 1995), pp. 206–9.

20 *Butlin's holiday pie*, p. 3.

21 C. Richard, 'So you want to be a pop star', in Spain, ed. *1962 Beaver annual*, p. 46.

22 North, *Butlin story*, pp. 61–2.

23 D. O'Connor, 'Enjoy yourselves', in E. Blyton, ed. *Butlin Beaver annual*, No. 3, (London: Fairhaven Books, 1964), 24. See also B. Spitz, *The Beatles: the biography* (New York: Little, Brown and Company, 2005), pp. 323–7.

24 Cheshire led a successful bouncing bomb raid on three key dams in the Ruhr Valley in the Second World War. The raids were made famous by the *The Dam Busters*, 124 mins, Warner Brothers Picture Distribution, 1954.

25 N. Spain, 'Hero of today', in *Beaver annual*, No. 2, pp. 14–16.

26 Butlin opened two additional hotels in 1955. 'Butlin's Margate, opens May 7', *Caterer and Hotel Keeper*, 2 April 1955, p. 23, 'Butlin's take over Metropole, Blackpool', *Caterer and Hotel Keeper*, 9 April 1955, p. 25.

27 'Eccentric millionaire's home becomes new holiday centre', *Caterer and Hotel Keeper*, 14 June 1958, p. 41.

28 'Hayling Island holiday centre sold', *Caterer and Hotel Keeper*, 1 August 1959, p. 25.

29 By 1962, Pontin owned fifteen camps. F. Pontin with P. Willsher, *Sir Fred Pontin: My happy life always thumbs up!* (South Molton, Devon: Solo Books, 1991), p. 59.

30 'Excitement of holiday camp life will affect staffing, says Bognor', *Caterer and Hotel Keeper*, 5 October 1957, p. 37.

31 J. Giles, *The parlour and the suburb: Domestic identities, class, femininity and modernity* (Oxford: Berg, 2004), ch. 2, and L. Johnson and J. Lloyd, *Sentenced to everyday life: Feminism and the housewife* (Oxford: Berg, 2004), p. 24.

32 The Catering Wages Act, March 1943 (London: HMSO, 1944), Cmd. 6509.

33 Editorial opinion, 'Staff shortage: where is the solution?' *Caterer and Hotel Keeper*, 29 October 1955, p. 17.

34 'Now the "Do it yourself" hotel: hotelier's idea for cutting costs', *Caterer and Hotel Keeper*, 8 September 1956, p. 41.

35 M. Philips and T. Philips, *Windrush: The irresistible rise of multi-racial Britain* (London: Harper Collins, 1999).

36 K. Paul, 'From subjects to immigrants: Black Britons and national identity, 1948–62', in R. Weight and A. Beach, eds *The right to belong: Citizenship and national identity in Britain, 1930–1960* (London: I. B. Tauris, 1998), pp. 223–48.

37 M. Bowley, *Britain's housing shortage* (London: Oxford University Press, 1944), M. Dresser, 'The colour bar in Bristol, 1963', in R. Samuel, ed. *Patriotism: The making and unmaking of British national identity* (London: Routledge, 1989), pp. 288–316, and W. Webster, *Imagining home: Gender, 'race' and national identity, 1945–64* (London: UCL Press, 1998), pp. 25–44.

38 'West Indians for British hotels', *Caterer and Hotel Keeper*, 27 August 1955, p. 19.

39 Buchi Emcheta reveals the problems that faced immigrants of colour in 1950 in securing accommodation, in her autobiography, *Head above water* (Oxford, 1986: Heinemann), and *Second class citizen* (London: George Braziller, 1994).

40 Adi, *West Indians in Britain*, ch. 6.

41 'Colour bar complaint to Huddersfield justices', *Caterer and Hotel Keeper*, 21 February 1959, p. 22.

42 'M.P. introduces Colour Bar Bill', *Caterer and Hotel Keeper*, 12 July 1958, p. 23.

43 'Colour bar complaint: statement by licensees', *Caterer and Hotel Keeper*, 9 May 1959, p. 45.

44 'MPs ask questions about colour bar in London hotels', *Caterer and Hotel Keeper*, 19 November 1960, p. 26.

45 'Hotels and colour bar problem', *Caterer and Hotel Keeper*, 6 September 1958, p. 19.

46 A. H. Pickwoad, letter to the editor, *Caterer and Hotel Keeper*, 11 April 1959, p. 25.

47 Adi, *West Indians in Britain*, ch. 6.

48 Philips and Philips, *Windrush*, p. 163.

49 The Notting Hill riots were the result of a confluence of problems in the area, but commentators at the time considered the underlying problem to be one of race.

50 V. Jenkins, 'Butlin's behind the scenes', in Blair, ed. *Butlin holiday book, 1949–50*, p. 56.

51 'Development and operation of holiday camps in Britain', *Caterer and Hotel Keeper*, 22 September 1956, p. 26.

52 W. Stewart in *Secret lives*.

53 R. Mason in *Secret lives*.

54 P. Everet in *Secret lives*.

55 V. Jenkins in *Secret lives*.

56 A. J. Marriot, e-mail correspondence with author, 19 July 2005.

57 D. O'Connor, *Bananas can't fly: The autobiography* (London: Headline Book Publishing, 2002), pp. 49–50.

58 Ibid.

59 A. J. Marriott, e-mail correspondence with author, 19 July 2005.

60 A. J. Marriott, e-mail correspondence with author, 21 April 2005.

61 A. J. Marriott, e-mail correspondence with author, 19 July 2005.

62 'Are British resorts too dull?' *Caterer and Hotel Keeper*, 11 August 1956, p. 33 and Barton, *Working-class organisations*, pp. 198–215.

63 'Dull resorts: Publicity man replies to disgruntled Briton', *Caterer and Hotel Keeper*, 25 August 1956, p. 31.

64 'BBC wetblankets caterers' hopes', *Caterer and Hotel Keeper*, 14 August 1954, p. 17.

65 'BBC Replies to Minehead hotels', *Caterer and Hotel Keeper*, 15 May 1954, p. 73.

66 Ibid.

67 'More campers at Butlins: on the Continent', *World's Fair*, 19 July 1952, p. 1.

68 Butlin's continental holiday brochure, 1957, Butlin's Travel Service Ltd.

69 By 1964 Pontin owned two other hotels in Majorca and Ibiza. Pontin with Willsher, *My happy life*, pp. 81–98.

70 'Mr. Butlin met the Duke of Bedford for camp-at-Woburn talks', *Caterer and Hotel Keeper*, 2 August 1958, p. 26.

71 'Butlin Bognor camp opposed', *Caterer and Hotel Keeper*, 11 January 1958, p. 26.

72 Butlin's Bognor Regis opened in 1961.

73 'Tourism – from tiny baby to high powered businessman', *Caterer and Hotel Keeper*, 18 March 1961, p. 103.

74 'Holiday camp profit', *Caterer and Hotel Keeper*, 30 September 1961, p. 25.

75 'Butlin's profits up 46 percent', *Caterer and Hotel Keeper*, 10 June 1961, p. 33.

76 Butlin's advert, *Blighty Parade*, 31 January 1959, p. 32 and Butlin's advert, *Illustrated*, 7 January 1956, p. 20.

77 'New Butlin camp approved by Minister', *Caterer and Hotel Keeper*, 22 July 1961, p. 29.

78 'Holiday camp dividend', *Caterer and Hotel Keeper*, 4 February 1961, p. 29.

79 A. Eperon, 'Holiday leisure', *Sun*, 2 January, 1965, p. 11.

80 Wendy Kilshaw, correspondence with author, 8 September 2005.

81 R. Mason in *Secret lives.*

82 Harry Warner died in 1964.

83 C. Lloyd, 'Holiday profits boom goes on', *Sun*, 18 January, 1965, p. 8.

84 T. Geoghegan, 'No place like holidaying at home', *BBC News Magazine*, http://newsvote.bbc.co.uk/mpappa/pagetools/print/news.bbc.co.uk/2/hi (accessed 2 November 2006).

Epilogue

Holiday camps appeared conventional as the counter-culture of the 1960s emerged. When former Butlin's Redcoat and teen idol Cliff Richard starred in the film *Summer Holiday* (1962), it signalled a shift in perceptions of the British seaside holiday. The star and his friends took a double-decker bus 'to the exciting Technicolour delights of "abroad" to escape from the monochrome dullness' of the British family holiday.[1] Singing and dancing their way through Europe, the film's characters criticised holiday camps as old fashioned and outdated. The youth of the 1960s, the film suggested, wanted to create their pleasure away from the entertainment developed for an earlier generation. By the mid 1970s, the all-inclusive holiday revolution begun in the 1930s appeared to be at an end.

Yet holiday camps continued to provide a familiar trope in mainstream culture. A 1973 film, based on the characters in a popular television series *On the Buses*, featured a Pontin's camp as the backdrop to the comedy, *Holiday on the Buses*. When Stan (Reg Varney) and his friend Jack (Bob Grant) took jobs as bus drivers at the Welsh camp, chaos ensued.[2] The pair pursued women unrelentingly – both guests and staff – for sexual pleasure and adventure. The riotous film reflected some of the most common stereotypes associated with the holiday-camp industry – a place for sexual freedom and immorality. This comedic familiarity gave way to a more scathing criticism of holiday camps in films like *That'll Be the Day* (1973) and Ken Russell's *Tommy* (1975).[3]

That'll Be the Day starred David Essex and Ringo Starr and revealed the seedier side of life in a 1950s camp. Filmed on location at Warner's Puckpool camp on the Isle of Wight, Essex's character transforms from a schoolboy into a sexual predator within the confines of the camp. Working as an entertainer, he rebels against the social rules as he straddles work and pleasure in the holiday camp. *That'll Be the Day* exposes the angst of the 1970s but relocates the counter-culture within the seeming 'conformity' of the 1950s.

Two years later, the rock opera *Tommy*, performed by contemporary icons of nonconformity The Who, directly satirised the mass appeal of the postwar holiday camps. Set in the immediate postwar years *Tommy* presented the holiday camp as a symbol of mass culture and one that stood in opposition to a more authentic culture and working-class experience. As war widow Mrs Walker and her son arrive at 'Bernie's Holiday Camp' they are met by rows of orderly wooden huts and groups of happy campers engaged in energetic and regimented 'keep fit' activities and non-stop entertainment. The critique centres on the seemingly mechanical and mindless actions of the campers, as well as the broader suppression of working-class culture in postwar Britain. The Who sought to expose the emptiness of the mass culture in which individuality was subsumed in endless group activities.

There was some truth to *Tommy*'s depiction of the holiday camps. They were regimented. Campers woke to the call of 'wakey-wakey' over the loud-speaker system and sat down to meals at times announced by dining bells. From the price schedules to the daily activities, holiday camps were successful, in large, part due to their predictability. Campers knew, from one camp to another, what to expect of a holiday-camp experience.

Yet life within the camps also fostered a unique culture of its own. Comedy and self-parody routines that simultaneously mocked and valorised working-class bodies and experiences were the hallmark of many of the camp activities. Knobbly Knees, Ugly Faces and Glamorous Granny competitions filled the camps' entertainment timetables and provided an alternative to the more glamorous beauty contests of mainstream culture. Camp entertainment also offered a venue for what would become quintessentially British humour in the post-Second World War years. Comedians such as Des O'Connor, Dave Allen, Jimmy Tarbuck, Frankie Howerd, Roy Hudd, Terry Scott, and Benny Hill performed for camp guests in the 1950s before enjoying later television and film fame. Their antics and brand of humour seemed to display the very nature of postwar British national identity – self-deprecating, innovative, and working class. All of these performers and the subsequent acts they inspired got their start in the holiday camps. Furthermore, holiday camps created a stage for the emerging youth culture of the late 1950s and 1960s. Singers and musicians such as Ringo Starr, Dusty Springfield, Georgie Fame, and Cliff Richard all began their careers as camp entertainers before rising to national and international fame as part of the music revolution of the 1960s counterculture. Thus, from Knobbly Knees to Cliff Richard, holiday camps provided an environment in which a unique post-Second World War culture emerged.

But if the holiday camps were such an integral part of postwar British national identity and culture, how does that explain The Who's assault on holiday-camp culture in the rock opera *Tommy*? In many ways, *Tommy* reflected the disenchantment of 1970s youth with the social policies of the postwar governments that holidays appeared to represent. The uniform public housing replicated in the camp buildings and the use of the school 'house' system and 'prefect-looking' Redcoats to maintain order felt repressive to the youth of the 1970s. Holiday camps appeared to be a visual expression of that postwar uniformity – the rows of chalets, the keep-fit activities and the constant herding of guests into crowded dining halls to eat or be entertained.

When Margaret Thatcher took office as the leader of the new Conservative government in 1979, the critique of the postwar culture continued. In 1980, the year Billy Butlin died, holiday camps were the subject of a long-running television comedy, *Hi-de-Hi!*[4] Inspired by the mass camps of the 1950s, the show's writers, David Croft and Jimmy Perry, centred the storyline on the employees and entertainers at the fictitious Joe Maplin's holiday camp, Crimpton-on-Sea. At Maplin's, the long-suffering campers endured seemingly endless jokes and tricks on the part of the camp's staff. Slap-stick humour abounded as Redcoats sought to supplement their pathetic wages in a bingo swindle or by selling private dance lessons and used tennis balls. The pilot programme introduced viewers to the camp's newly appointed entertainment manager, Jeffrey Fairbrother, a Cambridge University archaeologist who, in an attempt to find 'meaning' in his life, has given up his illustrious career gathering fossils to work among 'living' people. An obvious spoof of the attack on the Oxbridge-educated, ex-public-schoolboy establishment by the 'angry young men' of the late 1950s, Fairbrother's awkwardness, upper-class accent and morality are comic counterpoints to the frenetic and often disreputable activity of the rest of the working-class staff. Thus, *Hi-de-Hi!* featured a well-intentioned, but ineffective leader, unreliable and morally suspect camp employees who frequently cheated and mocked the very campers they were allegedly 'helping', and campers who seemed to be either oblivious to the swindles or apathetic about the ways in which the holiday camp fell far short of their expectations. Indeed, at the end of the pilot, two elderly campers thank Fairbrother for all the fun and games. Their week at Maplin's has been the best holiday of their lives. In fact, they can't remember when they had last 'had it so good'.

Most adult Britons watching the 1980 pilot would have recognised the reference to Prime Minister Harold Macmillan's 1957 assertion that most people had 'never had it so good'. The irony would not have been lost on them either. Stagflation in the 1970s had chipped away at the economic miracle and prosperity of the late 1950s and 1960s. Holiday camps, the cultural symbol of worker leisure and affluence, were in severe financial trouble and faced a serious image problem. The parody of holiday-camp culture in *Hi-de-Hi!* was as much a nostalgic look at the social and economic policies that had helped to create entities like 'Maplin's' as it was a parody of holiday camps as an institution.

The popularity of *Hi-de-Hi!* suggested that holiday camps were seen as part of the larger political, social, and cultural shifts of the twentieth century that served to construct working-class consumers of leisure as well as to develop the welfare system in Britain.[5] The mass camps that emerged in the 1930s provided a visual expression of a political desire to expand the basis of social citizenship. The provision of leisure and the welfare of workers and their families featured in popular and political campaigns for holidays with pay, and support for commercial leisure gave the holiday-camp industry political and social legitimacy. When the Second World War transformed British workers into 'the people', welfare emerged as the central tenet of the political and social policies of the postwar settlement. In this vision, welfare included the provision of pleasure. This offered holiday-camp entrepreneurs the opportunities and the resources to expand their facilities to meet the needs of British workers. Wage increases, full employment, nationalisation of major industries, and the expansion of holidays with pay facilitated the growth of the holiday-camp industry and underscored the cultural significance of the camps as leisure for the working class. Even as Britons looked to alternative leisure abroad in the late 1960s and 1970s, the major holiday-camp chains in Britain continued to expand both numerically and in accommodation.

By 1980, however, the postwar settlement and the mass holiday-camp industry had suffered a serious fiscal assault from both the economy and the radical policies of the Conservative government. Under the leadership of Margaret Thatcher, the Conservative policies that restructured and downsized Britain's major industries also restructured the working class. The process of deindustrialisation proved painful. The provisions of the post-1945 settlement and welfare state dissolved as unemployment rose to critical levels.[6] High unemployment affected the leisure industry significantly, as fewer workers could afford a holiday in Britain or abroad. The impact on the holiday-camp industry was particularly hard. The workers most affected by Thatcherite policies were those in the steel, coal, and transport industries – those living in urban centres and most likely to choose a holiday-camp holiday.

Holiday camps did not just suffer economically from deindustrialisation; they also suffered ideologically. Holiday camps and the culture they fostered had emerged at a moment when social, political, and cultural forces were transforming how the state and popular culture valued the worker. Supported by the unions and the Labour Party, mass holiday camps packaged the people's pleasure and identified themselves as part of working-class culture. When Margaret Thatcher's policies rationalised industry, they also streamlined the symbols of working-class identity – unions, working-men's clubs, and holiday saving's clubs – all supported and financed by workers' wages. The corporate alliance between employers and government against the unions transformed the culture of the workplace and the terms of employment. No longer could workers depend on the postwar institutions that had provided stability and affluence and a sense of group identity found in work.

Holiday camps offered a vision of Britain that was at odds with Thatcherite reconstruction because they physically and metaphorically represented a moment in the twentieth century that, by the mid 1980s, had disappeared. Developed in tandem with the welfare state, holiday camps embraced the opportunity to provide for workers' pleasure. Most importantly, this pleasure was recognised as a need not only that workers had the right to have met, but also that, when met, helped to ensure the well-being of the larger national community. In the 1980s, the image of communal and uniform living in the welfare state disappeared and a new identity based on a strident and individualistic capitalism emerged. The holiday-camp industry had to reinvent itself or expire.

The sons and heirs of the Butlin and Warner empires opted to sell out to the large leisure corporations, Rank and Haven.[7] Camps were demolished, restructured, and renamed, in much the same way as the Conservative government had dismantled and altered British industry. Many of Warner's original camps were demolished to make way for exclusive housing estates.[8] Once the backbone of family holidays, Warner's camps now excluded children, catering solely for adult holiday makers. With the camps now transformed into 'adult only' destinations, families were expected to holiday without children. When the Rank Corporation (later Bourne Leisure) bought the Butlin camps, it renamed them 'leisure centres' and 'holiday villages'. Although Rank later reversed this decision in order to take advantage of the product recognition afforded by Butlin's name, the heyday of the holiday-camp industry clearly had passed. Corporate ideas and designs now dominated British pleasure.

But British holiday makers did not completely abandon the packaged pleasure that they remembered from their childhoods and that had been permanently showcased in British popular culture through television, film, novels, and song. Despite the demolition of several of the older holiday camps, many remain, altered in style and decor and perhaps less spectacular than the early camps. Thousands of holiday makers continue to holiday at the camps each year, in the summer, or for 'weekend breaks', corporate conferences, and company parties. A core of holiday-camp fans remains. The three remaining Butlin camps, after seventy years, continue to accommodate 1.3 million guests each year.[9]

In 2002, Butlins Memories, an unofficial non-profit fan website dedicated to preserving some of the memories of the Butlin's holiday camps and hotels was established to bring this group of people together. The website posts pictures, interviews, camp and staff histories, and discussion forums as well as information about the camps today. Yet another community of collectors also exists, united by eBay auctions and the offline trading of Butlin, Warner, and Pontin memorabilia. Brochures, postcards, and badges from the 1950s, 1960s and 1970s sell for between £10 and £40 in the auctions. Nostalgia for the camps continues and many of the members of these unofficial fan clubs have become deeply involved in celebrating the memories, history, and fun of the holiday-camp culture of the last century. Their actions demonstrate the centrality of the holiday-camp experience to their lives in postwar Britain. At the same time, the efforts to preserve the memories of that experience attest to the enduring importance of holiday camps in twentieth-century British popular culture and national identity.

Notes

1 Walton, *British seaside*, p. 10.
2 *Holiday on the Buses*, 83 mins, Wham! USA, 1998.
3 *That'll be the Day*, 91 mins, Anglo Emi Films, 1973, and *Tommy*, 111 mins, Columbia Pictures, 1975.
4 The series ran for nine seasons from 1980 to 1988.
5 An estimated 12 million viewers watched *Hi-de-Hi!* each season.
6 For a discussion of Thatcherism and the working class see Blackwell and Seabrook, *A world still to win*, pp. 150–66.
7 Warner died in 1964 and his sons took over the company. Butlin died in 1980. His son, Bobbie, led the company from 1968.
8 Two of Warner's camps on Hayling were demolished to make way for housing in the 1980s.
9 W. Cook, 'The happy holiday we outgrew', *New Statesman*, 17 July 2006, pp. 44–5.

Select bibliography

Manuscript sources

National Repositories

British Library, St Pancras:
  Holiday Camp Review, vol. 1, no. 1–3 (April-June, 1938)
Colindale: National Newspaper Archive
The National Archives, Public Records Office, Kew: Ministry of Labour: LAB
  1/1, LAB 1/2, LAB 31/1, LAB 31/3 Ministry of Supply: SUPP 20/2, T161/1192

Local repositories

Bodleian Library, Oxford: John Johnson Collection
Hampshire Record Office, Winchester: 15M74/DDC 46, 15M74/DDC 140,
  15M74/DDC 247, 15M75 DDC/446, 114M90/2/1–8
Hayling Island Library: Local Studies Collection
National Fairground Archive, Sheffield University: *World's Fair*, 1919–1970
Portsmouth Central Library: Local Studies Collection, Warner ephemera
Wessex Film and Sound Archive, Winchester: AV 632/16/S1, AV 623/36/1–51

Newspapers and periodicals

Blighty Parade
Caterer and Hotel Keeper
Clacton News
Clacton News and East Essex Advertiser
Daily Express
Daily Herald
Daily Mail
Daily Mirror
Daily News Chronicle
Hampshire Telegraph
Harwich and Dovercourt Standard
Illustrated
Lansbury Labour Weekly

Ministry of Labour Gazette
News Chronicle
Picture Post
Skegness News
Sun
The Economist
The Times
World's Fair

Primary printed sources

An enquiry into people's homes: A report prepared by Mass Observation for the Advertising Service Guild (London: John Murray, 1943)
Beaver annual, 1962, N. Spain, ed. (London: Fairhaven Books, 1962)
Benson, T., *Sweethearts and wives: Their part in the war* (London: Faber and Faber, 1942)
Beveridge, W. *Social insurance and allied services* (London: HMSO, 1942)
Bowley, M., *Britain's housing shortage* (London: Oxford University Press, 1944)
Brown, W. J., *So far...* (London: George Allen & Unwin, 1943)
Butlin's continental holiday brochure, 1957 (Butlin's Travel Service Ltd)
'Butlin's for a REAL family holiday' (Butlin's advertisement flyer, c. 1940s)
Butlin's holiday pie (1946)
'Butlin's the perfect holiday for mother' (Butlin's advertisement flyer, c. 1940s)
'Camps Bill', 20 March 1939, *House of Commons Papers* (London: HMSO, 1939)
Dalton, H., MP, 'Labour's immediate programme', *The Labour Woman* (May 1937), 73–4
Deal, P., *Nurse at Butlins* (London: Arthur Barker Limited, 1961)
Dent, H. C., *Education in transition: A sociological study of the impact of war on English education, 1939–1943* (London: Kegan Paul, Trench, Trubner & Co. Ltd., 1944)
Drake, B., 'Starvation in the midst of plenty: A new plan for the state feeding of school children', *Fabian Tract* no. 240, December 1933
Evans, I. B. and M., *The arts in England* (London: Falcon Press, 1947)
Greene, G., *Brighton rock* [1938] (New York: Alfred A. Knopf, 1996)
Health and welfare of women in war factories, Third report from the Select Committee on National Expenditure, 1942–1943 (London: HMSO, 1942)
Holiday abroad: Summer 1939 (London: Frame's Tours Ltd., Southampton Row, 1939)
Holiday time at Butlins, 1950–51 (London: Butlin's Ltd, 1950)
Holidays in Spain, 1961, Frames Tours (London: Hendon Printing Works, 1961)
House of Commons Parliamentary Debates (London: HMSO, 1936–60)
Industrial relations handbook, Ministry of Labour and National Service (London: HMSO, 1944)
Kemsley, W. F. F. and D. Ginsburg, *Holidays and holiday expenditure* (London: The Social Survey, 1950)
Leavis, F. R., *Culture and environment* [1933] (London: Chatto & Windus, 1950)

———, *Mass civilization and minority culture* (Folcourt Press, 1930)

Le Gros Clark, F., *National fitness: A brief essay on contemporary Britain* (London: Macmillan and Co., Limited, 1938)

Make this year's holiday your best holiday at Warner's holiday camp, Warner Brochure (Dovercourt, Essex: Standard Printing Company, 1938)

Mensch J., MD, 'The urban worker's need for holidays', *The Labour Magazine*, Vol. X No. 11 (March 1932), 502–3

Ministry of Labour and National Service Report, 1939–1946 (London: HMSO, 1947)

Ministry of Labour Report, 1939–1946 (London: HMSO, 1947)

Murphy, T. *A History of the Showman's Guild, 1939–1948. Part II* (London: The Showman's Guild of Great Britain, 1950)

Ogilvie, F. W. *The tourist movement: An economic study* (London: Staples Press Limited, 1938)

Programme of attractions, Butlin's Filey, week commencing 7 September 1946

Programme of attractions: Butlin's Filey, week commencing 14 September 1946

Programme of attractions: Special grand celebrity week, Butlin's Pwllheli, week commencing 17 May 1947

Rowson, Guy, 'Holiday with pay', *N.F.R.B. Quarterly and Fabian Quarterly* (London: Fabian Publication, Ltd, 1937)

Seventeenth report from the Select Committee on National Expenditure, 1940–1941 (London: HMSO, 1941)

Summerskill, E. 'Conscription and women', *The Fortnightly* (March 1942), 209–14

The Butlin Beaver annual, No. 2, Nancy Spain, ed. (London: Fairhaven Books, 1963)

The Butlin Beaver annual, No. 3, Enid Blyton, ed. (London: Fairhaven Books, 1964)

The Butlin's holiday book, 1949–50, L. Blair, ed. (London: Butlins Ltd, 1950)

The Catering Wages Act, March 1943, Cmd. 6509(London: HMSO, 1944)

The challenge of leisure, W. Boyd and V. Ogilvie, eds (London: New Education Fellowship, 1936)

The holiday camp book (London: Clerke and Cockeran, 1949)

The holiday camp book, the official book of the National Federation of Permanent Holiday Camps (London: Brown & Bibby, 1949)

The new survey of London life and labour, Volume IX, *Life and leisure* (London: P. S. King & Son, 1935)

The travel log: A monthly magazine of travel and holidays at home and abroad and the journal of the Worker's Travel Association, Vol. XIII No. 1 (November 1938)

War begins at home, T. Harrisson and C. Madge, eds (London: Chatto & Windus, 1940)

War factory: A report by Mass-Observation (London: Victor Gollancz, 1943)

'Warner's Puckpool holiday camp, Ryde', Warner brochure insert (Dovercourt, Essex: Standard Printing Company, 1939)

Warner's Seaton holiday camp, Devon, Warner brochure (Dovercourt, Essex: Standard Printing Company, 1938)

Williams-Ellis, A., *Women in war factories* (London: Victor Gollancz, 1943)

'Workers' holidays', *Catering Wages Commission, First Annual Report, 1943–44* (London: HMSO, 1944)

Films and music

Carr, M., *At a holiday camp* (London: Peter Maurice Music, 1945)
Holiday camp, 97 mins, Gainsborough Films, 1947
Holiday on the buses, 83 mins, Wham! USA, 1998
Millions Like Us, 1943, 98 mins. dir. F. Lauder and S. Gilliat, Gainsborough Films
Secret lives – Billy Butlin, 52 mins, Praxis Films Ltd, 1997
That'll be the day, 91 mins, Anglo Emi Films, 1973
Tommy by The Who, 111 mins, Columbia Pictures, 1975

Interviews and correspondence with author

Harrison, J., interview, 14 September 2001
Houghton, O., interview, 14 September 2001
Hutt, A., e-mail correspondence, 25 April 2005
Kilshaw, W., correspondence, 8 September 2005
Marriott, A. J., e-mail correspondence, 20 April, 21 April and 19 July 2005
White, M., e-mail correspondence, 24 August, 21 September 2006

Online sources

Chambers, I., Bygone Butlins, www.bygonebutlins.com/stories/irene_chambers.html
Geoghegan, T., 'No place like holidaying at home', *BBC News Magazine*, http://newsvote.bbc.co.uk/mpappa/pagetools/print/news.bbc.co.uk/2/hi
'Skegred', Bygone Butlins Memories, www.bygonebutlins.com/forum/viewtopic.php?t=255

Secondary sources

Books

Abbott, M., *Family affairs: A history of the family in twentieth century England* (London: Routledge, 2003)
Addison, P., *The road to 1945: British politics and the Second World War* (London: Pimlico, 1994)
Adi, H., *West Indians in Britain, 1900–1960: Nationalism, pan-Africanism and communism* (London: Lawrence & Wishart, 1998)
Alexander, S., *Becoming a woman and other essays in 19th and 20th century feminist history* (New York: New York University Press, 1995)
Aron, C., *Working at play: A history of vacations in the United States* (Oxford: Oxford University Press, 1999)
Bailey, P., *Leisure and class in Victorian England: Rational recreation and the contest for control* (London: Routledge & Kegan Paul, 1978)
Barrows, S., *Distorting mirrors: Visions of the crowd in late nineteenth century France* (New Haven: Yale University Press, 1981)
Barton, S., *Working-class organisations and popular tourism, 1840–1970* (Manchester: Manchester University Press, 2005)

Baxendale J. and C. Pawling, eds, *Narrating the thirties: A decade in the making, 1930–the present* (Basingstoke: St. Martin's Press, 1996)

Beaven, B., *Leisure, citizenship and working-class men in Britain, 1850–1945* (Manchester: Manchester University Press, 2005)

Benson, John, *The rise of consumer society in Britain, 1880–1980* (London: Longman, 1994)

Bingham, A., *Gender, modernity and the popular press in inter-war Britain* (Oxford: Oxford University Press, 2004)

Birley, D., *Playing the game: Sport and British society, 1910–45* (Manchester: Manchester University Press, 1995)

Blackwell, T. and J. Seabrook, *A world still to win: The reconstruction of the postwar working class* (London: Faber and Faber, 1985)

Braggs, S. and D. Harris, *Sun, fun, and crowds: Seaside holidays between the wars* (Stroud: Tempus, 2000)

Braybon, G., *Women workers in the First World War* (London: Routledge, 1989)

Brooke, S., *Labour's war: The Labour Party during the Second World War* (Oxford: Clarendon Press, 1992)

Brown, Callum G., *The death of Christian Britain* (London: Routledge, 2001)

Bullock, A., *The life and times of Ernest Bevin: Trade union leader 1881–1940* (London: William Heinemann, 1960)

Burnett, J., *A social history of housing, 1815–1985* (London: Methuen, 1986)

Butlin, W. and P. Dacre, *The Billy Butlin story: A showman to the end* (London: Robeson, 1982)

Butsch, R., ed. *For fun and profit: The transformation of leisure into consumption* (Philadelphia: Temple University Press, 1990)

Childs, D., *Britain since 1945: A political history* (London: Routledge, 2002)

Church, R., *The rise and decline of the British motor industry* (Basingstoke: Macmillan, 1994)

Clarke, P., *Hope and glory: Britain 1900–1990* (London: Allen Lane, 1996)

Cohen, L., *Making a new deal: Industrial workers in Chicago, 1919–1939* (New York: Cambridge University Press, 1990)

Cole, M. and R. Padley, *Evacuation survey* (London: George Routledge & Sons, 1940)

Cole, M. A., *Holiday camp mystery* (London: Robert Hale Ltd, 1959)

——, *Another holiday camp mystery* (London: Robert Hale Ltd, 1967)

Conekin, B., 'The autobiography of a nation': The 1951 Festival of Britain, (Manchester: Manchester University Press, 2003)

Creasey, J., *The toff at Butlin's* (London: Hodder and Stoughton, 1954)

Cross, G., *Time and money: The making of consumer culture* (New York: Routledge, 1993)

Culleton, C. A., *Working-class culture, women, and Britain, 1914–1921* (New York: St. Martin's Press, 1999)

Davidoff, L. and C. Hall, *Family fortunes: Men and women of the English middle class, 1780–1850* (London: University of Chicago Press, 1991)

Davies, A., *Leisure, gender, poverty: Working-class culture in Salford and Manchester* (Milton Keynes: Open University Press, 1992)

Davin, A., *Growing up poor: Home, school and street in London 1870–1914* (London: Rivers Oram Press, 1996)

De Grazia, V., *Irresistible empire: America's advance through twentieth century Europe* (Cambridge, MA: Belknap, 2005)

——, *The culture of consent: Mass organization of leisure in Fascist Italy* (Cambridge: Cambridge University Press, 1981)

Deslandes, P., *Oxbridge men: British masculinity and the undergraduate experience, 1850–1920* Bloomington: Indiana University Press, 2005)

Donnelly, M., *Sixties Britain* (London: Pearson Longman, 2005)

Downs, L. L., *Childhood in the promised land: Working-class movements and the colonies de vacances in France, 1880–1960* (Durham: Duke University Press, 2002)

Drower, J., *Good clean fun: The story of Britain's first holiday camp* (London: Arcadia Books, 1982)

Dunleavy, P., *The politics of mass housing in Britain, 1945–1975: A study of corporate power and professional influence in the welfare state* (Oxford: Clarendon Press, 1981)

Dworkin, D., *Cultural Marxism in postwar Britain: History, the New Left, and the origin of cultural studies* (Durham: Duke University Press, 1997)

Edgerton, D., *Warfare state: Britain, 1920–1970* (Cambridge: Cambridge University Press, 2006)

Esty, J., *A shrinking island: Modernism and national culture in England* (Princeton: Princeton University Press, 2004)

Fielding, S., *The Labour Party: Continuity and change in the making of 'New' Labour* (London: Macmillan Palgrave, 2003)

Fielding, S., P. Thompson and N. Tiratsoo, *'England arise!': The Labour Party and popular politics in 1940s Britain* (Manchester: Manchester University Press, 1995)

Flanders, J., *Consuming passions: Leisure and pleasure in Victorian Britain* (London: HarperPress, 2006)

Fowler, D., *The first teenagers: The lifestyle of young wage-earners in interwar Britain* (London: Woburn Press, 1995)

Fryer, P., *The politics of Windrush* (London: Index Books, 1999)

Furlough, E. *Consumer cooperation in France: The politics of consumption, 1834–1930* (Ithaca: Cornell University Press, 1991)

Gardiner, J., *The children's war* (London: Piatkus Books, 2005)

Giles, J., *The parlour and the suburb: Domestic identities, class femininity and modernity* (Oxford: Berg, 2004)

——, *Women, identity and private life in Britain, 1900–50* (New York: St. Martin's Press, 1995)

Grafton, G., *The best summer of our lives: Derbyshire miners' holiday camp* (Derby: Breedon Books, 2000)

Graves, R. and A. Lodge, *Long week-end: A social history of Great Britain, 1918–1939* [1940] (New York: Norton, 1963)

Greaves, J., *Industrial reorganization and government policy in interwar Britain* (Aldershot: Ashgate, 2005)

Gullace, N., *The blood of our sons: Men, women, and the renegotiation of citizenship during the Great War* (New York: Palgrave, 2002)

Gunn, S., *The public culture of the Victorian middle class: Ritual and authority in the English industrial city 1840–1914* (Manchester: Manchester University Press, 2000)

Gurney, P. *Co-operative culture and the politics of consumption in England, 1870–1930* (Manchester: Manchester University Press, 1996)

Hassan, J., *The seaside, health and the environment in England and Wales since 1800* (Aldershot: Ashgate Publishing, 2003)

Hilton, M., *Consumerism in the twentieth century: The search for a historical movement* (Cambridge: Cambridge University Press, 2003)

Hoggart, R., *The uses of literacy* (New Brunswick: Transaction Publishers, 1998)

Howkins, Alun, *The death of rural England: A social history of the countryside since 1900* (London: Routledge, 2003)

Howson, S., *British monetary policy, 1945–1951* (Oxford: Clarendon, 1994)

Huxley, A., *Brave new world* [1932] (New York: HarperCollins, 1998)

Huyssen, A., *After the great divide: Modernism, mass culture, postmodernism* (Bloomington: Indiana University Press, 1986)

Inglis, R., *The children's war: Evacuation 1939–1945* (London: Collins, 1989)

Inman, P., *Labour in the munitions industries*, Civil Histories Series (London: HMSO, 1957)

Jacobson, L., *Raising consumers: Children and the American mass market in the early twentieth century* (New York: Columbia University Press, 2004)

Johnson, L. and J. Lloyd, *Sentenced to everyday life: Feminism and the housewife* (Oxford: Berg, 2004)

Jones, S., *Sport, politics and the working class: Organized labour and sport in interwar Britain* (Manchester: Manchester University Press, 1988)

Judt, T., *Postwar: A history of Europe since 1945* (New York: Penguin, 2005)

Kasson, J., *Amusing the million: Coney Island at the turn of the century* (New York: Hill & Wang, 1978)

Kingsley Kent, S., *Gender and power in Britain, 1640–1990* (London: Routledge, 1999)

——, *Making peace: Gender reconstruction in interwar Britain* (Princeton: Princeton University Press, 1993)

Kohan, C. M., *Works and buildings*, Civil Histories Series (London: HMSO, 1952)

Koven, S., *Slumming: Sexual and social politics in Victorian London* (Princeton: Princeton University Press, 2004)

Langhamer, C., *Women's leisure in England, 1920–1960* (Manchester: Manchester University Press, 2000)

LeMahieu, D. L., *A culture for democracy: Mass communication and the cultivated mind in Britain between the wars* (Oxford: Clarendon Press, 1988)

Light, A., *Forever England: Femininity, literature and conservatism between the wars* (London: Routledge, 1991)

Lloyd, T. O., *Empire, welfare state, Europe: English history, 1906–1992* (Oxford: Oxford University Press, 1993)

McKibbin, R., *Classes and cultures: England 1918–1951* (Oxford: Oxford University Press, 1998)

McLaine, I., *Ministry of Morale: Home front morale and the Ministry of Information in World War II* (London: George Allen & Unwin, 1979)

McQueen, R., *The Eatons: The rise and fall of Canada's royal family* (Toronto: Stoddart, 1999)

Marwick, A., *The home front: The British and the Second World War* (London: Thames and Hudson, 1976)

——, *The deluge: British society and the First World War* (London: Macmillan Press, 1965)

Matless, D., *Landscape and Englishness* (London: Reaktion Books, 1998)

Melman, B., *Women and the popular imagination in the twenties: Flappers and nymphs* (London: Macmillan, 1988)

Miall, A. M., *The holiday camp mystery* (Leicester: Brockhampton Press, 1950)

Mills, C., *The Bertram Mills Circus story* (London: Hutchinson, 1965)

Morgan, D. and M. Evans, *The battle for Britain: Citizenship and ideology in the Second World War* (London: Routledge, 1994)

Morgan, K. O., *The people's peace: British history 1945–1990* (Oxford: Oxford University Press, 1990)

——, *Labour in power, 1945–1951* (Oxford: Oxford University Press, 1984)

Morgan, N. and A. Pritchard, *Power and politics at the seaside: The development of Devon's resorts in the twentieth century* (Exeter: Exeter University Press, 1999)

Nevett, T. R., *Advertising in Britain: A history* (London: Heinemann, 1982)

Nicholas, S., *The echo of war: Home front propaganda and the wartime BBC, 1939–45* (Manchester: Manchester University Press, 1996)

Noakes, L., *War and the British: Gender, memory and national identity* (London: I. B. Tauris, 1998)

North, R., *The Butlin story* (London: Jarrolds, 1962)

Nott, J., *Music for the people: popular music and dance in interwar Britain* (Oxford: Oxford University Press, 2002)

Nye, R., *The origins of crowd psychology: Gustave Le Bon and the crisis of mass democracy in the Third Republic* (London: Sage Publications, 1975)

O'Connor, D., *Bananas can't fly: The autobiography* (London: Headline Book Publishing, 2002)

Olechnowicz, A., *Working-class housing in England between the wars: The Becontree estate* (Oxford: Clarendon Press, 1997)

Parker, H. M. D., *Manpower: A study of war-time policy and administration*, Civil Histories Series (London: HMSO, 1957)

Parratt, C. M., *More than mere amusement: Working-class women's leisure in England, 1750–1914* (Boston, MA: Northeastern University Press, 2001)

Paul, K., *Whitewashing Britain: Race and citizenship in the postwar era* (Ithaca, NY: Cornell University Press, 1997)

Pedersen, S., *Family, dependence, and the origins of the welfare state: Britain and France 1914–1945* (Cambridge: Cambridge University Press, 1993)

Peiss, K., *Hope in a jar: The making of America's beauty culture* (New York: Henry Holt, 1998)

——, *Cheap amusements: Working women and leisure in turn-of-the-century New York* (Philadelphia: Temple University Press, 1986)

Pelling, H., *The Labour governments, 1945–51* (London: Macmillan, 1984)

Philips, M. and T. Philips, *Windrush: The irresistible rise of multi-racial Britain* (London: Harper Collins, 1999)

——, *Keep on moving: The Windrush legacy: the black experience in Britain from 1948* (London: Voice Enterprises, 1998)

Pimlott, J. A. R., *The Englishman's holiday: A social history* [1947] (Sussex: Harvester Press, 1976)

Pontin, F. with P. Willsher, *Sir Fred Pontin: My happy life always thumbs up!* (South Molton, Devon: Solo Books, 1991)

Rappaport, E. D., *Shopping for pleasure: Women and the making of London's West End* (Princeton: Princeton University Press, 2000)

Register, W., *The kid of Coney Island: Fred Thompson and the rise of American amusements* (Oxford: Oxford University Press, 2001)

Reynolds, D., *Rich relations: The American occupation of Britain, 1942–1945* (London: Harper Collins, 1999)

Richards, J., *Films and British national identity: From Dickens to Dad's Army* (Manchester: Manchester University Press, 1997)

——, *The age of the dream palace: Cinema and society in Britain, 1930–1939* (London: Routledge, 1989)

Rose, D., *Villages of Surrey: Photographic memories* (Salisbury: Frith, 2004)

Rose, S. O., *Which people's war? National identity and citizenship in wartime Britain, 1939–1945* (Oxford: Oxford University Press, 2003)

Rosenzweig, R., *Eight hours for what we will: Workers and leisure in an industrial city, 1870–1920* (Cambridge: Cambridge University Press, 1983)

Ross, E., *Love and toil: Motherhood in outcast London, 1870–1918* (New York: Oxford University Press, 1993)

Ross, P., *Hayling Island voices* (Stroud: Tempus, 2000)

Rowbotham, S., *A century of women: The history of women in Britain and the United States in the twentieth century* (New York: Penguin, 1997)

Savage, C. I. *Inland transport* (London: HMSO, 1957)

Scanlon, J., *The Ladies Home Journal, gender, and the promises of consumer culture* (New York: Routledge, 1995)

Scannell, P. and D. Cardiff, *A social history of British broadcasting, Volume One 1922–1939: Serving the nation* (Oxford: Basil Blackwell, 1991)

Scott, J. D. and R. Hughes, *The administration of war production* (London: HMSO, 1955)

Seaman, L. C. B., *Life in Britain between the wars* (London: B. T. Batsford Ltd., 1970)

Sherry, N., *The life of Graham Greene, 1904–1939* Vol. I (New York: Viking, 1989)

Smith, G., *When Jim Crow met John Bull: Black American soldiers in World War II Britain* (London: I. B. Tauris, 1987)

Smith, M., *Britain and 1940: History, myth and popular memory* (London: Routledge, 2000)

Soffer, R., *Ethics and society in England: The revolution in the social sciences, 1870–1914* (Berkeley: University of California Press, 1978)

Summerfield, P., *Women workers in the Second World War: Production and patriarchy in conflict* (London: Routledge, 1989)

Steedman, C., *Landscape for a good woman: A story of two lives* (New Brunswick, NJ: Rutgers University Press, 1994)

——, *Childhood, culture and class in Britain: Margaret McMillan 1860–1931* (London: Virago, 1990)

Strasser, S., *Satisfaction guaranteed: The making of the American mass market* (New York: Pantheon, 1989)

Swinglehurst, E., *Cook's Tours: The story of popular travel* (Poole: Blandford Press, 1982)

Tabili, L., *We ask for British justice: Workers and racial difference in late imperial Britain* (Ithaca, NY: Cornell University Press, 1994)

Thompson, E. P. *Customs in common: Studies in traditional popular culture* (New York: Norton, 1993)

——, *The making of the English working class* (New York: Vintage, 1963)

Tinkler, P. *Constructing girlhood: Popular magazines for girls growing up in England, 1920–1950* (London: Taylor & Francis, 1995)

Todd, S., *Young women, work and family in England, 1918–1950* (Oxford: Oxford University Press, 2005)

Tosh, J., *A man's place: Masculinity and the middle-class home in Victorian England* (New Haven, CT: Yale University Press, 1999)

Urry, J., *Consuming Places* (London: Sage, 1995)

——, *The tourist gaze* (London: Sage, 1990)

Veblen, T., *The theory of the leisure class* [1899] (London: Penguin, 1994)

Vernon, J., *Hunger: A modern history* (Cambridge, MA: Belknap, 2007)

Walker, P., *Pulling the devil's kingdom down: The Salvation Army in Victorian Britain* (Berkeley: University of California Press, 2001)

Walton, John K., *The British seaside: Holidays and resorts in the twentieth century* (Manchester: Manchester University Press, 2000)

——, *Fish and chips and the British working class, 1870–1940* (London: Leicester University Press, 1992)

Walvin, J., *Beside the seaside: A social history of the popular seaside holiday* (London: Penguin, 1978)

Ward, C. and D. Hardy, *Goodnight campers! The history of the British holiday camp* (London: Mansell, 1986)

Waters, C., *British socialists and the politics of popular culture* (Manchester: Manchester University Press, 1990)

Webster, W., *Imagining home: Gender, 'race' and national identity, 1945–64* (London: UCL Press, 1998)

Williams, J., *Entertaining the nation: A social history of British television* (Stroud: Sutton Publishing Limited, 2004)

Withey, L., *Grand tours and Cook's tours: A history of leisure travel, 1750–1915* (London: Aurum Press, 1998)

Woolton, Lord, *The memoirs of the Rt. Honorable the Earl of Woolton* (London: Cassell, 1959)

Zweiniger-Bargielowska, I., *Austerity in Britain: Rationing, controls and consumption 1939–1955* (Oxford: Oxford University Press, 2000)

Journal articles and chapters in edited volumes

Adorno, T. W. and M. Horkheimer, 'The culture industry: Enlightenment as mass deception', in M. G. Durham, and D. M. Keller, eds *Media and cultural studies: Keyworks* (Malden MA: Blackwell Publishers Inc, 2001), 71–101

Aldgate, T., 'Comedy, class and containment: The British domestic cinema of the 1930s', in J. Curran and V. Porter, eds *British cinema history* (Totowa, NJ: Barnes and Noble Books, 1983), 257–71

Bandyopadhyay, P. 'The holiday camp', in M. Smith, A. Stanley and C. Smith, eds *Leisure and society in Britain* (London: Allen Lane, 1973), 252–65

Baranowski, S., 'Strength through joy: Tourism and national integration in the Third Reich', in S. Baranowski and E. Furlough, eds *Being elsewhere: Tourism, consumer culture, and identity in modern Europe and North America* (Ann Arbor, MI: University of Michigan Press, 2001)

Baxendale, J., 'You and I – all of us ordinary people: Renegotiating "Britishness" in wartime', in N. Hayes and J. Hill, eds *Millions like us? British culture in the Second World War* (Liverpool: Liverpool University Press, 1999), 295–322

Bennett, T., 'Ideology, hegemony, pleasure: Blackpool', in T. Bennett, C. Mercer and J. Woollacott, eds *Popular culture and social relations* (Milton Keynes: Open University Press, 1986), 135–54

Bland, L., 'White women and men of colour: Miscegenation fears in Britain after the Great War', *Gender and History*, 17:1 (April 2005), 29–61

Bullock, N., 'Re-assessing the post-war housing achievement: The impact of war-damage repairs on the new housing programme in London', *Twentieth Century British History*, 16:3 (2005), 256–82

Butsch, R., 'Leisure and hegemony in America', in R. Butsch, ed. *For fun and profit: The transformation of leisure into consumption* (Philadelphia: Temple University Press, 1990), 3–27

Buzzard, J., 'Culture for export: Tourism and autoethnography in postwar Britain', in S. Barbaowski and E. Furlough eds *Being elsewhere: Tourism, consumer culture and identity in modern Europe and North America* (Ann Arbor, MI: University of Michigan Press, 2004), 299–319

Catterall, P., 'The state of the literature on post-war British history', in A. Gorst, L. Johnman and W. S. Lucas, eds *Post-war Britain, 1945–64: Themes and perspectives* (London: Pinter, 1989), 221–41

Chase, L., 'Modern images and social tone in Clacton and Frinton in the interwar years', *International Journal of Maritime History*, 9:1 (June 1997), 149–69

Constantine, Stephen, 'The buy British campaign of 1931', *European Journal of Marketing*, 21:4 (1987), 44–59

Cross, G., 'Vacations for all: The leisure question in the era of the Popular Front', *Journal of Contemporary History*, 24 (1989), 599–621

Davies, A., 'Leisure in the classic slum, 1900–1939', in A. Davies and S. Fielding, eds *Workers' worlds: Cultures and communities in Manchester and Salford, 1880–1939* (Manchester: Manchester University Press, 1992), 102–32

Davin, A., 'Imperialism and motherhood', *History Workshop*, 5 (Spring 1978), 9–65

Dawson, S., 'Busy and bored: The politics of work and leisure for women workers in WWII British government hostels', *Twentieth Century British History*, 20:1 (2010), 29–49

——, 'Working class consumers and the campaign for holidays with pay', *Twentieth Century British History*, 18:3 (2007), 277–305

——, 'The battle for Beachlands: Hayling Island and the development of coastal leisure in Britain, 1820–1960', *International Journal of Regional and Local Studies*, 3:1 (2007), 56–80

Dresser, M., 'The colour bar in Bristol, 1963', in R. Samuel, ed. *Patriotism: The making and unmaking of British national identity* (London: Routledge, 1989), 288–316

Ellison, N., 'Consensus here, consensus there ... but not consensus everywhere: The Labour Party, equality and social policy in the 1950s', in P. Catterall and H. Jones, eds *The myth of consensus* (Basingstoke: Macmillan, 1996), 17–39

Farrant, S., 'London by the sea: Resort development on the south coast of England, 1880–1939', *Journal of Contemporary History*, 22 (1987), 137–162

Fowler, D., 'Teenage consumers? Young wage-earners and leisure in Manchester, 1919–1939', in A. Davies, S. Fielding and T. Wyke, *Worker's worlds: Cultures and communities in Manchester and Salford 1880–1939* (Manchester: Manchester University Press, 1992), 133–55

Francis, M., 'Not reformed capitalism, but ... democratic socialism: The ideology of the Labour leadership, 1945–51', in P. Catterall and H. Jones, eds *The myth of consensus* (Basingstoke: Macmillan, 1996), 40–57

Furlough, E., 'French consumer cooperation, 1885–1930: From the "third pillar of socialism" to a "movement for all consumers"', in E. Furlough and C. Strikwerda, eds *Consumers against capitalism? Consumer cooperation in Europe, North America, and Japan, 1840–1990* (Lanham, md: Rowman and Littlefield, 1999), 173–90

——, 'Making mass vacations: Tourism and consumer culture in France, 1930s to 1970s', *Comparative Studies in Society and History*, 40:2 (1998), 247–86

——, 'Packaging pleasures: Club Méditéranée and French consumer culture, 1950–1968', *French Historical Studies*, 18:1 (Spring 1993), 65–81

Gilbert, A., 'Buggery and the British navy, 1700–1861', *Journal of Social History*, 10 (1976), 72–98

Giles, J., 'Help for housewives: Domestic service and the reconstruction of domesticity in Britain, 1940–50', *Women's History Review*, 10:2 (2001), 299–324

Grant, M., 'Working for the Yankee dollar': Tourism and the Festival of Britain as stimuli for recovery', *Journal of British Studies*, 45 (July 2006), 581–601

Green, D. G., 'The Friendly Societies and Adam-Smith liberalism', in D. Gladstone, ed. *Before Beveridge: Welfare before the welfare state* (London: IEA Health and Welfare Unit, 1999), 18–25

Gurney, P., 'Labor's great arch: Cooperation and cultural revolution in Britain, 1795–1926', in E. Furlough and C. Strikwerda, eds *Consumers against capitalism? Consumer cooperation in Europe, North America, and Japan, 1840–1990* (Lanham, MD: Rowman and Littlefield, 1999), 135–72

Harper, S. 'The years of total war: Propaganda and entertainment', in C. Gledhill and G. Swanson, eds *Nationalising femininity: Culture, sexuality and British cinema in the Second World War* (Manchester: Manchester University Press, 1996), 193–212

Harris, J., 'Political thought and the welfare state 1870–1940: An intellectual framework for British social policy', in D. Gladstone, ed. *Before Beveridge: Welfare before the welfare state* (London: IEA Health and Welfare, 1999), 43–63

Hayes, N., 'More than music while-you-eat? Factory and hostel concerts, "good culture" and the workers', in N. Hayes and J. Hill, eds *Millions like us? British culture in the Second World War* (Liverpool: Liverpool University Press, 1999), 209–35

Hebdige, D., 'Towards a cartography of taste, 1935–1962', *Hiding in the light: On images and things* [1989] (London: Routledge, 1994), 45–76

Homer, A., 'Planned communities: The social objectives of the British new towns, 1946–65', in L. Black, ed. *Consensus or coercion? The state, the people and social cohesion in post-war Britain* (Cheltenham: New Clarion, 2001), 125–35

Huggins, M., 'Projecting the visual: British newsreels, soccer and popular culture, 1918–39', *The International Journal of the History of Sport*, 24:1 (2007), 80–102

Hughes, D., 'The spivs', in M. Sissons and P. French, eds *The age of austerity* (Westport, CT: Greenwood Press, 1976)

Jeffreys, K., 'Social class, affluence and electoral politics, 1951–64', in S. James and V. Preston, eds *British politics since 1945: The dynamics of historical change* (Houndmills, Basingstoke: Palgrave, 2001), 51–76

Jones, S., 'Working class sport in Manchester between the wars', in R. Holt, ed. *Sport and the working class in modern Britain* (Manchester: Manchester University Press, 1990), 67–83

——, 'Trade union policy between the wars: The case of holidays with pay in Britain', *International Review of Social History*, 31 (1986), 40–55

——, 'Sports, politics, and the labour movement: The Workers Sports Federation, 1923–1935', *British Journal of Sports History*, 2 (1985), 154–78

Land, H., 'Eleanor Rathbone and the economy of the family', in H. L. Smith, ed. *British feminism in the twentieth century* (Amherst: University of Massachusetts Press, 1990), 104–23

Leventhal, F. M., 'The best for the most: CEMA and state sponsorship of the arts in wartime, 1939–1945', *Twentieth Century British History*, 1:3 (1990), 289–317

Lowe, R., 'The Second World War, consensus, and the foundation of the welfare state', *Twentieth Century British History*, 1:2 (1990), 152–92

Lowerson, J., 'Battles for the countryside', in F. Gloversmith, ed. *Class, culture and social change: A new view of the 1930s* (Sussex: Harvester Press, 1980), 258–80

Mackey, R., 'Safe and sound: New music in wartime', in N. Hayes and J. Hill, eds *Millions like us? British culture in the Second World War* (Liverpool: Liverpool University Press, 1999), 179–208

Marquand, D., 'The end of postwar consensus', in A. Gorst et al., eds *Post-war Britain, 1945–64: Themes and perspectives* (London: Pinter, 1989)

——, 'Sir Stafford Cripps', in M. Sissons and P. French, eds *Age of austerity* (Westport, CT: Greenwood Press, 1976), 167–88

Mercer, H., 'Industrial organization and ownership, and a new definition of the postwar "consensus"', in P. Catterall and H. Jones, eds *The myth of consensus* (Basingstoke: Macmillan, 1996), 139–56

Nicholas, S., 'Being British: Creeds and cultures', in K. Robbins, ed. *The British Isles, 1901–1951* (Oxford: Oxford University Press, 2002), 103–36

Newman, B., 'Holidays and social class', in M. Smith, S. Parker and C. Smith, eds *Leisure and society in Britain* (London: Allen Lane, 1973), 230–40

Paul, K., 'From subjects to immigrants: Black Britons and national identity, 1948–62', in R. Weight and A. Beach, eds *The right to belong: Citizenship and national identity in Britain, 1930–1960* (London: I. B. Tauris, 1998), 223–48

Poole, R., 'Oldham Wakes', in J. K. Walton and J. Walvin, eds *Leisure in Britain* (Manchester: Manchester University Press, 1983), 71–98

Potts, A., 'Constable country between the wars', in R. Samuel, ed. *Patriotism: The making and unmaking of British national identity*, Vol. III (London: Routledge, 1989), 160–1

Prynn, D., 'The Clarion Clubs, rambling and the Holiday Associations in Britain since the 1890s', *Journal of Contemporary History*, 11:2/3 (1976), 65–77

Rabbinovitz, L., 'Temptations of pleasure: Nickleodeons: amusement parks, and the sights of female sexuality', *Camera Obscura*, 23 (May 1990), 71–88

Rieger, B. 'Fast couples: Technology, gender, and modernity in Britain and Germany during the 1930s', *Historical Research*, 76:193 (August 2003), 364–88

Rose, S. O., 'Sex, citizenship and the nation in World War II Britain', *American Historical Review*, 103:4 (1998), 1147–76

——, 'The "sex question" in Anglo-American relations in the Second World War', *International History Review*, 20 (December 1998), 884–903

Ross, E., 'Not the sort that would sit on the doorstep: Respectability in pre-WWI London neighborhoods', *International Labor and Working Class History*, 27 (Spring 1985), 39–59

Sladen, C., 'Holidays at home in the Second World War', *Journal of Contemporary History*, 37:1 (2002), 67–89

Smith Wilson, D., 'A new look at the affluent worker: The good working mother in post-war Britain', *Twentieth Century British History*, 17:2 (2006), 206–29

Spry Rush, A., 'Imperial identity in colonial minds: Harold Moody and the League of Coloured Peoples, 1931–50', *Twentieth Century British History*, 13:4 (2002), 356–83

Thane, P., 'The working class and state "welfare" in Britain, 1880–1914', in D. Gladstone, ed. *Before Beveridge: Welfare before the welfare state* (London: IEA Health and Welfare Unit, 1999), 86–112

——, 'Population politics in post-war British culture', in B. Conekin, F. Mort, and C. Waters, eds *Moments of modernity: Reconstructing Britain 1945–1964* (London: Rivers Oram Press, 1999), 114–33

——, 'The women of the Labour Party and feminism, 1906–1945', in H. L. Smith, ed. *British feminism in the twentieth century* (Amherst, MA: University of Massachusetts Press, 1990), 124–43

Vernon, J., 'The ethics of hunger and the assembly of society: The techno-politics of the school meal in Britain', *The American Historical Review*, 110:3 (June 2005), 693–725

Walton, J. K., 'Popular entertainment and public order: The Blackpool carnivals of 1923–24', *Northern History*, 34 (1998), 170–88

——, 'The Blackpool landlady revisited', *Manchester Region History Review*, 8 (1994), 23–30

——, 'The world's first working-class resort? Blackpool revisited, 1840–1975', *Lancashire and Cheshire Antiquarian Society* (1994), 23–30

——, 'The demand for working-class seaside holidays in Victorian Britain', *The Economic History Review*, new series, 34:2 (May 1981), 249–65

Weight, R., 'Building a new British culture: The arts centre movement, 1943–53', in R. Weight and A. Beach, eds *The right to belong: Citizenship and national identity in Britain, 1930–1960* (London: I. B. Tauris, 1998), 157–80

Welshman, J., 'Evacuation and social policy during the Second World War: Myth and reality', *Twentieth Century British History*, 9:1 (1998), 28–53

Wilkinson, H., 'The new heraldry: Stock photography, visual literacy, and advertising in 1930s Britain', *Journal of Design History*, 10:1, 1997, 23–38

Yates, N., 'Selling the seaside', *History Today*, 38:8 (1988), 24

Zweiniger-Bargielowska, I., 'Consensus and consumption: Rationing, austerity and controls after the war', in P. Catterall and H. Jones, eds *The myth of consensus* (Basingstoke: Macmillan, 1996), 79–96

Index